Crown and Nobility in Early Mo

European History in Perspective
General Editor: Jeremy Black

Benjamin Arnold *Medieval Germany, 500–1300*
Ronald Asch *The Thirty Years' War*
Christopher Bartlett *Peace, War and the European Powers, 1814–1914*
Robert Bireley *The Refashioning of Catholicism, 1450–1700*
Donna Bohanan *Crown and Nobility in Early Modern France*
Patricia Clavin *The Great Depression, 1929–1939*
Mark Galeotti *Gorbachev and his Revolution*
David Gates *Warfare in the Nineteenth Century*
Martin P. Johnson *The Dreyfus Affair*
Peter Musgrave *The Early Modern European Economy*
J. L. Price *The Dutch Republic in the Seventeenth Century*
A. W. Purdue *The Second World War*
Christopher Read *The Making and Breaking of the Soviet System*
Francisco J. Romero-Salvado *Twentieth-Century Spain*
Matthew S. Seligmann and Roderick R. McLean
Germany from Reich to Republic, 1871–1918
Brendan Simms *The Struggle for Mastery in Germany, 1779–1850*
David Sturdy *Louis XIV*
Peter Waldron *The End of Imperial Russia, 1855–1917*
James D. White *Lenin*

European History in Perspective
Series Standing Order
ISBN 0–333–71694–9 hardcover
ISBN 0–333–69336–1 paperback
(*outside North America only*)

You can receive future titles in this series as they are published by placing
a standing order. Please contact your bookseller or, in the case of difficulty,
write to us at the address below with your name and address, the title of the
series and the ISBN quoted above.

Customer Services Department, Macmillan Distribution Ltd
Houndmills, Basingstoke, Hampshire RG21 6XS, England

Crown and Nobility in Early Modern France

DONNA BOHANAN

palgrave

First published 2001 by
PALGRAVE
Houndmills, Basingstoke, Hampshire RG21 6XS and
175 Fifth Avenue, New York, N.Y. 10010
Companies and representatives throughout the world

PALGRAVE is the new global academic imprint of
St. Martin's Press LLC Scholarly and Reference Division and
Palgrave Publishers Ltd (formerly Macmillan Press Ltd).

ISBN 0–333–60971–9 hardback
ISBN 0–333–60972–7 paperback

This book is printed on paper suitable for recycling and made from fully managed and sustained forest sources.

A catalogue record for this book is available from the British Library.

Library of Congress Cataloging-in-Publication Data
Bohanan, Donna, 1954–
    Crown and nobility in early modern France / Donna Bonahan.
        p. cm.—(European history in perspective)
    Includes bibliographical references and index.
    ISBN 0–333–60971–9—ISBN 0–333–60972–7 (pbk.)
        1. Nobility—France—History—17th century.   2. Central–local government relations—France—History—17th century.   3. Elite (Social sciences)—France—Political activity—History—17th century.
    4. Monarchy—France—History—17th century.   5. Patronage, Political—France—History—17th century.   6. Elite (Social sciences)—France —Political activity—History—17th century—Case studies.
    I. Title.   II. Series.

HT653.F7 B64 2000
305.5'2'0944—dc21   00-053085

10 9 8 7 6 5 4 3 2 1
10 09 08 07 06 05 04 03 02 01

Printed in China

For Frank M. Smith
and
in memory of
J. Russell Major

Contents

Acknowledgements

I first learned about the complexities, importance, and mercurial nature of the dynamic relationship between crown and nobility when I was an undergraduate at Hendrix College. In a class on early modern Europe, Garrett McAinsh presented this historical issue and its significance for state and society in such a compelling way that it has since become the major theme of my own research. It took me from Hendrix to graduate school at Emory University where I studied with J. Russell Major, an extraordinary mentor and scholar whose imprint on this book should be quite obvious to the reader.

The research and writing of this book were made possible by the financial support of various institutions. The American Philosophical Society funded a trip to the archives in Grenoble. The Auburn University Humanities Fund, the Auburn University Professional Improvement Leave program, the College of Liberal Arts and the History Department funded trips to Paris, Rennes, and Aix.

I have also benefitted enormously from the support of various friends and colleagues. Among those who did their utmost to promote the completion of this manuscript are Larry Gerber and Daniel Szechi. As department chair, Gerber did his best to design my schedule so that I might have the time to finish the research and to write. Szechi, my fellow early modernist at Auburn, very generously read parts of this project and offered his unfailingly perceptive comments. Hines and Joy Hall, Joseph Kicklighter, Carol Harrison, and Gerry Gryski have also been endless sources of advice and encouragement.

At Palgrave, I found a group of colleagues that operated with the greatest professionalism and yet were able to show me infinite understanding and patience. My series editor, Jeremy Black, and my project editor, Terka Bagley, tolerated my tardiness and allowed me to work according to my own schedule. I can never adequately express my gratitude for their humane and sympathetic approach to publishing deadlines. And to Katy Coutts, my copy-editor, I owe special thanks for a splendid job of editing and correcting my manuscript.

Finally, my parents and my family, as always, have been my stalwart support team. While I was working in the Grenoble archives, my sister and brother-in-law, Cindy and Paul Ackermann, graciously provided a hospitable retreat by opening their home to me weekend after weekend.

In the end, I owe my biggest debt to my husband, Frank Smith, who edited the manuscript and, more important, makes me laugh.

Introduction

This book is about relations between the central government of France and the provincial nobility during the early modern period. It focuses specifically on the Bourbon monarchs of the seventeenth century and their efforts to extend a measure of control over the semi-autonomous peripheral provinces and the nobilities that dominated them. I have chosen as illustrations the provinces of Provence, Dauphiné, and Brittany, which were the objects of royal designs to siphon off greater revenues in the form of taxation. In each of these *pays d'états*, royal policy provoked resistance and rebellion on the part of the nobility – or, more accurately, on components within the nobility – which in turn exposed the fundamental contours and structures of provincial society.

There are several important underlying assumptions about crown and nobility that have shaped my approach to these provinces and their great moments of resistance. Chapter 1 offers a view of the early modern nobility that is dynamic, enlarged, invigorated, and substantially more complex and sophisticated than its medieval progenitor. From the late fifteenth century through the seventeenth century, upward social mobility infused the French nobility with the vital forces needed not only to sustain it through to the Revolution but to expand its role in French government, society, economy, and culture. The seventeenth century was the age of aristocracy, which should in no way be taken to suggest that I see the nobility as a monolith; rather I would urge their dominant role in French society, especially in the provinces. Arranged according to their constituent parts, each provincial nobility had the potential of being divided along those same lines.

Chapters 3, 4, and 5 offer a vision, province by province, of what those constituent parts may have been and how the monarchy responded to

1

them. In Provence, the urban and Mediterranean circumstances of the nobility largely eliminated a functional or occupational division and diminished the effects of antiquity. Instead, factionalism and the vertical ties of patronage organized the elites of the region into distinct, separate, and rival groups. In Dauphiné, the antiquity of a noble family acquired greater social meaning as locals debated noble tax exemption and where to set the lines of demarcation between taxed and untaxed elements in provincial society. In Brittany, institutional politics and the seigneurial regime would superficially separate the nobility along the functional lines of sword and robe. Beneath the surface lay the horizontal solidarities associated with class.

These various ways of carving up and typing nobility imply another fundamental and operative assumption – that old and new, sword and robe are categories that work in more than simply dichotomous ways. Instead of dissecting provincial nobles with the blunt instruments of sword vs. robe, old vs. new, I would propose including them in a more elaborate schema for elite society. Regrettably untidy, this vision of provincial nobles asks the reader to juggle sword and robe, old and new, in and out of favor, as the essential categories of the defining matrix for provincial nobility. Traditional historians envisioned and limited categories to sword/old and robe/new. Let us consider some other possibilities in the provinces: sword/new and robe/old. Or, what about the combinations of sword/robe/new and sword/robe/old? Then, factor in the dynamic effects of patronage, faction, alignments and realignments – in favor or out of favor, clientele A or clientele B – and we find that the permutations of essential categories are extraordinarily complex. Perhaps it would be useful to view provincial nobilities through a lens that involves simultaneously an axis and a matrix:

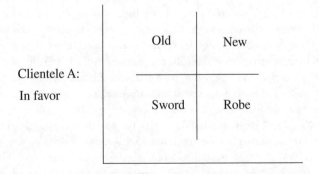

Clientele B: Out of favor

Now factor into this nearly byzantine system of nomenclature the galvanizing hand of the state, and it rapidly becomes apparent that generalizations about the relationship of crown and provincial nobility are at best simple and at worst misleading and even untrue. This book will attempt to portray the crown as a dynamic force of change, but one that was entirely sensitive to the particularity of the province. Provincial nobilities operated within their unique institutional contexts to affect the outcome of royal policy. In some instances they obstructed royal goals, and in other instances they were agents of the royal will. Either way, their involvement, their opposition and their complicity reveal the limits of royal power in seventeenth-century France.

With these limits in mind, my approach to Chapter 2 has been influenced by the more recent wave of historians who question the existence of absolutism, though some may still value it as a useful construct. Roger Mettam has persuasively argued for an alternative view of the relationship between Louis XIV and his subjects. He writes about 'absolutist historians' who have seriously overstated the extent of royal power, the modernization of administration, and the reliance on new government agents. Instead, Mettam's view of the monarchy under the Sun King sees it operating through the careful manipulation of patronage and factions, that is, through very traditional means.[1] As classically defined, absolutism never really existed in these three provinces. Instead, what evolved over the course of three reigns was a system of governance in which provincial elites, or a component therein, sided with the crown. Indeed, these crucial components became the accomplices of the crown, or, at the very least, they stood by, having carefully exempted themselves, and allowed the crown to drain the province of what it needed. This view of royal authority as it radiated to the periphery sees it as pragmatic, flexible, accommodating and even compromising rather than doctrinaire, reformist, centralizing, and modern. It is a view that attributes to the state some growth in power, but not at the expense of the locality or its elites. In each province, a group of nobles came out ahead or survived unscathed to prosper under the *ancien régime*.

By 'prosper' I refer to the benefits of patronage and/or the avoidance of taxation and its economic effects on investments. Patronage and taxation provided the system of rewards and punishments that motivated provincial nobilities. As such, they are fundamental to an analysis of state and society, and they offer historians two analytical tools to be used on the gross anatomy of the body politic and the body social. Sharon Kettering has described for us the mechanics and the operative principles of the patron–client system as it functioned at the various intersections of state and society. James Collins and Daniel Hickey have shown us the mechanics and operative principles of taxation as negotiated at the provincial level. The painstaking and thoughtful works of all three historians have informed this book; they have supplied both interpretative insight and substantive information.[2]

Patronage and taxation were not only the carrot and stick of royal policy: patronage had the capacity to achieve the state's objectives even as provincial estates debated matters of taxation. Provence, Dauphiné, and Brittany were *pays d'états*, which meant that their provincial estates had the right to approve taxes, to choose their form, and to collect them. For this reason the institutions of the provincial estates figure prominently in the story of the three provinces. Here I have relied heavily on the scholarship and perspective of J. Russell Major, the historian of France's representative assemblies who made clear the consultative and limited nature of the Renaissance state and who described the process of building the absolutist state as a series of conflicts and negotiations with the *pays d'états*. For Major, absolutism did indeed exist by the 1670s, because there were no theoretical limits on royal authority, but he freely acknowledges the crown's dependency on the vertical and practical ties of patronage.[3] Absolutism, if we can use the term, required the cooperation of provincial elites.

The idea of cooperation, even collaboration, on the part of provincial elites lies at the heart of William Beik's richly detailed and formative study of state and society in seventeenth-century Languedoc. Although Languedoc is not one of the examples used in this work, Beik's book has had a profound effect on the way I view the relationship between crown and provincial nobility. His book appeared in 1985 and made a very persuasive case for the idea that absolutism rested on collaboration and mutually beneficial deals. Beik's work is also important in that he uses the concept of class as an interpretative device by which to describe the Languedocian elite. Beik rejects the concept of social orders, articulated by Roland Mousnier, to advance a case for the role of economic interests in shaping society and behaviors.[4]

I have also been persuaded by David Parker's argument for a class-based analysis of French society.[5] Like Parker, I believe that wealth was indispensable to the seventeenth-century nobility. Nobles enjoyed honor and esteem in part because their wealth made possible a lifestyle that marked them as honorable. Ennoblement was not possible without lots of money. Moreover, seventeenth-century society attached a great deal of cultural and social value to the newest features of aristocratic life. Ambition, self-construction, *politesse*, *honnêteté*, education, connoisseurship, distinction, and the consumption of an increasingly elaborate and exotic material world all required money. To cultivate these aspects of the aristocratic life required levels of income that set nobles apart from the rest of society. It also meant that nobles would have to give greater attention to their investments.

Thus, in certain instances I invoke the notion of class to describe the behavior of elite society. Unlike Beik and Parker, however, I do not use class as a consistent frame of reference. Rather, I have taken my cue from Collins whose work on Brittany advances a convincing argument for the simultaneous existence of orders and classes. Certain issues make apparent the ongoing existence of a society of orders, based on function, esteem, and honor. Others bring to the fore the faint contours of class. Collins maintains that Breton society functioned within two hierarchical systems, order and class, depending on the issue. I am persuaded by Collins that this is true for Brittany, and I have chosen to apply the idea of class to Dauphiné in the debate over the *taille*. In Provence, there were also moments in which class interest erupted to drive or derail the narrative of revolt, though I am convinced by Kettering that factional intrigue and competition were even more important.

Finally, my decision to focus on three outlying provinces, all *pays d'états*, demands explanation. It was based on the fact that such provinces presented the greatest obstacles, both practical and theoretical, to monarchical power. Their locations at the periphery had traditionally sheltered the provinces to some extent from the grasping fiscal reach of central government. Logistics and communications difficulties set real limits on what the king was able to do in such remote areas. More important, as *pays d'états* the three provinces were able to claim political rights that afforded them a measure of autonomy. Their local estates retained the right to approve, assess, and collect taxes, in this way setting institutional and constitutional limits on the king's power within the locale.

When, in the seventeenth century, the costs of Bourbon foreign policy forced the crown to seek more resources on the periphery, it faced a variety of adversarial responses from the local nobilities. Arlette Jouanna maintains that the political culture of nobility in general and the vertical ties that bound one nobleman to another in particular virtually mandated revolt. The patron–client system provided the means by which they organized and engineered their resistance. In the course of their opposition to royal policy, the provincial nobility took up the constitutional cause of mixed monarchy and institutional limits on royal authority.[6] They were also able to advance their own self-interest, a cause that was entirely compatible with their resistance ideology because it placed them on the same side as the cause of provincial rights.

In Provence and Dauphiné, aristocratic opposition to tax reforms guaranteed the destruction of the local estates. In Brittany, the cooperation of the local estates ensured their survival. There it was the provincial parlement that paid the price of resistance. In each province, the local nobility survived, and some of its components emerged from the fray substantially better off. In no two provinces did this happen in precisely the same way. Central government's success in raising more money from the *pays d'états* depended on its ability to juggle a set of different strategies, each conceived according to the particularity of the social, political, and institutional context of the province. Provence, Dauphiné, and Brittany offer three examples of how relations between crown and provincial nobility could vary significantly and yet produce for both the desired results for most concerned.

Chapter 1: Nobility: Metamorphosis

For some time modern historians wrote about a crisis of the nobility in fifteenth- and sixteenth-century France. By 'crisis' they were referring to a decline in aristocratic power, wealth, and number. Such a decline had for these historians broad political implications because it effectively removed the primary obstacle to monarchical power – a recalcitrant, essentially independent warrior nobility – to be replaced by a rising middle class, a group whose political strength derived from the supportive role in which it had been cast by virtue of its alliance with the monarchs of the sixteenth century. For the crisis historians, the decline of the aristocracy was paralleled by the rise of the middle class and was *ipso facto* accompanied by the growth of monarchical power.

Though rejected by most historians today, the 'crisis' interpretation is not entirely without merit. On the contrary, the changes observed by the older generation of historians suggest a profound transformation of elite society and its relationship to the crown. What distinguishes older 'crisis' theories from more recent revisionist interpretations is primarily the conclusions drawn from these observed changes. The revised view sees a major and life-saving transformation of the aristocracy based on an infusion of new blood, new money, and new talents from below. Crisis then becomes a matter of upward social mobility, a historical phenomenon that preserved the nobility, though in an altered and enlarged form, and inhibited the development of a bourgeois class consciousness. Moreover, a reinvigorated nobility at times constituted a significant check on monarchical authority and limited the expansion of royal power.

Why is it that historians have reached such vastly different conclusions about these changes in elite society? How could the same historical phenomena be interpreted earlier in terms of crisis and decline, while later

7

historians would characterize them in terms of evolution, revitalization, adaptation, and preservation? What changes inspired such divergence of opinion?

Crisis Interpretation

Among the challenges faced by the nobility of France in the late Middle Ages, none was more threatening to its *raison d'être* than the military revolution. Europe experienced in the late medieval and early modern periods a revolution in warfare based largely on the rise of infantry tactics. The Hundred Years War had seen the introduction of these first in the use of the longbow and then in the use of gunpowder. The advantages of new technology and the infantry tactics that accompanied them were clear after the battle of Crécy in 1346. Over time the mounted warrior noble was supplanted by the common foot soldier, who could be trained in less time with less expense. Warfare came to rely more on this man and less on the mounted knight. Gone then was the dominant military rationale for a fighting nobility and for its privileged place in European society.

These changes in military technology and tactics unfolded at the very time that many noble families were becoming extinct. The late Middle Ages was a period of demographic crisis for the nobility and noble families frequently saw their last male heir die in battle. The Hundred Years War took a major toll on aristocratic families in bringing to an end the male line, which in turn meant the end to their claims to nobility. As fiefs escheated back to the feudal overlord and crown, aristocratic numbers dwindled. And this, combined with the chance extinction of families brought on by their failure to produce a male heir, meant that the nobility lost significant numerical strength.

What demographic strength it retained was diluted by the increasing incidence of marriage with the bourgeoisie. In the fifteenth and sixteenth centuries, the number of exogamous (outside their social group) marriages grew as noble families began to select partners from the growing middle class. Why would a social group that had for so long practiced endogamy begin to look for spouses from the ranks below? The answer is simple but very important and revealing. They looked to highly successful bourgeois families for brides who brought the wealth of handsome dowries. Their approach to marriage was mercenary, and it reflected the values of European society in the late Middle Ages and early modern periods. Their calculating approach to marriage was consistent with prevailing notions of family priorities and criteria for such unions. Among the criteria for a good match were the social status of both families and the wealth that each could contribute to the marriage. As financial problems dogged the nobility, money often surpassed status as the major criterion in the decision-making process.

Money, or the size of a dowry, assumed even greater importance in marriage deliberations as more noble families fell upon hard times. The economic dislocation associated with the great catastrophe of the bubonic plague had seen aristocratic fortunes erode. In reducing the population of western and central Europe by nearly one-third, the plague caused demand for agricultural commodities to drop and simultaneously created a scarcity of agricultural labor. Those whose fortunes were based on land – the nobility – were in trouble: their wealth generated substantially less income. Moreover, the crisis of the plague era was not alleviated by the recovery of the population in the late fifteenth and sixteenth centuries. Although this recovery generated growing demand, when combined with the vast influx of bullion from the Americas, it created the inflation of the so-called Price Revolution. Economic historians have debated the causes of this inflation and its effects; what is known with certainty is that there was an inflationary trend in the sixteenth century and that it was to the disadvantage of those whose incomes were price inelastic, that is, those whose income was based on land (occupied by peasants with long-term – 100-year – leases). Noble families experienced the crisis of inflation and declining real income to such an extent that the *hoberaux*, broken down and impoverished noble families, became a feature of the French countryside, at the time that bourgeois families had begun to make fortunes in domestic and overseas trade.

But they still had political power as the lords of feudal estates – or did they? Here too they were losing ground. The sixteenth century saw the rise of the modern bureaucratic state in which political power was increasingly wielded by those occupying the growing number of government offices. Officeholding presupposed an education in law, a condition that disqualified the sons of many noble families. Instead, it was the sons of wealthy merchant families who acquired the requisite training to move into the courts. Called to government service as a means of improving the social standing of his family, the bourgeois son was an agent of upward social mobility. Officeholding became an important avenue of ennoblement, as certain offices conferred nobility instantly and others conferred it over the course of three generations. In this way an officeholding nobility, the famous *noblesse de robe*, emerged to rival and oppose the political power of the old warrior nobility, the *noblesse d'épée*.

What would become of the old warrior nobility, excluded from political power by their own ignorance and by the virtual monopoly of government posts held by the emerging robe? Its last major stand would come during the Wars of Religion. The nobility would seize the opportunity presented by civil war to revolt against the crown and to gather whatever it could. In the process, the nobles would do irreparable harm to their reputations, and the excesses committed during the wars would bring them into disrepute. The very ideal of nobility came into question in the late sixteenth century. After all, nobility, many argued, was the way in which one conducted oneself – it meant virtue. And yet the old noble families of France had run amok during the wars; their behavior had been far from virtuous. They had disgraced themselves, and in the process they had revealed themselves to be ignoble. They were no better than anyone else now, or so many critics argued.

Here we have it – the various crises experienced and confronted by the French nobility in the fifteenth and sixteenth centuries. For traditional historians, these problems added up to decline. Numerical decline, economic hardship, dilution from intermarriage, the erosion of political power, and the disappearance of a noble rationale all combined with the criticism of the rest of society to bring to an end the period of aristocratic dominance.

More Recent Interpretations

For most historians working more recently, these problems and changes have taken on a different meaning and significance. They are viewed as part of a tranformation of the nobility, an evolution that enlarged and preserved this elite, albeit in a more complex form. How might these changes be viewed as the metamorphosis of the nobility?

Let us begin with the military revolution and its implications for the nobility. It is undeniable that warfare was changing substantially during the early modern period and that the common infantryman would become the backbone of armies. But who would command these units, what type of individual was best suited to lead in warfare? The noble – the individual with a family tradition of warfare, the person who came from a culture of warriors. In short, the nobility retained control of matters military as the officer corps of the early modern army. Although military technology and tactics may have changed in revolutionary ways, methods of recruiting troops changed only gradually. Recruitment in the early modern army was still essentially medieval, that is, personal and based on ties of dependency. For this reason, the noble was indispensable. He staffed the army with his clients, his relations, and his peasants, all individuals bound to him by one sort of obligation or another. Furthermore, military service, by providing access to royal patronage, remained one of the most successful means of advancing the interests of one's house and one's clients.[1]

Although military service might bring royal favors, the financial reality of leadership and recruitment was that often these aristocrats were forced to bear much of the expense of maintaining the units that they had called to arms. That nobles continued to fulfill a military role, even at the risk of great personal expense, is testimony to the social importance of military service. The profession of arms continued to carry social prestige and privilege.[2] For this reason its appeal was not limited to the old families who had been fighting for generations: more recently ennobled families also sought military positions for their sons. In so doing, they sought the prestige that success in warfare would bring to their houses. In seventeenth-century Aix-en-Provence, approximately equal numbers of both old and new families placed their sons in the profession of arms. Moreover, both kinds of families seemed to move easily in and out of the military, as circumstance dictated. Sons could serve in the army or navy while waiting to take over their fathers' government positions. Commissions were passed from father to son. The ease with which these families shifted from the sword to the robe, and vice versa, challenges the idea of a great occupational and cultural barrier between the professions.[3]

With the expansion of the army that occurred during the reigns of Louis XIII and Louis XIV, opportunity abounded for young nobles to serve.[4] From the reign of Henry IV to 1683, the peacetime royal army increased by ten times, and its officer corps was overwhelmingly noble. Although their preference for military service varied significantly from one province to the next, their dominance as officers is indisputable.[5] Warfare continued to be a major part of aristocratic culture, but what it was to be a nobleman had become much more complex.

By the second half of the sixteenth century, it was widely believed that the nobility occupied an elevated position in society as a result of the natural order of the universe in which human beings were arranged hierarchically. There was a natural explanation for the existence of social elites – it was part of the natural order, and their purpose was to use their advantages for the welfare of the rest of society. Such conduct required education and cultivation, and it was possible to inculcate virtue in the nobility because of their natural predisposition or proclivity to it. Implicit in this understanding of social hierarchy was the idea that lineage, *race*, lay at the heart of nobility. Through the concept of race, ideas of nobility were reconciled with the social reality of nobility by birth. What Arlette Jouanna refers to as the mythic concept of race involved the belief that noble families merited being on top because of their inherited qualities and the good things they did, with a little instruction and guidance, for the rest of society.[6]

What were the properties of aristocratic virtue? What forms did it take? Closely associated with traditional ideas of nobility was that it was a profession of valor and that nobles acted virtuously on the battlefield. Their job was to defend society in battle with courage, honesty, and loyalty to one's commander. The problem was, however, that this idea of nobility ran counter to the social realities of the late sixteenth century when most nobles enjoyed their privileged status by birth and when, in fact, they often acted less than virtuously. The period of the Wars of Religion in France saw nobles act in ways that ultimately provoked a great debate of a moralist nature about the nature and meaning of nobility. Moreover, the sixteenth century saw many critics emerge to write about the nobility's ignorance and anti-intellectualism. The backwardness of the traditional nobility was the subject of numerous pamphlets and treatises in the period, and many nobles lamented their loss of political power and offices to those who were better educated. Apologists proposed a program for the rehabilitation of the nobility, and some pronoble authors were, in fact, nobles who saw education as the only way to restore virtue and to retain political power.[7]

An important outcome of this discourse was that noble apologists redefined what was meant by nobility in ways that better accommodated social reality. By the end of the sixteenth century, some authors began to describe virtue in more inclusive terms, in ways that would justify a place for the robe within the privileged rank. Aristocratic excesses during the Wars of Religion had brought disrepute to the nobility and undermined its claims to inherited virtue, indeed its claims to meritocracy. The wars enlivened social antagonisms between elites and the common people, and elites closed ranks in a common defense based on race to maintain a natural and hierarchically ordered society. Both sword and robe relied on concepts of natural superiority/inferiority to retain their privileged status and to defend themselves against the threat of disorder from those situated beneath them.[8]

What then was the meaning of nobility by the seventeenth century? There were now a number of signs of nobility, in addition to the profession of arms. As society evolved, money, office, and education provided access to noble status and privilege, so that warfare became only one of several *marques de noblesse*. One could become a nobleman by letters of ennoblement or by occupying certain government offices; money proved the crucial ingredient in both cases and education proved important in the latter. Jean-Marie Constant found that in seventeenth-century Beauce officeholding became the most common path to ennoblement, replacing fiefholding and military service to a considerable extent.[9] Officeholding also offered families access to nobility in places like Aix, Grenoble, and Rennes, the seats of sovereign courts. Many entered the nobility by these paths, thereby contributing to the transformation of ideas of nobility and aristocratic virtue.

How was virtue taught? A young nobleman first learned the art of warfare, and in the lessons of war he encountered the great lessons of life. This was true because warfare required a knowledge of the past, particularly of the ancients, a belief universally accepted by the seventeenth century and one that reflected the impact of Renaissance humanism. Also, by the late sixteenth century a body of literature had emerged that addressed the compatibility of arms and letters and urged nobles to profit from the knowledge and experience available in classical literature and history.[10] This view suggested that successful engagement of the enemy demanded an empirical approach to warfare and to human affairs. In this way the study of war led to 'a powerful engagement with contemporary intellectual life'.[11] As the technology of warfare changed, so did the psychology and mentality employed on the battlefield. Gunpowder undermined chivalry as a code of battle; conduct was determined by effectiveness, not honor or ethics, and effectiveness was the result of rational calculation requiring training and formal preparation.[12]

In what institutional and social context could the young nobleman learn the scientific and moral lessons of warfare? One short-lived place was in the new academies for nobles. Noble apologists, concerned about the apparent loss of virtue during the Wars of Religion, advocated formal education as a means of inculcating virtue in the young nobleman. Specifically, they called for the union of arms and letters in the education of the gentleman, and some argued for the creation of academies strictly for the education and preservation of the nobility.[13]

The curriculum of noble academies reflected the traditional relationship between the nobility and the military, but it also emphasized letters.

In fact, military subjects provided access to letters, since students read about riding and the equestrian arts. They studied mathematics in order to learn the science of fortification. The academies also taught history, music, and other subjects that reflected the humanist influence and Renaissance concepts of the perfect gentleman and served to redefine the nobility in cultural terms. Indeed, culture itself became a new *marque de noblesse*.[14] The nobility came to value education as a new means of distinguishing itself from the rest of society. In this context, language assumed special importance. The ideal aristocrat would be a well-spoken individual who was adept at the fine art of conversation, the product of a very specific educational program. To fashion such an individual required the classical humanities, but the goal was to produce, rather than erudite scholars, 'knowledgeable spectators able to decode the mythological references of court ballets or the Latin mottos carried by riders in equestrian festivals'.[15] Such concerns suggest that the nobility used the classics for the superficial attributes that they conferred on the student and not to cultivate an empathetic understanding of the sources themselves. Certainly, the ambitions of noble families did not always conform precisely to the loftier goals of the humanists whose educational programs guided them, but humanism contributed more than just civility and urbanity to the meaning of what it was to be noble. Among those families destined to hold office, the humanist program was taken to heart for the emphasis it gave to Latin, rhetoric, and Roman law, all essential by the late sixteenth century for a career as a magistrate.

For court aristocrats and provincial magistrates, the culture of the nobility evolved significantly from the sixteenth century through the seventeenth century. As we have seen, this evolution took place in response to noble critics and apologists and came to reflect the basic social reality that birth had replaced valor as the basis of nobility. But other, broader, social and cultural forces also propelled this evolution.

Historians have argued that elite society was self-consciously refashioned in an effort to achieve separation and distinction from popular culture. In other words, elites purposefully pulled away and distanced themselves from popular culture in a variety of ways. Literacy and formal education played an obvious role in this process, but there were other, more subtle, behavioral changes as well. Manners, or the way in which people comported themselves, was another means by which elites sought to achieve distance from the lower orders. They created distinction through complex codes of etiquette and civility. Underlying the immense social power of etiquette was the fact that early modern Europe was to a considerable extent a society of orders in which aristocratic identity rested on honor and esteem, that is, on social opinion. One's behavior and society's response to it was definitive, and it was the rest of society that viewed nobles as honorable and conferred privileges upon them.[16] Etiquette became a major force in the society and culture of the French nobility because it allowed them to reinforce the ideas of distinction and honor. Nobles behaved in distinctive and prescribed ways. With the court as the model, civility evolved as an elaborately codified means by which to display publicly the rank or status of an individual.[17] Table manners served as a social marker; nobles ate with knives and forks. It was not simply a matter of abundance, though the bounty of the table certainly brought distinction upon a house; it was also a matter of how one actually consumed food in the presence of others.

But early modern ideas of civility extended beyond the capacity to manipulate table utensils. They came to involve the much broader concept of *honnêteté*, which incorporated a moralistic quality. *Honnêteté* referred to refinement *and* virtue, and it appears to have developed in opposition to court society which some criticized for its excesses. In contrast, *honnêteté* reflected restraint and the idea of *proper* behavior.[18] In the *honnête homme*, or honest man, one finds more than just charm and grace: the *honnête homme* exhibited a defining moral and intellectual quality.[19] By the early seventeenth century, nobles had access to a large and growing etiquette and *honnêteté* literature which included the prototype, Castiglione's *Courtier*, as well as Nicolas Faret's widely read *The Honnête Homme, or, The Art of Pleasing at Court*. Provincial nobles, as well as the court aristocracy, found this literature indispensable when they instructed their children in the decorum that brought honor and esteem to their families. As generations were reared to seek distinction through education and civility, the culture of nobility evolved as one of sophistication and cultivation, which replaced to some extent the culture of valor.

Education also had the additional and very practical benefit of preparing nobles for service to the state.[20] This involved the occupation of offices in the rapidly expanding bureaucracy of the early modern monarchy. The size of government began to expand significantly during the reign of Francis I, who, for reasons of financial expediency, created offices, some of them useless, in order to sell them. As the state became more bureaucratic, so did the means by which political power was exercised. To gain and maintain political power in this context, it was essential to hold and control government offices. As the nobility observed bourgeois and upwardly mobile families occupy and infiltrate government, it became apparent to them that offices offered new access to power. They responded by acquiring offices at all levels of government and at an increasing rate. It was in the context of rapidly growing government, political opportunities, and the public sphere that the nobility came to define itself not only in terms of lineage, but in terms of personal ambition and success as well. By the seventeenth century nobles used the language of ambition and self-construction to describe their lives. Their memoirs celebrated their individual successes, and their libraries included an expanding how-to literature which offered guidance to the ambitious young nobleman who hoped to rise beyond his modest origins by his own talents and ambition. Even the son of a wealthy family was expected to construct for himself a life of public service. Ambition could find expression in the spheres of both sword and robe, but the growth of the state created political opportunities that were largely new to the nobleman.[21]

It was particularly true that old noble families in the provinces embraced these new opportunities, and they moved rapidly into the various provincial parlements. In Rouen during the sixteenth century, the parlementaires often came from established noble families, and many had been recruited by the great aristocracy who used powers of patronage to secure these positions for their clients.[22] In seventeenth-century Aix, where the occupational distinctions between sword and robe were non-existent, approximately the same proportion of old and new noble families occupied offices in the provincial courts.[23] And in the Parlement of Brittany, almost equal numbers of sword and robe families held office during the seventeenth century.[24]

If government office brought old nobles of the sword together with the newer nobles of the robe, then marriage drew them even closer. The marriage patterns of elite society served to promote upward mobility, to narrow the gap between sword and robe, and to some extent compensated for a family's lack of antiquity. Among provincial elites, intermarriage was widespread, and old and new families intermarried routinely. By 1695 the urban nobility of Aix was a complex mixture, because 70 per cent of the new noble families and 73 per cent of the old noble families had intermarried at least once since 1500.[25] Similar patterns occurred in Bayeux during the period 1430–1669. Here new nobles married more often with old noble families than they did within their own social group.[26] By regular intermarriage, assimilation occurred between old and new families. As their family trees became enmeshed and intertwined, it was harder for old families to hold those more recently ennobled in contempt. Intermarriage promoted cohesion, but it did not eliminate hierarchy.

Just as society was arranged hierarchically, so the nobility itself was organized according to rank and status. Several factors gave shape to this hierarchy: titles and antiquity, wealth, and family connections. The history of an aristocratic family and its claims to nobility, as well as the titles held by that family, influenced in obvious ways its status within the bounds of elite society. Wealth also contributed to status or the perception of status. It enabled a family to engage in conspicuous consumption, which over the course of the sixteenth century became itself a *marque de noblesse*. Expenditure on homes, furnishings, and fashions set the nobility apart from the poorer classes and at the same created distinctions or levels within the nobility. How much wealth did it take to engage in conspicuous consumption, and how did nobles obtain such wealth?

The economic changes of the sixteenth century had seen the impoverishment of many noble families. Still, most were not poor, and some were enormously wealthy. It was the middling nobles who tended to grow in number and to increase their share of national wealth over the course of the early modern period.[27] And their financial success was the result of their willingness and ability to adapt to changing economic circumstances. Specifically, it was this middle rung that most completely made the transition to a capitalist economy. Although much of their wealth continued to be tied up in land, they exploited their realty in an aggressively capitalistic manner, that is, in a manner that reflected the development of a market economy and production for that market. First, this meant managing and cultivating the domain directly, rather than just collecting feudal revenues, and, when possible, expanding the domain. Second, it meant cultivating and producing for a market. Following the ebb and flow of the market, the population and its patterns of consumption, nobles produced accordingly.[28]

There were other forms of capitalist investment open to nobles in early modern France. *Rentes*, or government bonds, offered the opportunity to loan money at interest by investing in the royal debt. Traditionally, nobles in most of France had not engaged in commerce or moneylending; in fact, to do so meant risking derogation, or the loss of noble status, because handling and making money at another's expense was considered conduct beneath a nobleman. *Rentes*, on the other hand, opened the door to a socially acceptable form of moneylending that did not place one's noble status in jeopardy. The growth of the state and government spending on warfare increased royal indebtedness and gave rise to a public debt. By purchasing these bonds and funding the public debt, the nobleman was considered to be performing an act of civic virtue.[29]

The money made on such public investments could be reinvested in more land, in government offices, in strategic marriages, in discreet commercial adventures, and on the lifestyle of a nobleman. In this way, wealth made plain the levels of nobility and a family's position in that hierarchy. To a broader public, rank was displayed through possessions: the country house, the *hôtel* or town house, their furnishings, and the opulence of one's wardrobe. These were the insignia of nobility that communicated one's rank within the elite and society as a whole.

Patrons and Clients

By the very nature of hierarchy, a noble's rank was, of course, relative to those above and those below. In fact, rank depended to a great degree on the specific connections that one held with patrons above and clients below, as aristocratic society was organized by a series of vertical ties known as the patron–client system.[30] The nature of such relationships has been examined and debated by a small group of historians, and there is significant variation in the way in which they have interpreted the emotional content of clientage connections. This book relies on Sharon Kettering's vision of the patron–client relationship which argues that its ties, or personal connections, were based upon 'obligatory reciprocity', a relationship in which '. . . a patron was obliged to reward the loyal service of a client if he wanted to retain his service, and a client was obliged to repay a patron's material generosity with loyal service if he wanted patronage in the future'.[31] These relationships were personal and informal. Their reciprocal nature meant that they were negotiated on an ongoing basis. The contributions of the client were evaluated together with the rewards of the patron; if serious neglect or deficiencies occurred on either side, the relationship could be, and often was, dissolved. Patrons could easily recruit new clients, and clients could enlist with new patrons, though such shifts in affiliation were generally easier for the patron as a result of his or her greater rank and resources. Patrons had greater flexibility in that they had more to give, and the rewards they distributed were tangible and often material, in contrast to the services provided by a client.[32]

Kettering's explanation conveys variations in this complex system. Within the patron–client spectrum, she argues that some connections involved a much greater degree of friendship and loyalty, the so-called *fidèles*, and were often formed as a result of family or pre-existing personal ties. Some relationships advanced significantly the administrative career of the client, or *créature*, so that he owed everything to his patron or protector. And some relationships, simply known as clients, brought together neighbors or colleagues and were less personal and less dependent. A clientele could exist within a great noble household, or it could exist within a province and its institutions. Or, it could extend to both.[33]

What sorts of things could a patron provide for a client to enlist his loyalty and service? Patrons tended to the material needs of their clients. Often this meant securing a government office or a commission in the army, and in return the client was supposed to serve the patron's interests. Effective and loyal service could mean additional rewards for the client and even for other members of his family. A patron who found a devoted and able client was more likely to recruit the client's family on the assumption that the whole clan would conduct themselves similarly.[34] Henri de Séguiran, sieur de Bouc and first president of the Cour des Comptes in Aix, was a client of Cardinal Richelieu. Thanks to the largesse of his patron, Séguiran was made a naval lieutenant-general in 1632 and was dispatched on a rather celebrated inspection of the coastal fortifications along the Mediterranean. A devoted client, Séguiran asked the cardinal to make his son and brother captains of galleys. Richelieu obliged him by bestowing these positions on his family, and then went on to reward Séguiran himself further. Good service brought good rewards.[35]

Patronage might also mean a place in the household of the patron. The size of a noble household reflected its degree of rank within the nobility. In this sense, a household and the patronage opportunities that it offered were a form of aristocratic conspicuous consumption. The greater the house, the greater its household. The royal court served as the model for noble households, and just as it grew over the course of the sixteenth and seventeenth centuries, so the households of the French nobility also increased in size and complexity.[36] 'Such households created material interdependence of the great and more modest noblemen within it.'[37] And the population of a household was not stable – there were some nobles who remained in the patron's company on a regular basis, but others came and went. This was true also of the commoners who constituted an important and large element within the household. As one historian of nobility writes, 'The term "household" describes the environment in which prominent nobles always lived, surrounded by a group of attendant noblemen and commoners. This environment was thoroughly portable ... It consisted of people of varying ranks who lived together intermittently but with easy familiarity, providing concrete services for each other.'[38]

Not all patron–client relationships were this direct or straightforward. There also existed a three-party version in which a broker mediated between patron and client. The broker brought together patrons and clients who would otherwise never have been joined because of geographic or social separation. The broker negotiated the transfer of rewards for service, and enhanced these rewards with his own resources. This meant that brokers commanded significant resources and clienteles of their own which they could put at the disposal of those greater than themselves. In assisting superiors in arranging more expansive networks of clients, the broker brought more honor, power, and status upon himself. To function as a broker, a noble needed sufficient *crédit*, or reputation, status, clients, and material resources, to attract a patron and to make the system work. The successful broker was also a very important component in the story of the state in seventeenth-century France.[39] As Kettering writes:

> The society and government of early modern France was organized loosely in layers of clienteles reaching vertically to the king at court. One man's patron was another man's client, and brokers bridged the distances between patrons. When clienteles pyramided as they did when expanding horizontally and vertically, brokers handled the exchanges between levels of patrons and clients separated by distance, place, and rank. The pyramiding of clienteles produced, besides layers and layers of patrons and clients, the need for a third but not necessarily distinct role, that of broker who linked the layers.[40]

Seventeenth-century clienteles came in two forms: those constructed around the household of a great noble, and administrative clienteles constructed through institutions and around men of political and institutional power. Over the course of the seventeenth century, the provincial version of the administrative clientele would prove particularly useful to the crown and its ministers. Central government relied on provincial brokers and their administrative clienteles to effect reform and to control the periphery.[41] Manipulation of provincial clienteles was not a simple prospect. These complex networks and layers of relationships, or clienteles, were dynamic and constantly changing. Some relationships were permanent and others lasted only briefly because one party or the other was dissatisfied or found a more promising connection elsewhere.

In 1636 the same Henri de Séguiran left the clientele of Richelieu because the cardinal had not secured for him a position that he was most anxious to acquire – the office of first president of the Parlement of Aix. Séguiran felt neglected by the cardinal, that the cardinal had fallen short on reciprocity, and so he departed Richelieu's service.[42]

The frequency with which realignments took place suggests that self-interest was the overriding consideration in patron–client relations. This does not preclude the possibility of fidelity binding person to person; rather, it means that more often these ties were self-serving and impermanent. For this reason, the patron–client relationship is not simply a later incarnation of the feudal relationship. Moreover, the fact that these vertical ties were not fixed or permanent meant that early modern government could redirect them in its own interests.[43] In this process, the broker played the crucial role. In the sixteenth century, brokers were recruited from the ranks of *les grands*, that is, from the greater nobility, because it was they who held the positions of provincial governors and lieutenants-general. They used their authority to create extensive clienteles that assisted them in governing the provinces, and they dispensed royal patronage to their clients in the provinces. This ultimately proved tremendously problematic for the central government, because it enabled *les grands* to form huge clienteles that could be directed in ways contrary to the interests of the crown. In the second half of the sixteenth century, the French crown fell victim to the competing interests of these great clienteles and the opposing religious communities for which they spoke.[44]

In the seventeenth century, this situation changed dramatically in ways that served the interests of the crown and the provincial nobilities, and in ways that limited the power of *les grands*. Cardinal Richelieu constructed his own clienteles in the provinces and did not use the provincial governors as brokers. He did not eliminate the role of broker; instead, he chose his brokers more carefully. He avoided the governors and focused on officials in provincial and municipal institutions. These men became his clients and his brokers, and proved more loyal than the governors. Most came from less important older houses or from new houses. Prominent in a provincial context, but obscure to court society, these individuals headed their own clienteles that had fully infiltrated provincial and municipal institutions. Richelieu's less illustrious brokers harnessed local and provincial institutions to the crown, and the crown would ultimately succeed in using the provincial nobility to strengthen its hold on the realm.[45] The provincial nobility was, as we shall see, crucial to the interests of the crown and state-building. As local elites they held the key to monarchical control of the provinces, especially at the periphery. It was the more remote provinces, such as Languedoc, Provence, Dauphiné, Normandy, and Brittany, that had resisted vigorously the intrusion of central authority, and it was their elites that would enter into a collaborative arrangement with the crown to effect absolutism.

Provincial Nobility

What was the provincial nobility and where did it fit in the greater scheme? By provincial nobility we mean a group largely separated from the court nobility and *les grands* by geography, wealth, and lifestyle. It is important to recognize, however, that a portion of the provincial nobility was tied to the court nobility through patronage. Provincial nobles dominated the region politically, economically, and socially. They were big fish in a smaller – though not small – pond, and they held the keys to controlling the province. For Jean-Marie Constant and Laurent Bourquin there was a hierarchy within the provincial nobility that defined those families that were prominent and powerful within the provincial context separately from the lesser nobility. This provincial upper crust constituted what Constant first classified as *la noblesse seconde*: families that might be tied to the grandees but that commanded their own clientele of lesser nobles in the province.[46] They exercised political control through the traditional seigneurial regime, through the military, and through provincial administrative institutions such as the parlements, the financial bureaucracy, and the provincial estates. Often they dominated town councils and municipal institutions as well. These were the individuals involved in the routine affairs of governing the province. Some of them were provincial power-brokers. It was the provincial nobility of Languedoc, for example, that constituted much of the ruling elite of that region. William Beik has given us an elaborate description of the ruling elite of Languedoc, including how they controlled the region and how they struck deals with the central government in the second half of the seventeenth century. As he describes this group, 'Their position might derive from inherited status, from control of the resources needed to dominate production on the land, or from a privileged relationship to the state machine; usually it involved all three. Most nobles, old and new, were included . . . '[47] Beik estimates this group to have numbered about 10 000 of a total provincial population of between 1 000 000 and 1 500 000, which is a fraction of 1 per cent of the population. Within the ruling elite, there were 223 'truly influential powers' based on political and social power, and, of these, Beik describes 51 as 'chief power-brokers'.[48]

Languedoc's chief power-brokers held offices that positioned them strategically to control the province. In Table 1.1, Beik lays out the provincial positions in which real power resided. Their minuscule number is evidence of the very hierarchical nature of early modern society and explains how a few strategically placed choices of clients could open the door to provincial influence and control.

The wealth of the Languedocian ruling elite formed in part the basis of their power, and that wealth ranged from families among the richest in the kingdom to families on a par with successful bourgeois and small-time

Table 1.1   The 'truly influential powers' (in descending order of importance)

1. Archbishop of Narbonne	1	
2. 21 other prelates	21	
3. Governor	1	
4. First president of the Parlement	1	
5. First president of the Comptes	1	
6. Treasurer of the bourse	1	
7. Intendant	1	
8. Présidents à mortier of the Parlement	11	
9. Presidents of the Comptes	10	
10. 3 lieutenant-generals of the province	3	
Subtotal	51	chief brokers of power
11. 20 most influential councillors from the Parlement + the 3 royal prosecutors	23	
12. 20 most influential councillors from the Comptes + the 3 royal prosecutors	23	
13. 3 syndic-generals for the province	3	
14. 20 leading treasurer-generals of finance	20	
15. 22 diocesan syndics 'en exercice'	22	
16. 9 seneschals and baillis	9	
17. 10 barons of the estates who attended regularly	10	
18. 20 officers from sénéchaussée courts	20	
19. 20 consuls attending the estates	20	
20. 22 diocesan receivers 'en exercice'	22	
Subtotal	172	other influential powers
Total	223	individuals

Source: William Beik, *Absolutism and Society in Seventeenth-Century France: State Power and Provincial Aristocracy in Languedoc* (Cambridge, 1985), p. 44.

country squires.[49] This was true of provincial nobilities in general, and there were tangible social markers that, regardless of wealth, indicated to the rest of society that a family enjoyed noble status. Obviously, the style, size, and decor of a domicile said something about the social status of its occupants. Nobles lived in country houses, and in most parts of France this was their primary or only (depending on income level) residence.[50]

The *château*, or country house, evolved during the sixteenth century from a medieval fortification to a structure that was designed and decorated according to Renaissance aesthetic values. Many *châteaux* were conglomerations of medieval fortification and more modern additions and redecorations.[51] As the size and magnificence of the *château* reflected the wealth and status of the family, so did the quantity and quality of its furnishings. In one of the few studies made of the material settings of aristocratic households, Kristen Neuschel has analyzed the structure and contents of the *châteaux* of high-ranking noblemen in sixteenth-century Picardy. One outstanding fact is that the design of the *château* and its contents allowed for great flexibility. This was essential because the provincial nobility, with the means to do so, hosted a population that constantly fluctuated. Guests, clients, and servants routinely came and went. The most stable element in the household population were the domestic servants and guards, and their presence remained constant, but they were joined by others whose number ranged enormously. The household had to be equipped to handle large numbers of people with little notice.[52]

To accommodate changing numbers of people, nobles provisioned their households with portable furniture. This included various kinds of sleeping arrangements, among them numerous beds, pallets, and camp beds (often brought along by the visitor). And when beds were not used for their primary purpose, they could be used as seating. The household also included stools, chairs, and benches for flexible seating; trunks, dressers, and buffets for storage; and trestle tables allowed for greater or lesser numbers of people to be served at mealtimes.[53]

By the seventeenth century the furnishings of *châteaux* and urban town houses had become significantly more elaborate and numerous because the interior of the home came to assume even greater importance to the family. It offered concrete evidence of a family's wealth, station, taste, and refinement. We find a proliferation of items and greater concern with their decorative features. Notaries who conducted testamentary inventories took special care in describing foreign and exotic items. Their meticulous descriptions of materials and origins highlight the fact that connoisseurship had become a hallmark of elite society. For example, in 1668 Anne de la Croix, widow of Abel de Simiane, president to the Chambre des Comptes du Dauphiné, died, and her heirs commissioned a local notary to conduct an inventory of the contents of her household. Starting with the room in which she died, the notary painstakingly recorded and described every item. His list was extensive and detailed, and he was careful to mention the country of origin for imported items. Among the decorative elements recorded were tapestries from Flanders, Turkish rugs, coverlets from Catalonia and as far away as India, and table coverings in tapestry from Bergamo in Italy.[54] A few years later similar items appeared in the inventory of the estate of Abel de Buffevant, a councillor in the Cours des Comptes in Grenoble. His well-appointed home contained several Bergamo tapestries, a Turkish rug, toile draperies from Holland, and table linens from Venice.[55]

The consumption patterns of noble households are important because they suggest a desire to display social and economic status through careful choices of possessions and sometimes through the mere weight of their ability to consume. By choosing imported items, families sought to create a subtle kind of distinction that incorporated a taste for the foreign and the exotic. Imported elements offered evidence of a family's wealth, and the preference for such possessions reflected a worldliness that defined the seventeenth-century nobility as an elite whose cultural evolution had taken it well beyond the warrior culture of its medieval predecessor. Whether every provincial noble family that owned oriental rugs appreciated their aesthetic qualities or the culture that produced them is, of course, doubtful, but the desire to own such an item is very significant. Through their patterns of consumption, provincial families participated, to varying degrees, in a culture of nobility that was marked by advancing levels of education, refinement, and civility.

Among the household possessions, libraries were a blueprint of refinement. To suggest that nobles bought books merely to cultivate an aura of connoisseurship would be misleadingly reductionist, because intellectual curiosity on the part of a better-educated elite prompted in many cases their desire for books. But a geniune interest in the world of ideas did not preclude the possibility that noble men and women were aware of the social benefits that book acquisition might confer. Their desire to possess the written word would have been driven by both intellectual forces and social forces, with one reinforcing the other. By their choices of books, nobles indicated the subjects and ideas that they considered most important, for both their intrinsic intellectual value and their acquired social and cultural value. Of course, not all provincial nobles owned a full library; many households included only a cabinet's worth, a few dozen books or less.[56]

Book ownership in late seventeenth-century Paris tended to be greater among parlementaires and families occupying important administrative positions than it was among the old nobility and lower level officials.[57] There was a highly predictable relationship between career, education, and book ownership, and this was also the case in the provinces. In seventeenth-century Aix-en-Provence, where both old and new noble families pursued careers in the courts and were similarly educated, the contents of their libraries were also much the same. Legal writings figured prominently in the inventories of their libraries, and they also owned a wide array of classical authors, humanist works, and historical literature. Clear indication of the nobility's concern with the construction of social image was their consumption of the seventeenth-century's growing etiquette, *honnêteté*, and comportment literature.[58]

The literary tastes of the Aixois were not unlike those of other provincial nobles. The estate of François de Simiane de la Coste, president of the Parlement of Grenoble, included an impressive selection of Greek and Roman titles ranging from Homer and Herodotus to Virgil and Titus Livy. His list of Renaissance and contemporary authors was also extensive: Petrarch, Boccaccio, Guicciardini, Machiavelli, Bodin, Ficino, Erasmus, Rabelais, Hobbes, and Descartes, among others. And the library held enormous historical, legal, and religious literatures as well as titles on science and mathematics (including Euclid, Ptolemy, Copernicus, and Galileo). The president also acquired (or inherited) a number of books on architecture and the art of fortification, among them the works of Alberti and Vignola. Fortification literature was standard fare for military nobles, and the fact that a president in a parlement owned such works is indicative of the kind of professional mobility that existed in the provinces. Simiane's family had pursued military as well as judicial careers. He inherited his office as president from his father, who had previously been *intendant des armées et commissaire des guerres*. Although Simiane himself does not appear to have held a commission in the army, two of his sons did.[59]

This was the social world of an early modern elite. Enlarged and made more complex by upward mobility, they dominated society through political office and exploitation of an emerging capitalist economy. Money gave them access to power, education, and refinement; society bestowed upon them the honor and esteem that were the basis of noble privilege.

As the highest-ranking member, the king's interest coincided with that of the nobility. As the head of the body politic, the king's interests at times were diametrically opposed to those of the nobility.

Political Culture of Nobility

Crown–noble relations in early modern France involved motives that, unlike centripetal and centrifugal forces, could act alternately, rather than simultaneously, to bring together and to drive apart. This is true of the crown's relations with both the great nobility and the provincial nobilities. The sixteenth century saw France torn apart by religious and civil wars in which components of the nobility were at odds with the crown or those in control of the crown. The first half of the seventeenth century was punctuated by great noble insurrections and the efforts of provincial nobles to resist the expansion of royal authority and the elimination of provincial rights.

What justified acts of aristocratic violence against the crown? On what basis did nobles claim to act and to legitimate their conduct? Was their violence and obstruction simply a matter of self-interest, of gathering for themselves and their clients all the pay-offs and power that they could? For Arlette Jouanna, Denis Crouzet, and Jean-Marie Constant aristocratic behavior cannot be explained solely or even primarily in terms of material benefits or self-aggrandizement.[60] These historians have argued instead for an ideological basis. In looking at the period of the Wars of Religion, Crouzet describes how religious ideology propelled aristocratic violence. Jouanna focuses on the relationship between aristocratic behavior and the birth of the modern state during the period 1559–1661. Specifically, she analyzes the conjunction of the patron–client system and noble political ideology during the late sixteenth and early seventeenth centuries.

The political culture of nobility involved the belief that authority resided not only in the king, but in the nobility and the people as well. The king represented the head of the body politic and provided direction for the state, but he did not do so without consultation, because sovereignty rested with the entire body politic. This notion of shared sovereignty was reinforced by contemporary notions of kingship which involved the theory of the king's two bodies.[61] The king possessed an individual body that would someday perish because it was subject to the limitations of the human condition. But the king also had a second, political, body, a sort of mystical body. His individual body was the head, but the three estates constituted the remainder of the mystical body. This second body was therefore incomplete without the other members. In the context of the religious violence of the late sixteenth century, if the individual body of the king were a prisoner, or if the officers of the crown were engaged in policies and activities that were injurious to the political body, the members were justified in defending the body. In this way, by taking up arms against his individual body, they were fighting not against, but for the political body of the king.[62]

The theory of the king's two bodies complemented the theory of mixed monarchy that gained currency with humanists and classically inspired political theorists during the sixteenth century. Responding to Aristotle's *Politics*, theorists constructed a historical case for the French constitution being a mixed monarchy. It combined a fundamentally monarchical character with an aristocracy and an Estates-General (an element of democracy) to arrive at shared sovereignty. The aristocracy was a 'natural' elite that was fundamental to the body politic; through the royal council they influenced policy and exercised their power. The idea of shared power, or mixed monarchy, appears prominently in the political texts of the period of the Wars of Religion, when authors invoked notions of *patrie* and the public good (*le bien public*) to justify rebellion against the individual body of the king and the threat of absolutism. As the 'natural' elite of the body politic, it was the duty of the nobility to reject policies that did not seek the public good.[63]

In describing the political theory behind aristocratic resistance, Jouanna admits that rebellion often served the personal goals of those who rebelled, but she argues that this did not preclude the political culture of the nobility providing an ideological basis and legitimacy for taking up arms against the king. She argues that the cause of mixed monarchy served the nobility. It served the grandees that led rebellion, and it served to mobilize their clients beneath them. Defending the concept of shared sovereignty might bring tangible material benefits, but their lure did not outweigh the nobles' sense of duty.

In the early seventeenth century, the ideology of rebellion became more complex. The notion of the public good continued as an operative principle, but increasingly the literature justifying aristocratic rebellion turned to the idea of the 'relief of the people' ('*soulagement du peuple*'). Rather than addressing threats of absolutism, aristocratic authors lamented the weakness of government under the regencies and expressed sympathy for the king's subjects who endured the growing burden of taxation.

Why the change from concern over a king with absolutist tendencies to concern over a king who was too weak? For Jouanna the answer lies in the fact that the religious wars evolved political theory beyond limits that were tolerable for the nobility. Evolution from mixed monarchy to contractual monarchy was not difficult. The Monarchomaques, among others, began to write about the sovereignty of the people rather than the natural superiority of the nobility. Their tracts elevated the role of law and left no place for the personal bonds of fidelity that were the glue of the early modern state. They celebrated a contract between the king and his subjects, and in Mornay's *Vindicae contra Tyrannos* (1579), magistrates are to represent all their subjects, including a nobility, with no special relationship based on fidelity ties. Alarmed by the egalitarian implications of these ideas, the nobility produced texts that argued the need for a stronger monarch. The authoritarian tone of their political treatises was also promoted by the Politiques, who had earlier maintained that a strong central government was a necessary antidote to anarchy.[64]

The period of the Fronde also produced justifications for aristocratic rebellion. The great body of pamphlets and treatises associated with the Fronde are known as Mazarinades in recognition of the fact that the chief minister, like Richelieu before him, was known as the great public enemy. In terms of the theme of royal power, this literature does not contain new ideas, but grapples instead with the various constitutional and political principles raised in the late sixteenth and early seventeenth centuries. They too pointed out the weaknesses of the regency. One author wrote in support of what Jouanna calls the new absolutist orthodoxy: that royal power is divine; that the king is above the law; and that the people are not above the monarch. The same author argued, on behalf of Gaston d'Orléans and the princes, that, after 1651 and his majority, Louis XIV was perfectly capable himself. Hence, no need for a regent or chief minister.[65]

Not all nobles embraced absolutist theory during the civil wars of the Fronde. Indeed, internal divisions developed between the princes and grandees on one hand and the parlementaires and provincial nobles on the other. For the grandees, the period of the regency produced instability and political disequilibrium as a result of the rise of favorites. Cut off from power and patronage, they responded violently in a *coup d'état*. The goals of the grandees were absolutist in that they hoped to see Louis XIV firmly in control so that he might restore a system of court life and politics that preserved their privileged position. The middle and lower ranks of the nobility, in contrast, produced the constitutional arguments and demands most associated with the Fronde. They wrote in defense of aristocratic privilege, but they did so along earlier constitutionalist lines. Their arguments were discredited at court and among the grandees by association with the stigma of 'la *"province"* '. The Fronde revealed the chasm that separated the great nobility from the rest, from those who resided in the provinces.[66]

The 'second nobility' also produced political and resistance theories based on Christian stoicism. Constant writes about Henri de Campion, a nobleman from Normandy, who supported the count of Soissons' uprisings against Richelieu. Both Campion and his brother Alexandre wrote to justify their involvement in some of the great aristocratic revolts, and their work is representative of a corpus that emerged from the lower ranks of nobles who followed the grandees into rebellion. For Constant, the Campions' ideas comprise an early form of liberalism inspired by the morality of Christian stoicism, and which to an extent anticipates the liberal ideas of the Enlightenment. The count of Montrésor, who also opposed Richelieu, argued that the king must respect the consultative tradition, its institutions, and the law. By failing to do so, he becomes a tyrant. Constant notes that these are not precursors to Locke and Montesquieu, as nowhere do they talk about separation of powers. But their ideas were based on the belief that the prince should exhibit a stoical virtue, that he should know how to balance severity and kindness, justice and mercy. For these authors, everything rested on the character and morality of the monarch. He must not violate their freedom of speech or their political traditions.[67]

Alexandre de Campion used a historical base for his arguments and wrote with great reverence for the power of institutions to guarantee freedom. For him the Roman senate was a virtual rampart against tyranny. He wrote about the three members of the body of the Roman state, the people, the nobles, and the consuls, about how they exercised diverse kinds of authority and obedience, and functioned in harmony and equilibrium thanks to the equitable distribution of power. For Campion, the ministry of Richelieu had disrupted the equilibrium that should have existed in France's body politic. By concentrating power exclusively in his hands and in the hands of the king, he had deprived the other members of their normal and traditional role and had brought about a great crisis for the monarchy.[68]

It was the lesser nobility, whose society and culture was based on 'la province', that presented the most persistent obstacle to monarchical control of the realm. The process of dealing with the provincial nobilities was complex, spanned three reigns, and produced varied and highly localized results. This was particularly true in provinces that were *pays d'états* and in provinces located at the periphery. In central government's struggle to subdue the periphery, it was necessary to bring provincial nobilities on board, and it was this allegiance, between crown and provincial noble, that effected absolutism in seventeenth-century France.

Chapter 2: Crown: State-building

Just as historians have revised interpretations of the changes that occurred within the early modern nobility, so they have offered alternative and more finely nuanced analyses of the construction of the early modern state. Over the course of the sixteenth and seventeenth centuries, central government struggled, ultimately with a measure of success, to extend its authority from the center to the periphery of the realm. This was not a steadily deterministic process, and there were major setbacks along the way, not the least of which were decades of religious and civil war that tore the country apart at its very seams. The expansion of monarchical authority brought central government into direct conflict with the many groups, duly constituted bodies, and regions in whose interest it was to oppose and obstruct the process of state-building. Within these various expressions of regionalism, constitutionalism, and traditionalism, aristocratic voices clearly resonated. Indeed, the provincial nobilities of France figured prominently in the great episodes of conflict and resistance to reform. Finally, their complicity made possible the relations with central government that have subsequently been called absolutism.

In the Middle Ages, the relationship between the French crown and the nobility placed the monarch in the complex and circumscribed role of both suzerain and sovereign. Kings attempted to control the realm in the dual capacity of feudal overlord and monarch, relying alternately on one source of authority or the other, as historical circumstances dictated. As F. L. Ganshof writes, 'until the late twelfth century the French king could exercise power outside the royal domain only in a feudal capacity'. He is quick to point out that feudal institutions did not necessarily detract from royal authority, and he argues that elements of feudal law actually assisted the development of sovereignty.[1] Nevertheless, the limited development of royal government placed important constraints on sovereignty in the medieval period.

The Renaissance Monarchy

By the sixteenth century, the French monarchy had seen some important changes. First, many of the great semi-independent fiefdoms or provinces had come into the royal domain, which meant that in theory they fell directly under royal control. In reality, however, they still functioned nearly autonomously and they were certainly not firmly within the royal grasp. To obtain the allegiance of his new subjects, the king made concessions, including pledges to observe the traditional rights and privileges of the province. In this way, the realm, though greatly expanded, remained highly decentralized and lacked legal and institutional uniformity. For example, as a province came into the realm the king might agree to recognize its provincial parlement as a sovereign court rather than impose the Parlement of Paris as the sole court of appeals. This is particularly significant because provincial parlements exercised a legislative and administrative role; they could veto royal decrees that ran counter to provincial rights and privileges. In addition, the various parlements had the right actually to make laws, or *arrêts*, and it was this authority that saw them become involved in almost every area of governance.[2] By the very way in which the Renaissance kingdom came together, much governmental power resided at the local level.

The institutional decentralization of the Renaissance monarchy referred not only to the judicial institutions of the realm, but to the representative assemblies as well. The trend over the course of the Renaissance was for the Estates-General to meet less and for local assemblies to meet more. The tradition of assemblies was an old one that dated back to the Franks, but feudalism played the formative role in the development of representative institutions based on the fact that a lord could ask aid and counsel of his vassals. It was from the feudal custom of counsel that the idea of institutionalized representation and consultation evolved. During the Hundred Years War, because of evident necessity, meetings of these assemblies were tied to the need for taxation. The reign of Charles VII (1422–61) was particularly important in this regard. Charles abandoned the Estates-General and played to local interests by seeking approval for taxes from the provincial and local estates. His policies left France with a system of consultation and taxation that was decentralized and lacked uniformity. As J. Russell Major, the authority on representative assemblies, has shown, Charles consulted provincial assemblies in those areas already accustomed to approving taxes voted earlier by central assemblies. Conversely, he did not consult local assemblies in those regions whose estates 'had not become sufficiently established to be regarded as essential to the preservation of their privileges and to the maintenance of low taxes'.[3] In this way, a complex system was born in which the king consulted some local estates (Normandy, Brittany, Languedoc, Guyenne, Perigord, Provence, Dauphiné, and Burgundy) and not others. Those parts of France in which the tradition of the local estates persisted became known as the *pays d'états*, in contrast to those provinces where the tradition eroded. The latter became known as the *pays d'élections*, a designation that refers to the tax-collecting district presided over by the *élus* or royal tax collectors.[4]

As specific and localized as this system was, it was made even more complex by the many ways in which the main tax, the *taille*, was assessed. Northern France was subject to the *taille personnelle*, which was levied against non-noble individuals. Much of southern France was the land of the *taille réelle*, which was assessed against non-noble property (allodial property, or that which is held without overlordship and feudal obligations) regardless of the social status of the individual who owned it. Beyond this fundamental distinction in the two parts of the realm, there were other important variations. Dauphiné, for example, was a sort of hybrid region in which the mountainous areas paid the *taille réelle* and the rest of the province paid the *taille personnelle*. In Brittany, nobles were exempted from either form of the *taille*. It was also true that many towns had bargained for exemptions from the *taille*, thereby adding considerably to the complexity of the system.[5] These institutional parameters set practical limits on the power of the Renaissance monarchy.

Royal authority was not, however, solely dependent on the characteristics and effectiveness of the institutions of government. As David Potter writes, 'Rather, ritual should be seen as an important adjunct to the manipulation of power.'[6] Through symbolism kings sought to convey the sacral nature of monarchy to their subjects and make plain the divine origins of their authority. Drawing upon traditional rituals, many of which had been only recently invented, in the fifteenth and sixteenth centuries, Renaissance monarchs participated in ceremonies that served as a 'flexible vehicle for inculcating the idea of loyalty to the state embodied in the person of the king'.[7] Take, for instance, the ceremonial pageantry that occurred the first time a French king chose to enter one of the great cities of the realm. These ceremonies developed to express the bond between king and citizens in which he would respect their local traditions and privileges and they would pledge their loyalty. Municipalities celebrated a royal entry with processions, speeches, the staging of living tableaux, and the construction of all sorts of visual symbols and edifices. By the sixteenth century, cities preferred classical imagery, reflecting the influence of humanism, but biblical images were still commonplace. The king's arrival might be likened to Christ's epiphany or he might be represented as a Gallic Hercules. Whatever the choice of images, classical or biblical, the royal *entrée* was an occasion on which city fathers and the crown could symbolically represent as compatible the potentially incompatible ideals of monarchical power and urban autonomy.[8] In this sense, the royal entry was the symbolic representation of a contract.

The idea of a contract gained prominence in the political theory of the period, a trend that was closely related to the growth of self-government. The theory of contractual government derived from a number of Renaissance intellectual traditions, but its specific political context was the consultative tradition of the New Monarchies. In conferring with assorted estates and assemblies, French monarchs had confirmed the existence of a contract. Implicit in this relationship was the recognition that subjects had certain rights and privileges, among them the right to consent to taxation. But what benefits did the king derive from consultation and the limits on royal authority implied therein? Actually, the monarchy gained significant advantages as a result of consultation. First, Renaissance monarchs, sometimes finding their own bureaucracies insufficient for the task at hand, enjoyed the practical benefit of relying on the estates and their officials to perform some of the bureaucratic functions of government. Second, by conferring with these assemblies, monarchs enjoyed the theoretical advantage of securing the support of their people. What many Renaissance theorists argued was that popular support was essential to monarchical power. As consultation was the crucial means by which to insure popular support, and popular support was essential to the strength of the monarchy, 'the growth of self-government paralleled the growth of monarchical government'.[9] The tradition of consultation was not incompatible with the rise of the New Monarchies. By consultation and the manipulation of popular opinion, Renaissance monarchs attempted – with considerable success – to expand their authority.

In the sixteenth century, the role of sovereign expanded and developed along more bureaucratic lines, and as a result the monarch's relationship with the nobility changed. The reign of Francis I (1515–47) inaugurated the era of the 'New Monarchies' in France. By 'new' historians are referring to an institution that was considerably stronger than it had been during the Middle Ages and that operated through a burgeoning bureaucracy. As traditional checks on royal power eroded, new institutional means became available to the king; such changes led earlier historians to conclude that Francis I and his contemporaries were absolute monarchs.

R. J. Knecht has written extensively and most recently about the reign, and Professor Knecht attributes significant innovation to Francis. For him, however, the reign was one of only 'limited absolutism'.[10] Absolutism referred not only to the practical aspects of royal power, it also involved an alternative doctrine or body of theory that circulated in Renaissance Europe. Shaped by the sixteenth-century revival of Roman law, absolutist theory maintained that power resided with one individual who had the 'sole right to legislate, to dispense justice, to revoke all lawsuits to his court, to levy taxes and to create offices'.[11] According to Knecht, Francis I drew upon this theory as he set the monarchy on a new course. In his relations with the Parlement of Paris, for example, Francis acted in ways that became increasingly authoritarian. Moreover, he refused to call a meeting of the Estates-General, in this way undermining the consultative nature of the French monarchy which had for some time seen the king share the decision-making process with the representatives of the nation.

Beyond the attempts it saw to concentrate more authority in the hands of the king, Francis's reign is important for the administrative and bureaucratic changes that established important precedents for the centralization of government. By his reforms of the royal treasury, Francis set in motion a series of administrative changes possibly designed to centralize institutions in Paris and make uniform their agencies in the field. In this sense he began a process that would climax in the reign of Louis XIV. Specifically, in 1523 Francis established the *trésorier de l'Epargne* as a central treasury official. Eventually the king designated the treasurer as the official to whom all the royal revenues went (after local expenses had been deducted). Although the Epargne did not become the central repository that Francis had hoped it would be, it was for a time the locus of a large portion of royal revenue.[12]

Knecht has built a strong case for the authoritarian tendencies of Francis I, but he would not push the issue of royal authority too far. The survival of the provincial estates, the political privileges of many towns, the king's reliance on fiscal expedients such as the sale of offices, and the persistence of aristocratic power as expressed through the patron–client network all combined to set very real limits on the authority of the king. Still, there were changes under Francis that set this reign apart from those of his Valois predecessors and anticipated those of his Bourbon successors.[13]

J. Russell Major prefers to emphasize to an even greater extent the limits on Francis's authority. The resulting differences between the interpretations of Major and Knecht have a great deal to do with historical perspective and amount to degrees rather than fundamentally different opinions. Knecht has described them best when he writes: 'Historians, who have attempted to label the monarchy of Francis I, may be divided into two camps: those whose standpoint has been the centre of the realm, looking outwards, and those who have approached it from the periphery. The first group have seen it as "absolute"; the second as "contractual" or "popular and consultative".'[14] Major represents those historians who argue that the reign of Francis was still popular and consultative, that the New Monarchies were indeed new, but that they were defined by characteristics unique to the period of the Renaissance and that these very traits set limits on the strength of the crown. Major is opposed to the view that Francis was an absolutist; instead, he sees absolutism coming about in the seventeenth century in a rather slow, evolutionary way. Starting with the reign of Henry IV and climaxing with the reign of Louis XIV, the absolutist state emerged slowly through the reforms and negotiations of three reigns. For Major it is highly significant that in 1542 Francis redirected his strategy for tax collection by forgetting the Epargne and dividing the realm into 17 *généralités*, or regional districts for fiscal administration. As the treasurers resided in these units, it appears that Francis had abandoned his policy of centralization. Major, in fact, argues that it was never actually his intention to centralize the treasury, that he was merely trying to create a war chest in Paris.[15]

The monarchy's mounting debts and fiscal vulnerability, brought on by the wars in Italy and the inflation of the sixteenth century, caused Francis to borrow from bankers and eventually to set up *rentes sur l'Hôtel de Ville*. Using the credit of the city of Paris, *rentes* were another means of borrowing. *Rentes* served as annuities or bonds sold by the government and guaranteed by the city of Paris.[16] They provided a means of raising revenue without raising taxes and they became part of a huge royal debt that contributed to the instability of the crown on the eve of the Wars of Religion.

In his exhaustive study of royal finances under Francis I, Philippe Hamon makes it clear that the policies of Francis were pragmatic in nature rather than reformist, and in this way Francis's reign anticipated those of Henry IV and the Bourbon monarchs of the seventeenth century. Rather than seeing it as part of a grand centralizing design, Hamon views Francis's use of expedients as an attempt to gain greater control over finances by relying on regionalization – the *généralités* – rather than on the upper echelons of financial administration, financiers whom he no longer trusted.[17]

In the end, these developments were important not only because they reflected actual limits on the power of this king, but also because, as mere expedients, they created unforeseen problems for later kings. The expedient most closely associated with the Renaissance monarchy was the venality of office. By treating government offices as private property and putting them up for sale, Francis found a way to raise additional revenue without raising taxes. This seemed a reasonable solution to the financial problems of the crown, and it meant the growth of government as offices and officeholders proliferated. Although the idea of venal offices existed in the fifteenth century, it did not become a major feature of government until the reigns of Francis I and Henry II.[18] Ultimately, all but a few financial and judicial offices were for sale. The unforeseen problem inherent in the venality of office was the independent and often unreliable government that resulted from it. Financial officials and judges who owned their offices viewed them as private property to administer as they pleased. To be sure, families struggled to retain control of this property through succession from fathers to sons. The crown's response to this inevitable consequence of venality was to find additional ways to cash in, specifically by the 40-day rule. When a man resigned his office in favor of an heir or the highest bidder, he had to survive the transaction by 40 days. If he should die before 40 days, then the office reverted to the crown, only to be sold again. To avoid the 40-day stipulation, the officeholder could pay a fee that would enable him to direct the office to the individual of his choice. In either case, the crown made money.[19] But the lasting effect was to create a government in which officeholders enjoyed security and a high degree of independence that allowed them on many occasions to oppose the policies of the crown.

The Wars of Religion

Despite these various means of raising funds, by the end of the reign of Henry II (1547–59) the monarchy was approaching bankruptcy. Its financial weakness and the fiscal choices to which Francis I and Henry II had resorted created political instability on the eve of the Wars of Religion; the wars would in turn put the monarchy through a great ordeal.

The causes of the French Wars of Religion have been the subject of much historiographical debate. For some time historians emphasized the political motives that led the nobility of France to use religion to promote the interests of one faction or another. They wrote about the weakness of the monarchy as the fundamental cause of disorder, and they assessed religious conversion in the most calculating and secular terms. In contrast, most of the historians writing in the past decade have chosen to emphasize religion as the driving force in the conflict of the second half of the sixteenth century.[20] This is not to suggest that the pendulum has swung to another extreme in which political, social and economic factors are neglected or are considered merely contextual to a great clash of competing theologies. Instead, recent works focus on the essentially religious nature of society and polity in sixteenth-century France. By looking at religion as a 'body of believers rather than the more modern definition of a body of beliefs',[21] they have offered interpretations that reveal the essentially religious foundation of early modern Europe. As such they have offered more nuanced and compelling explanations for actions taken by the crown and the nobility in this period.

The Wars of Religion presented the French crown with its greatest crisis before the Revolution. Henry II's death in 1559 revealed clearly the limits on royal authority and the monarchy's susceptibility to factional control. Francis II (1559–60) was too young to manage the various clienteles and factions that had formed and been enlarged as a result of the widespread sale of offices during the previous two reigns. His marriage to a member of the Guise family presented that faction and their clients with the opportunity of tipping the balance of power decidedly in their favor. The king's council was dominated by the duke of Guise and his brother, the cardinal of Lorraine, a situation that produced factional rivalries of the first order. The Guise headed one of three dominant factions, the other two being the Bourbons and the Montmorency. To say that these three factions were dominant is not to suggest that all of the French nobility had been enlisted into one or another of these three clienteles, as there were 'noble families which did not belong to the clientage systems of the three families, and even in the provinces where they were most powerful they had numerous opponents'. Still, they were individually large and powerful, and for the Guise to obtain control of the royal council held enormous implications for the distribution of power among them.[22] As the three factions aligned themselves confessionally, they came to play major roles in the impending Wars of Religion. The importance of factional rivalry to the policies of the monarchy and the politics of religious conflict is not to be underestimated, and explains why historians have traditionally placed great emphasis on the political causes of the wars and the political and economic uses of conversion. Still, the fact that clientage networks converted or remained Catholic does not eliminate the possibility of genuine devotion. As Mack Holt has suggested, such patterns tell us more about networks of transmission and communication than about motives.[23] Certainly, there were many people, noble and non-noble, who converted to Calvinism for political gain and personal profit, but many others embraced the reformed faith because of a genuine change in religious conviction. Conversely, those who followed the house of Guise did not always remain Catholic to improve their financial or social lot in life.

The works of Denis Crouzet and Barbara Diefendorf make clear the central role of religion in the conflicts of the late sixteenth century. For Crouzet religion is singularly important in understanding these conflicts and the nobility's role in them.[24] He argues that the violence of the wars offered the nobility a soteriological experience – the opportunity to encounter God and therefore to experience salvation. Furthermore, Crouzet finds a critical link between the wars in Italy during the earlier part of the century and the religious wars that began in France in 1562. The literature and memoirs from the Italian campaigns refer to these events in religious terms, seeing the wars as a messianic gesture; nobles writing about their experiences described the violence in soteriological terms – that through war they acted as His protagonists and they encountered God. The Treaty of Câteau-Cambrésis in 1559 interrupted the wars without real conclusion, thereby denying noble warriors a soteriological encounter with God and undermining their very identity. It was the French Wars of Religion that provided an opportunity for them to redeem their honor and their souls. Some did so as crusaders against heretics; others chose to become reformed soldiers of God. All found honor and redemption in their deeds.[25]

From the monarchy's perspective the wars represented a total breakdown of the body politic. Confronted with rival and warring clienteles, the crown tried to use clientage to restore order. Catherine de Medici, regent for Charles IX (1560–74), struggled to create some kind of equilibrium through a more equitable distribution of patronage. Her policy, though seemingly judicious, proved highly unsuccessful, because the crown lacked the financial resources to make it work, and the house of Guise resented sharing power.

At the provincial level the monarchy's failures saw governors, given the dearth of rewards to distribute from the crown, find their own alternatives to anarchy. Without the means to recruit adequate numbers of troops, provincial governors turned to one or the other church and its respective army for assistance. They also used their influence within provincial institutions to place their clients or to recruit clients from within. Ultimately, the fact that there was less patronage to distribute from the crown contributed to disorder, as clients shifted from one patron to another if they felt their needs were not being adequately addressed. In short, the monarchy had failed to maintain adequate control of clientage to maintain order. Provincial governors and the great nobility had sufficiently redirected vertical ties in the interest of one faction and church or the other that the body politic lay wounded.[26] The monarchy suffered enormously during the course of these wars, especially during the reign of Henry III (1574–89). One of its lowest points occurred in 1588 when, after the famous Day of the Barricades, Henry III was forced to sign the Edict of Union, a document that conferred tremendous authority on the duke of Guise as lieutenant-general of the realm.[27]

The financial problems of the monarchy significantly limited its ability to address the conflict between confessional communities. It was one of these communities, the Huguenots, which as a disaffected minority would produce another major challenge to monarchical authority, indeed viability, in the form of resistance theory and republican political rhetoric. The St Bartholomew's Day Massacre in 1572 brought dissident political ideas to the surface. In 1573 François Hotman's *Francogallia* put forth the idea of elective monarchy, that kings were traditionally chosen by an assembly, which ran counter to any theory of divinely ordained kingship. The next year Theodore Beza's treatise *On the Right of Magistrates* took a more radical turn in that he argued for resistance against kings that had offended God. Subsequent works went even further to explain the fundamentally contractual nature of government and the sovereignty of the people.[28]

In addition to the political rhetoric of the Huguenot minority, the crown was the subject of criticism in the sermons of Catholic preachers. The most notable examples were the sermons of Simon Vigor, who preached in Paris during the 1560s. According to Diefendorf, Vigor expounded a 'logic of sedition' that viewed heresy as a threat to the entire social order. Underlying this logic was the sixteenth-century tendency to practice religion as a 'body of believers' rather than a 'body of beliefs', which resulted in collective notions of salvation. By tolerating the infection of heresy, the community would share in the responsibility, so Vigor and others argued: God punishes collectively as well as individually. The sacral nature of monarchy meant that it was the responsibility of the crown to shepherd the community towards collective salvation by making sure that it did not tolerate heresy in its midst. And, if the monarch failed to rid the community of this pollutant, he deserved to be deposed.[29] So went a Catholic logic of sedition that posed as real a challenge to monarchical authority as Protestant resistance theory; this was made clear during the early reign of Henry IV when Catholic elements refused to recognize him as king.

The Reign of Henry IV

In fact, the issue of Henry of Navarre's succession as Henry IV (1589–1610) became a matter of great public debate in 1584 when François, duke of Anjou, heir to the throne, died. According to Salic law, his death left Henry of Navarre next in line. Bourbon succession was obviously more than problematic for most of France, as the house of Bourbon had for almost three decades directed the Protestant movement. Much of France was committed to opposing this king. Catholics argued against Salic law (which stated that the French crown must pass through the male line) and in favor of consanguinity (which emphasized the closeness of connection rather than the male or female lines, and was based on Roman law). Relying on the principle of consanguinity, Catholics advanced the claims of Navarre's uncle, Charles, cardinal of Bourbon. They also made a very strong case for the sacral nature of the monarchy. The mystique of monarchy was based on its divine origins and its relationship to the Catholic Church; this mystique was reflected in the fact that the king, after the religious ceremony of coronation, was imbued with the power to heal scrofula and had the authority to appoint bishops. Traditionally in France kingship had derived much of its authority from its 'Catholicity'.[30]

The case advanced by Catholics was a compelling one. Henry IV would, in fact, recognize the Catholicity of the French monarchy and abjure his Protestant church. Though he chose not to do so immediately, a strategy that was itself evidence of his political acumen, he would in due course recognize the essentially sacral nature of the French monarchy by reuniting France under one faith and one king. His conversion in 1593 made it possible for Catholics to accept his reign and for Henry and his advisors to attempt to heal the body politic. Of course, his Protestant supporters reacted to his decision with disappointment and antipathy, and in 1598 Henry appeased them with the Edict of Nantes. By its terms, Protestants were allowed to worship freely in those cities and towns that were essentially Huguenot strongholds. The edict also protected the civil rights of Huguenots and guaranteed their right to fortify and defend themselves. What the edict did not do, however, was to guarantee complete religious freedom or toleration in the realm. It was a document that allowed for coexistence but that recognized the fundamentally Catholic nature of the realm. As conceived, the edict was to provide a temporary solution to the religious conflict so that the king could ultimately bring France together again as a Catholic nation. It was part of a longer-range plan to put the realm on a steady course that recognized the Catholicity of the French crown.[31]

Well before the end of the religious wars, in 1593, Henry attempted to find that steady course for the monarchy. His most urgent problems were the Spanish presence in France and the financial crisis of the crown, made worse by the fact that he spent a fortune on bribing nobles and towns into submission. By 1596 the crown was nearly bankrupt. The question that confronted him was what course the monarchy should follow as it struggled to create solvency and to restore political stability. According to Major, Henry had two choices before him: he could restore the Renaissance monarchy, or he could attempt reforms that would break the power of the estates and the great magnates of France. In other words, he could restore order by relying on tradition and recognizing the limits of royal authority, or he could innovate by a policy of centralization and absolutism. Following the advice of his minister, Pomponne de Bellièvre, Henry embarked first on a course that would have meant the restoration of the Renaissance state. Bellièvre sought to resolve some of the financial problems of the crown in a way that he hoped would not produce great resistance. This meant cutting expenses and managing revenues better. The first part of this plan proved the most risky. Specifically, Bellièvre proposed lowering interest rates on *rentes*, reducing the number of pensions and salaries, and transferring part of the tax burden from the countryside to towns. He also proposed a Council of Good Order to manage half of the royal revenues. Finally, to avoid controversy and to secure approval for the plan, Henry deferred to the consultative tradition of the monarchy by calling an Assembly of Notables.[32]

The Assembly of Notables approved most of Bellièvre's proposals, and it appeared that France would experience a restoration of the Renaissance monarchy. This course was, however, interrupted in 1597 when the Spanish took the city of Amiens. Military disaster meant that the government needed a lot more money, and soon. There would be no time for Bellièvre's thoughtful strategy; the crown would have to resort to some of the old expedients. More to the point, the crown would have to act forcefully in order to collect the revenues necessary to repel the Spanish. The military crisis was the beginning of the end of Bellièvre's career, and it marked the ascendancy of Maximilian de Béthune, known as the duke of Sully. It was the policies of Sully that would eventually put the monarchy on a different, seemingly reformist, course.[33]

Sully came from a minor noble family that had converted to Protestantism. His own rise to power started in 1572 when he entered the clientele of Henry IV. In 1595 and 1596 he acted as a delegate of the privy council in investigating the administration of the *élections*. Sully could be ruthless in fulfilling the obligations of his position. Certainly, he impressed the king with his thoroughness and enthusiasm, and by 1598 he was Henry's superintendent of finance. From this position he consolidated his authority and took bold steps to remedy the monarchy's financial crisis. He cleverly renegotiated the royal debt through various means, the terms of which usually proved favorable to the king. For instance, Henry IV's marriage to Marie de Medici in 1600 was calculated for the financial relief that it might bring. Henry had borrowed from, among several others, the grand duke of Tuscany, and his debt was enormous; dowry negotiations resulted in its reduction.[34] From one debt to the next, Sully and Henry attempted to make various kinds of arrangements, some of which meant essentially the elimination of the debt. In this way the 'Antichrist of ingratitude' managed to scale down the burden.[35]

Even more important to the monarchy from an institutional perspective were Sully's intiatives in the realm of taxation. Here we see his energetic and direct style at work, resulting in changes that have been labeled 'absolutist' in nature. Sully sought to collect more money in a variety of ways, not the least of which was by imposing the *élection* on parts of France where it had not previously existed. This policy brought him into conflict with the representative institutions of the *pays d'états*. According to Mark Greengrass, Sully was not an exponent of absolutist theory;

rather, he operated with a 'style that was more military and abrupt'. The results of Sully's approach constituted important precedents for centralization and reform. By introducing the *élections* to Guyenne, Sully started the process of creating greater uniformity in the provincial system of tax collections. The plan was to introduce similar changes in Provence, Burgundy, Languedoc, and Dauphiné. His intentions were not uniformity for uniformity's sake, but simply to collect more money from provinces that had managed hitherto, based on provincial privilege, to avoid the full extent of the tax burden.[36] But the decision to introduce the *élection* and its corresponding bureaucrats, the *élus*, provided important precedents for later reforms under Louis XIII and Cardinal Richelieu.

Another major development was the *paulette*, which was an attempt to affect greater control over the bureaucracy by undermining its control by patrons. The specific way in which the *paulette* worked was by allowing the officeholder, for a price, to avoid the 40-day rule and name the individual to succeed him at any point in time. Previously, an officeholder had had to survive at least 40 days after he had designated his heir or the individual to whom he had sold the office. Failing the 40 days, the office reverted to the possession of the crown. In 1604, Henry IV and Sully devised the *paulette*, an annual tax of one-sixtieth of the official or assessed value of the office, paid by the officeholder to ensure that the office went to the individual of his choice. In short, it confirmed, for a fee, the hereditary nature of the French bureaucracy, the ultimate purpose of which was to instill some loyalty to central government and to weaken the bonds of loyalty between patron and client. It was a measure designed to counteract the unfortunate consequences of venality, the independence of the bureaucracy, by providing a reason for loyalty to the king and by undermining loyalty to the patron whose influence and wealth might have originally procured the office for the magistrate. It also carried the additional advantage of raising some much-needed revenue for the crown, though this was not its primary purpose.[37]

The intent and indeed the results of the policies of Henry IV and Sully were to restore financial solvency and to promote greater efficiency in government. When a Catholic fanatic, Ravaillac, assassinated Henry in 1610, there was a surplus in the treasury and a measure of uniformity had been imposed on France's system of taxation. These were changes of enormous significance, a fact that did not escape contemporaries eulogizing Henry at the time of his death and the many historians who have written about the reign. Just what is the significance of the reign of

Henry IV? The eulogies predictably constructed the 'legend' of the first Bourbon king by celebrating the peace and political stability that he had brought to France. Both religious communities contributed to the legend: for Protestants, he was the source of their security; for Catholics, he was a king who acted in the interest of his people's welfare. As a legend, his representation by those who celebrated the reign was drawn much larger than life. His accomplishments and his concern for his subjects, the king who wanted to see a chicken in every peasant's pot, would become the dominant themes in the collective memory of Henry IV. Why was it that this king would become France's favorite son? Why not his predecessor Francis I or Louis XIV? Certainly, to some extent it had to do with the way in which he came to his end and the memory of his assassination. But Henry III, also struck down by a Catholic fanatic, did not benefit from such sympathetic views as a result of his violent death. Clearly, the way in which Henry IV was represented had much to do with the policies of his reign, and particularly the resulting political stability. His policies brought to an end one of the worst crises experienced by the realm, and for this he became a legend.[38]

Legendary though they became, the policies of Henry IV and Sully were pragmatic in nature and appear to have been conceived not in accordance with an absolutist theory, but in purely empirical terms. Despite his brusque manner, Sully was no doctrinaire absolutist; instead, he appears the hard-working, practical Calvinist, a man who was guided by the principle of feasible solutions to very immediate problems. These policies inspired further consideration and implementation during the reign of Louis XIII. It was this king's reign, and his collaboration with Cardinal Richelieu, that made plain the practical limits on state-building in seventeenth-century France.

The Reign of Louis XIII

Louis XIII (1610–43) was not yet nine years old when his father was assassinated. His mother, Marie de Medici, served as his regent during the early reign of the young king. As is nearly always true of regencies, this was a period when the monarchy was vulnerable to attempts by *les grands* to control government and to gather for themselves all the largesse that they might. They began to jostle and intrigue for France's most desirable military, royal-household, and ecclesiastical posts, as well as for pensions, hoping to take advantage of both the royal minority and the huge treasury surplus Sully had amassed.'[39] The principal figure in this great conflict of self-promotion was Louis' cousin, Henri de Condé, who in 1614 took the internecine squabbles of the court and the king's council to a more violent level by leading an exodus of supporters from court to the country where they would raise troops against the crown. Sully had long since departed from court and there had been no love lost between him and Marie; his insistence on frugality had met with opposition, especially since Marie needed pensions to placate the nobility. As regent, Marie responded to the rebels by mobilizing the royal guard and some Swiss mercenaries, but she declined to deploy them against the rebel headquarters. This left her little alternative but to negotiate. Among the concessions that she and the council made to the grandees was to call a meeting of the Estates-General. Condé hoped that he could manipulate the Estates-General into confirming his own claims to power.[40]

When some of the rebels persisted in their activities, Marie agreed to an offensive against them in western France. With her son, the king, in tow, they engaged in what might be described more as a public relations campaign than as a military campaign against insurgents. As the entourage made its way across the country and the king's subjects got to view him for the first time, France fell in line. Lloyd Moote, Louis' most recent biographer, notes that this was a tactic that Louis would employ throughout his reign, 'making him the most traveled and most accessible king within France of any French king'.[41] The net effect of this western tour was to influence in the king's favor the election of deputies to the upcoming Estates-General. It was a major victory for Marie and it inspired the rebels to forget military resistance; Condé was, in fact, less than enthusiastic now about the impending meeting.[42]

The meeting of the Estates-General would be a significant one, not for the reforms that resulted, as there were none, but because it was the last meeting before the much more famous convocation in 1789. More important, the deputies of the three estates debated and recommended the abolition of venality of office and the *paulette*. Their reasons for doing so varied, not surprisingly, according to estate. For the nobility and the clergy the issue was not the problems for government inherent in venal offices and a hereditary bureaucracy; rather, they were distressed at the way in which prices of offices had inflated since the introduction of the *paulette*. By confirming and insuring the hereditary nature of offices, the *paulette* had caused their prices to soar, a fact that the nobility particularly resented because they regarded officeholding as their prerogative. The third estate opposed venality on more philosophical grounds, but, since many of their deputies were actually officeholders themselves, they had some personal and self-serving reservations about the idea. To make the proposed reform more palatable, the third estate attached a request that the *taille* be reduced significantly.[43]

In the end these initiatives failed, but they remain important to historians for the light they shed on the relationship between the monarchy and the nobility. The noble deputies were members of the provincial nobility; they were not grandees or magnates. What becomes apparent from their *cahiers* is that they preferred favor directly from the king, because to 'bind themselves to a prince to receive a royal office or a pension might lead to their being required to follow their patron down the dangerous road to rebellion'. In their *cahiers*, they asked specifically 'that no pensions, offices, or other gifts be given in the future through the intercession of the princes and seigneurs of your kingdom, so that those who have them will be bound entirely to your majesty'.[44] Their reluctance in 1614 to serve a patron, who would act as intercessor in obtaining venal offices or commissions, and their obvious preference to receive largesse directly from the crown, made it clear to some how the monarchy should operate to instill greater control from the center.

Among those sensitive to the opportunities at hand if the monarchy redirected its powers of patronage and bypassed the greater magnates to distribute awards directly to provincial elites was Villeroy, a secretary of foreign affairs who had become the dominant presence on the council in matters both foreign and domestic. But Villeroy's influence waned, and in 1616 he and two others were dismissed and replaced by the ascendant Concino Concini, an Italian whose stock with Marie had risen rapidly due not in small part to the fact that his wife, Leonora, was a favorite in Marie's household. Concini was not the only rising star; it was during this period that the bishop of Luçon, later known as Cardinal Richelieu, was also gaining political prominence. He first came to the attention of Marie and others as a deputy of the clergy to the Estates-General; from there he went on to cultivate a relationship with Marie and her Italian favorite; and eventually he was named secretary of state. There is obvious irony in the fact that the man who would later be so closely associated with the king rose to prominence thanks to the patronage of Marie and Concini, two individuals whose influence and power Louis would struggle to throw off.

The young king's effort to rule without the domination of his mother and her circle was a long and highly conflicted one. In 1614, at the age of thirteen, by a *lit de justice* before the Parlement of Paris, Louis declared his majority. Predictably, his mother continued to wield power as a sort of *de facto* regent. Over time Louis resented her influence and consciously acted to assert both his independence and his authority. In the course of claiming power for himself, Louis was assisted by first his royal falconer, Luynes, and second the secretary of state, Richelieu. Originally, it was Luynes who encouraged the king to distance himself from Marie, and it was Luynes who orchestrated the assassination of Concini.

Richelieu's relationship with young Louis began inauspiciously. The king perceived him as much too authoritarian, and he was, of course, tainted by the fact that he had risen as a client of Marie. With the assassination of Concini, Richelieu even lost his position on the council. When the king proceeded to act aggressively against Marie by banishing her to the Château of Blois, Richelieu cast in his fate with the former regent and joined her at Blois as president of her council. From this position Richelieu worked in very calculating, though seemingly erratic, ways to regain his position at court. First he tried to curry favor with Luynes by reporting as a spy on the activities of Marie and her followers; then, sensing the suspicion and distrust that resulted from this approach, he withdrew to his diocese. He would re-emerge during the great episodes known as the Wars of the Mother and the Son.[45]

The story of this major power struggle between Marie and Louis began on 22 February 1619 when she escaped by ladder from the Château of Blois. Carrying a box that contained a fortune in jewelry, she led six companions away in the middle of the night to plot her return to power. Specifically, she wanted to remove Luynes from his coveted position as the closest advisor to the king, a place that she hoped to reclaim for herself. In March the king recalled Richelieu whom he ordered to rejoin Marie in the role of mediator in hope that he might exert some kind of moderating effect on the queen mother and her entourage. Richelieu did mediate and helped mother and son reach an agreement in which Marie was left free and in control of Anjou and related strongholds. But the settlement proved ephemeral, as Marie and her circle of magnates continued to feel shut off from power; their resentment and sense of exclusion produced yet another coalition against Luynes and the king.[46]

This time Marie managed to enlist the service of many more supporters. In addition to the duke of Epernon, who had been with her from the beginning, she recruited Louis' illegitimate half-brothers, the duke of Vendôme and the grand prior of France, and his cousins, the count of Soissons and the duke of Longueville. They were joined by a number of

other magnates and their clients, and Richelieu played a significant role
in putting together Marie's opposition forces. The result of this coalition
was that the armies of the mother and the son met in 1620 at a place near
Angers known as the Ponts-de-Cé. There Louis led his army against that
of Marie, though he did not confront her directly. 'Louis prepared the
battle scene himself, stayed seventeen hours in the saddle, and carried
the day.' In the treaty negotiations that followed the son's victory over
his mother, Marie was obliged to swear off such activities, but she was in
turn given the opportunity to explain and justify her behavior. Motivated by what Moote has described as his profound sense of justice, Louis
dealt with the grandees who had supported his mother by denying them
any role in his service.[47]

According to Major, the significance of the revolt has to do with the
relationships between Marie and her clients, as the entire episode is actually most instructive for what it reveals about patronage and clientage and
the implications therein for the monarchy. As a patron Marie exhibited
steadfast loyalty, but the same could not be said about all of her clients.
After seeing that the king's troops outnumbered those of Marie and
hearing that negotiations were in progress, the duke of Retz withdrew
his troops. Moreover, the magnates who brought their clients on board
to serve Marie did not always protect the interests of the men they had
enlisted. In short, what we can learn from the Wars of the Mother and
the Son is that self-interest played a significant, if not dominant, role in
the formation and dissolution of the vertical ties of the patron–client system. There would now be important opportunities in the future for the
crown to harness these ties in its own interest. Such opportunities would
be even more certain given that provincial nobles had already expressed
in 1614 their reluctance to sign on as client to a great magnate, prefer-
ring instead to receive largesse directly from the king himself.[48]

The conflict between Marie and Louis brought Richelieu back into the
limelight; the death of Luynes in December 1621 would eventually leave
him on center stage. This did not happen overnight, because Louis still
believed Richelieu to be untrustworthy. Louis appointed Marie to his
council, partly because of the void left by Luynes's death and partly to
satisfy Marie so that she ceased to be the troublemaker. Marie's influence
and perseverence gained for Richelieu the title of cardinal in 1622, and
then obtained for him another position on the council in 1624. Once
installed on the king's council Richelieu went instantly about ousting
his most important rival, La Vieuville, thereby making way for his own
ascent to the position of chief minister, all of which transpired in 1624.[49]

The next decade was crucial in the history of the monarchy. The under-lying and most pressing problem that confronted royal government was how to extend control over the army, the judiciary, and the collection of taxes. The issue of the control and effectiveness of central government was in turn fundamental to dealing with the problems of the Huguenots and domestic instability on the one hand, and the Habsburgs and foreign conflict on the other.[50]

In response to the need for governmental reform, Richelieu renewed several proposals that had been put forward, without result, in the Estates-General meeting of 1614 and in an Assembly of Notables meeting in 1617. To win the acceptance of elites, Richelieu persuaded Louis to convoke another Assembly of Notables and to seek their approval for the reforms. The assembly met in 1626-7. Michel de Marillac, co-superin-tendant of finances and keeper of the seals, addressed the assembly about the financial exigencies created by internal revolts and foreign conflicts. Marillac made it abundantly clear that the monarchy's expenses exceeded by far its revenues and that something had to be done to restore solv-ency. All present were sensitive to the fact that the peasantry could not withstand an increase in their tax burden, and therefore other means of generating revenue would be necessary. There was, predictably, much discussion and support for the idea of curbing expenses and creating economies, but the deputies also addressed reform of the administrative apparatus. What followed this convocation was a major attempt to make the government, particularly financial administration, operate more effectively.[51]

It was in this context that the government under Louis XIII began to extend the *élections* and the *élus*. In an effort at centralization and uni-formity in the realm of tax assessment and collection, the government designated four of the great provinces within the *pays d'états* to be carved into *élections*. Provence, Dauphiné, Burgundy, and Languedoc became the foci of reform, and the response of locals to this initiative was to resist. In the cases of Provence, Dauphiné, and Burgundy, it resulted in open rebellion.[52] This assault on the traditional privileges of the *pays d'états* does not appear to have been Richelieu's idea. Not only was he aware that there would be massive resistance if the government tried to impose royal institutions on parts of the realm that had traditionally been exempted, he also realized that certain *pays d'états* already generated a fair amount of revenue for the crown. For example, he never tried to impose on Brittany in this way. Although Brittany was taxed signifi-cantly below the rate at which the *pays d'élections* were taxed, Richelieu knew that a not insignificant amount was already being channeled from the Bretons to the royal treasury. Collins also tells us that Brittany provided handsomely for the cardinal himself and his clients: Richelieu became governor of Brittany in 1630 and during his governorship the Breton Estates paid him and his clients 1.2 million *livres*.[53]

The cardinal was not a reformer; rather than by an ideologue of absolutism, he was motivated by pure pragmatism. Given Richelieu's *modus operandi*, it appears that the individual behind the extension of the *élections* was Marillac, whose desire for system and order was well known. It was Marillac who had drafted the failed Code Michau, an ordinance that he composed in response to the grievances voiced at the 1626–7 Assembly of Notables. The code, or the Ordinance of 1629, has been called France's first code of law, though certainly it was not received in this spirit as it prompted resistance sufficient to undermine it completely. Still, the Code Michau is important as a representation of reformist sentiments, especially those of Marillac, who in writing this compilation attempted to regulate the affairs of the realm.[54] By reform, Marillac hoped to extend the control of the center to the periphery, and his vision was driven by his 'personal sense of religion and morality, a sense of rectitude and integrity that he thought was widely lacking among royal servants and provincial officials and that only a well-coordinated monarchy could ensure for the kingdom of France'.[55]

Marillac's personal sense of religion also shaped his views on foreign policy and the problem of the Huguenots. At court, there circulated two factions with contrasting perspectives on these issues. First, there were the *bons Français*, among them Cardinal Richelieu, who were motivated primarily by concern for the security of France in the wake of conflict with the house of Habsburg. For the *bons Français* the most pressing issue was the threat of Spanish hegemony, and to eclipse the Spanish they were willing to put aside religious issues, namely the success of the Counter-Reformation. Opposing Richelieu and the Good Frenchmen were the *dévots*, among them Marillac and Marie, who placed top priority on the revival of Catholicism within France and Europe. In the interest of the Counter-Reformation, the *dévots* were willing to undertake alliance with Spain. The contest between these two factions eventually produced a great rivalry between Richelieu on the one hand and Marillac and Marie on the other. Although these factions separated clearly and primarily over the inseparable issues of religion and foreign policy, their respective views reverberated also in debates over taxation and reform. For Richelieu the object was to collect the money, by whatever means and without provoking domestic turmoil and conflict, and to pursue successfully an anti-Habsburg foreign policy. For Marillac the objects were reform and the Counter-Reformation; the latter meant a pro-Spanish foreign policy and war against the Huguenots at home, and the former was to provide the money for these policies.[56]

Richelieu was no friend to the Huguenots; nor was he indifferent to the Counter-Reformation. As bishop of Luçon he had made a genuine effort to introduce the reforms of the Catholic Reformation. His opinion on the Huguenots was, quite simply, that heresy was sedition, and Richelieu was certainly not one to tolerate sedition. But, as Holt writes of him, 'Richelieu was a man of much broader vision than a mere Huguenot fighter, however, and he recognized that the authority and security of the French crown hinged to some degree on the outcome of international events that were quickly overtaking most of Europe'. Though not a man without principles, Richelieu's pragmatic side realized that it would be impossible to wage war on two fronts – at home and abroad. Indeed, the war abroad was itself not conceived without principles; it was after all a struggle to preserve the French monarchy. And it was the issue of sedition that compelled Richelieu finally to take strident action against the Huguenots. When Louis and Richelieu moved to lay siege against the Huguenots of La Rochelle in 1627–8 it was because Protestant antics amounted to 'explicit rebellion against the crown'. By receiving support from England, including an English fleet under the command of the duke of Buckingham, the Huguenots were seditiously engaged in their own separate foreign policy and rebellion, which violated the terms of the Edict of Nantes.[57]

Having remedied this particular threat to internal instability, Richelieu, the *bon Français*, was free in 1629 to counter the Habsburg threat by entering the Thirty Years War. This intensified factional debate, and the court became a hotbed of conflicting opinions. It was apparent to all concerned that someone would have to go, and to many it was obvious that it would be the cardinal. The great climax came on 11 November 1630 in what has been remembered as the Day of the Dupes. The context was that the king had recently been ill (he even received last rites on 29 September), which left him emotionally susceptible to his mother's influence. Marie and Marillac urged peace with Spain. Moreover, Marie had come to feel that Richelieu, who had risen as her client, was a total ingrate and completely untrustworthy. She relieved him of the positions that he occupied in her household, and she railed against him to her son. Relations between Marie and Richelieu, and presumably between Louis and Richelieu, deteriorated to the extent that observers were confident that this would be the end of the cardinal's career. In a gesture that was representative of Louis' capacity for independent and self-reliant action, he surprised everyone by siding with Cardinal Richelieu. The Day of the Dupes meant the end for Marillac, who was placed under arrest, and the beginning of the end for Marie; France would henceforth pursue a consistently *bon Français* course.[58]

Thus began the collaboration between king and chief minister. From this point Louis and Richelieu forged a partnership that allowed them to embark on initiatives of enormous significance both domestically and internationally. Moote has examined this partnership very closely to conclude that it was indeed a collaboration, that 'Richelieu formulated policy suggestions in the lucid manner of contemporary scholastic reasoning by giving the pros and cons, then left the proper inference to be drawn by his monarch'.[59] Together they arrived at the policies that historians traditionally regarded as absolutist, policies that now appear to have been fundamentally pragmatic in nature and would inspire a similarly pragmatic approach to governance during the reign of Louis XIV.

What were these so-called absolutist policies? First, there was the use of the infamous *intendants*. The *intendants* were officials dispatched to the provinces in the interest of creating more reliable, efficient government. Specifically, they were a response to the problems of venal officeholding and the costs of foreign policy; they were salaried officials (that is, they did not purchase their office), and the occupants were to respond directly to central government. The *intendants* were not a new idea; they had been used sporadically, on an *ad hoc* basis, to carry out specific tasks during the sixteenth century. Richard Bonney makes clear that Richelieu did not at the outset use the *intendants* in any systematic way. Rather, he deployed them in response to various crises. In due course, they became a permanent feature of Louis XIII's government, and their administrative role expanded significantly. Drawn generally from the Parisian *noblesse de robe*, the *intendants* exercised judicial and financial authority at the provincial level. By the nature of their commissions, their authority could vary to meet changing circumstances. They served as watchdogs over provincial officials; they acted on behalf of the crown in instances of rebellion; they controlled troops; and they attempted to eliminate corruption in tax collection. For Bonney the financial exigencies resulting from France's involvement in the Thirty Years War drove the expansion of the *intendants'* power. Increasingly, authority for tax assessment and collection in the *pays d'élections* was transferred to the *intendants*. They rapidly became objects of resentment on the part of officeholding nobles who lost authority to them, felt restricted by them, and were often ready to coalesce against them.[60] Though their effectiveness has been debated, the *intendants* have been viewed as agents of absolutism and centralization. Certainly, local responses to them would suggest that contemporaries saw them this way.

Closely associated with the intendancies was the initiative to eliminate or undermine the provincial estates. Under Louis XIII, central government took aggressive action to bring the *pays d'états* more firmly under control. This was not an innovative policy; again, Henry IV and Sully were the first to challenge provincial privilege when they introduced the *élus* and *élections* to Languedoc and Guyenne. Nor did Richelieu enthusiastically endorse the idea. Marillac was the reformer who wanted to impose one system of tax collection on France. Richelieu simply resumed the effort because of financial exigency, and in the process he often encountered resistance. The end result was not uniformity; outcomes varied widely from one province to the next. In view of the opposition, Richelieu, the pragmatist, negotiated settlements province by province. Some provinces came out better than others. The Estates of Burgundy, Languedoc, and Brittany survived; the Estates of Normandy and Dauphiné were eliminated; and the Estates of Provence were replaced by the more manageable Assembly of Communities.[61]

Richelieu was also responsible for changes in the army, initiatives that were driven by conflict with the Habsburgs. These changes were essentially twofold. First, he extended the size of the army. Second, he attempted to centralize control of the army. He was more successful in the former than in the latter. Royal government would not delegate sufficient authority to unit commanders. Specifically, France, in contrast to other countries, did not recruit and maintain armies by what has been referred to as entrepreneurship, a system in which an 'entrepreneur would raise and maintain an army at his own expense against subsequent reimbursement by the government concerned'. The advantages to this system were that it was easier to recruit greater numbers of troops, and that commanders were more likely to run an efficient operation since they were actually investors in their units. Rather than rely on entrepreneurship, Richelieu and Louis XIII used military offices as a source of patronage, and they were given to individuals who wanted the status and were willing to raise and maintain forces without the promise of reimbursement. This approach placed a financial burden on commanders that was only made worse by the fact that they were not actually allowed proprietary rights over their units; a unit could be transferred or eliminated without reimbursement. The end result was an officer corps that was not salaried and yet could not view its units as investments, a situation that produced absenteeism among the dispirited and corruption among those officers who sought their own unofficial forms of reimbursement. Even *intendants*, whom Richelieu dispatched to inspect provincial units, proved unreliable and went over to the other side by becoming clients of the nobles who served as commanders.[62]

Richelieu's policies toward the parlements, both provincial and the Parlement of Paris, inspired contemporaries and historians to comment on the authoritarian nature of this regime. Traditionally, the parlements could affect law by registering royal edicts or remonstrating against them. If the Parlement of Paris chose to protest an edict by remonstrance, the king had the recourse of a *lettre de jussion*, which directed the parlement to register the controverial edict without further discussion, or he could invoke a *lit de justice* ('bed of justice') in which he appeared in person and supervised the registration. The *lit de justice* was obviously a more stringent tactic and was generally employed after a *lettre de jussion* had failed. Kings did not use the *lit de justice* routinely, and it was a great event when they did. This relationship between monarch and parlements changed under Louis XIII and Richelieu. In 1641 a royal edict forbade parlements to remonstrate against edicts of a political nature unless invited to do so, which amounted to telling the parlements that they could no longer comment on state affairs.[63]

In addition to restricting their right to remonstrate, Louis also eclipsed the power of the parlements by the use of judicial commissions. Although the commissions were not a new concept, Richelieu developed them more fully and used them more systematically. He turned over those accused of commiting *lèse majesté*, or treason, to special commissions, and in this way eliminated his political enemies. Most prominent among them were the grandees who had been a regular source of instability during the early reign. For this alone he acquired the reputation of a despot. Yet the cardinal took none of these steps without historical precedent and without the full knowledge and complicity of the king. Moote's study of the reign makes a very good case for the idea that many of Richelieu's policies were inspired by the king himself, especially by his own profound sense of justice.[64]

Of all the cardinal's policies, the most significant was his use of the patron–client system, and it was his reliance on clients of his own making that created the illusion of centralization and reform. Much of his success depended on his manipulation of clientage, and for recent historians clientage has become the key to state-building in the seventeenth century. Cardinal Richelieu established control through an elaborate and carefully constructed ministerial clientele. This network began in Paris and was extended into the provinces where his judicious choice of loyal and effective clients allowed Richelieu to instill an important measure of control.

Richelieu began construction of a clientele by using his proximity to the king to direct royal patronage to his own men. After the Day of the Dupes Richelieu was in effect a *créature* of Louis XIII. As the client of the king, he was able to direct patronage to others whose support he enlisted on behalf of Louis. Still, these were Richelieu's men, this was truly a ministerial clientele, and he invested lavishly from his own resources and sinecures. Often his clients were already officeholders who sought connection to advance their careers. Nor did the cardinal hestitate to dole patronage out to members of his family. He preferred the security of surrounding himself with family, and his relations benefitted astoundingly from his largesse and his reliance on them. Many of his clients were placed in high positions, including the secretaries of state. Even the recalcitrant prince of Condé came to enter a relationship with Richelieu by marrying his son into the cardinal's family.[65]

As we saw earlier, the notion that patronage and clientage might be effectively harnessed by the monarchy was not a new idea. It is widely undertood now that sixteenth-century kings governed through patronage by making the great nobles provincial governors. Grandees who served in this capacity then brokered the king's patronage to their clientele who assisted them in governing the region. The problem with this use of clientage was that it enabled great nobles to build huge power bases in the provinces which they would later put to use in civil war. Richelieu's innovation was to create an enormous, far-flung clientele that remained loyal. He did this by choosing very carefully a series of provincial brokers who were prominent among provincial elites and would channel patronage to their clients or others in provincial government. In this way, he successfully bypassed and outmaneuvered the great nobility. As Kettering writes, 'the ministerial policy of diverting part of the flow of royal patronage to their own administrative networks in the provinces was a direct challenge to the political power and privileges of the great nobles, who were provincial governors and had traditionally brokered royal patronage in the provinces'. In terms of its effectiveness and long-term consequences, the real innovation associated with Richelieu and Louis XIII was not the *intendant*, nor was it the special judicial commission; rather, it was the way in which the crown made use of patronage and clientage. As we shall see, the fundamental underpinning of so-called absolutism was cooperation between the crown, its ministers, and provincial elites.[66]

The Reign of Louis XIV

The deaths of Cardinal Richelieu (1642) and Louis XIII (1643) left the monarchy in vulnerable circumstances. Succeeding as king was the five-year-old Louis XIV (1643–1715), and control of his government instantly became the basis of competition among the princes of the blood, the regent, Anne of Austria, and her chief minister, Cardinal Mazarin. In its most destructive and violent phase, this great power struggle would play out at mid-century in the civil war known as the Fronde (1648–53). But the Fronde was not simply a contest of competing personal ambitions; some historians have argued that the role of the Parlement of Paris amounted to a revolutionary effort to effect fundamental constitutional changes in France. At the very least, the Fronde was a complex episode, and its imprint on Louis XIV was significant. It was propelled by a variety of motives and by an assortment of participants who sometimes, despite their divergent aims, acted in concert, thereby defying any sort of monocausal explanation.

The context in which the Fronde began included a regency government that, in continuing the policies of the previous reign, brought growing disfavor and distrust upon itself. Its efforts to fund the war with the Habsburgs saw the crown resort to a series of desperate fiscal expedients which resulted in near bankruptcy and widespread hostility to the government. It was ultimately the fiscal policies of the crown and Particelli d'Emery, the financier most closely associated with abuse, that catapulted France into crisis in 1648. His first approach to financial crisis was to reduce expenditures by cutting the interest due on *rentes* and reducing the salaries of officeholders. Soon he was forced to raise taxes and demand forced loans from officeholders. In pressuring the judges of the Parlement of Paris to approve the forced loan he threatened not to renew the *paulette*; then, in 1648, he renewed the *paulette*, but at a price – he suspended salaries for officeholders in the sovereign courts. The judges of the Parlement of Paris were made an exception to the four-year suspension, probably in the hope that this would alienate them from the other officers. But the plan failed miserably. Emery's policy amounted to an attack on the property of venal officeholders and it ignited a powder keg of united opposition and unconcealed resentment towards the crown. This was playing tough, and the parlement responded in kind.[67]

At issue was what the parlement perceived as the unlawful extension of the council's power and jurisdiction. The council was making decisions without observing the custom of consulting the parlement or the appropriate court. New taxes were introduced without the parlement's verification. New tax-farming contracts were issued without consulting the Chambre des Comptes and the Cour des Aides. In a variety of ways, the council and ministers appeared to usurp prerogatives and to violate jurisdictions.[68] In May 1648 the parlement created the Chambre Saint-Louis, an assembly of delegates from the four sovereign courts of Paris, the parlement, the Chambres des Comptes, the Cour des Aides, and the Grand Conseil. This action gave the Fronde ideological and revolutionary overtones, and the revolutionary rhetoric that emanated from this assembly was even more profound. The purpose of such a meeting was to discuss the crown's fiscal policies, but the implication was much more significant. A meeting of this nature would provide a forum for other criticisms of the government and the very institution of the monarchy. Those assembled in the chamber drew up a list of 27 articles or changes in policy they demanded of the crown. The contents of these articles referred to the need for fiscal reform and reduction in taxes, as well as the desire to eliminate the *intendants* and to end corruption in government. The response of the king's council was at first to give in, but then, following Condé's much needed victory at Lens, to resist. In August the royal government arrested the leaders of parlementary opposition, including Broussel, a senior and highly regarded judge. Their arrests met with a predictable response from the Parisians, who proceeded to orchestrate another Day of the Barricades by taking to the streets.[69]

The violence in Paris forced Mazarin and the royal government to back down in its opposition to the parlement and to negotiate. Despite the fact that the regency government made significant concessions to its opponents, the conflict continued and, in fact, escalated into civil war. The descent into open violence occurred for a variety of reasons, not the least of which were Mazarin's reliance on intrigue and the grandees' commitment to self-advancement and control of the throne. What ensued was an incredibly complex narrative of alignment and realignment in which Frondeur grandees sided with the parlement to oppose

Mazarin, Mazarin sought the opportunity to form temporary alliances with various Frondeurs and to play one off against the other, and all parties contributed to popular rebellion. In the countryside royal authority virtually crumbled, and provincial populations seized the opportunity to make clear their resentment towards its fiscal policies and the threat of centralization. Between 1648 and 1653 France drifted to the brink of total anarchy. The Fronde came to an end in much the same way that it was propelled, by intrigue and the realignment of factions. Mazarin defeated his opponents as much because of their own weaknesses and divisions as by his own political acumen, and he also resorted to the use of brute force when necessary.

What is the significance of the parlementary Fronde in French history? Historians differ in their interpretations. For some it constituted a failed attempt at revolution, and its revolutionary agenda produced visions of limited monarchy in which sovereign courts consented in matters of legislation and taxation.[70] Other have seen it as an attempt to dismantle the state or 'para-state' constructed by Louis XIII and Cardinal Richelieu and to reconstruct the state of Henry IV.[71] Alternatively, there is the view that the Fronde lacked a revolutionary agenda, that it was not a revolt against absolutism or an effort to limit monarchy, but a struggle among various factions to control the existing government. On the part of the parlement it was an effort to protect its own financial interests, to bring about fiscal reform, and to end the abuses of Mazarin's regime.[72] Some have made an even greater distinction between revolution and reform. They view the parlementaires as reformers, not revolutionaries, because they never sought fundamental social, economic, or constitutional change. The parlementaires have even been compared to the English Long Parliament in the early 1640s because they managed to reduce taxes, overthrow ministers, and make fiscal expedients subject to their approval. They also rid France of most of the hated *intendants*, at least for a while. And all of this they accomplished by legalistic arguments and by legal means.[73] Rather than increase the authority of the parlement, their goal was to reform royal government's style of administration. They advanced the argument that finances were subject to judicial authorities; they maintained their right of judicial review; and they argued that the parlement's authority placed it above the council.[74]

Whatever the accomplishments of the parlementary Fronde, the politics of the parlement in the post-Fronde decade confirm the limits of centralization and absolutism. For Mazarin the immediate problem was funding the ongoing war with Spain. Faced with financial crisis and few revenue-generating options, he continued to resort to objectionable financial means and to skirt the parlement's authority. The judges responded by obstructing the cardinal's initiatives in a variety of ways, not the least of which were remonstrating and instructing lower courts to ignore governmental orders. At points, it appeared that the kingdom might be on the verge of another Fronde. Mazarin, anxious to avoid the resumption of open conflict, backed down or altered policies to accommodate the court's wishes time and time again. And, by playing to the judges' own vested interests, it was possible to allay their concerns.[75]

Revolutionary or not, ideological or not, the Fronde constituted a powerful image during the remainder of Louis XIV's reign. And in no one's mind was this memory more vivid than it was in that of the young king. His attitudes towards the nobility were fixed by the Fronde, and herein lies its real significance in the long run of French history, or certainly in the run of France's longest reign. In terms of the state, Louis was not a reformer. This is not to suggest that changes were not made; certainly the abuses and unpopular practices associated with the regency were abandoned. But, as Robin Briggs notes, those in charge conceived of such practices as only temporary and undesirable in the end, and the government of Louis XIV was actually conservative and disinclined to innovate.[76] His successes were based less on innovation and more on his skillful uses of the traditional means at hand. Among the means available to Louis were his nobility and the elements of their political culture.

Louis' relationship with his nobility amounted to a highly successful collaboration which formed the backbone of the absolutist state. The order and control effected by this reign were the result of vastly improved relations between the king and his nobility. Emerging from the chaos of the Fronde, both king and nobles came to realize that cooperation could prove mutually advantageous. After decades of revolts and conflict, this realization came nearly as an epiphany to both sides, and it produced a dramatically different posture between the two. Deals were struck. Offices, honors, and titles were dispensed. Ties of dependency were reinforced. But how would this approach to monarchical/aristocratic relations differ from what had come before? The difference was in the more careful and thoughtful management of patronage. And if there was an innovation in the reign of Louis XIV, this was it – to take the Renaissance state and manage it to greater effect.

Louis' more thoughtful approach to administration began with the court nobility. Drawing upon an image of the court that dated back to the reign of Francis I, Louis constructed a more elaborate and more loyal version of the Renaissance court. Historians have been fascinated by the court and daily life at Versailles, to the extent that its importance may have been exaggerated. Nonetheless, it represents an important achievement and aspect of the reign. The most obvious feature of court society under Louis was its size. The number of aristocrats who circulated in and out of court increased dramatically during this reign, and the construction of the great baroque palace made this logistically possible. The king and his court took up residence at the palace in the mid-1680s, though construction was not yet complete. Those who comprised court society included the royal family, high-ranking nobles, leading officials, and individuals who had managed to curry the king's favor. They came to court for access to power and prestige, but court life also had its own intrinsic appeal, which derived in part from the Renaissance model of court life found in Castiglione's very popular handbook, *The Courtier*. Courtliness had been a cultural ideal that itself served to draw the upper echelons of the nobility to court.[77]

In the end, however, it was access to patronage and political power that siphoned these elements from the aristocratic population to court society. By residence at court, the most prominent families of France were able to promote the power and wealth of their kinsmen and clients. In short, the political implications of residence at court reverberated through the provinces, as clienteles reaped the benefits of their patrons' proximity to the king.[78]

Predictably, court society was highly competitive, because it, like all of aristocratic society, was organized into factions or cliques, each struggling to promote its own interests. These factions were forged by family ties, marriages, and the bonds between patrons and clients. According to Roger Mettam, court society was distinguished from greater elite society in that loyalty and gratitude were not components of such relationships. Instead, it was a milieu in which relationships changed quite abruptly according to one's political capital and usefulness, making 'cunning and deceitfulness' essential to survival. As Mettam writes:

> When the star of a courtier appeared to be rising, it was for each man to decide whether his own ends were better served by aiding or thwarting this process. No one wanted any faction to be too powerful, unless it was his own. It was therefore as vital to disguise the strategems of your own clique as it was to uncover those of others. The result was a society dominated by bluff and counterbluff, in which it was imperative to be a step ahead of everyone else.[79]

To manage this highly dynamic but unstable court, Louis attempted to balance factions, which had the effect of encouraging competition. Louis made it plain that he would always give a request for patronage a fair hearing, which in turn propelled the competition at court. By keeping his courtiers constantly in a state of competition, Louis was able to maintain a balance of factional power and therefore to effect control. Crucial to this process were the ritual, courtesy and etiquette that constituted essential features of daily life at Versailles.[80] But the use of ceremony and courtesy by the state was not new. Cardinal Richelieu recognized in courtesy a means by which he might control France's most powerful and frequently most unruly subjects. By enforcing the rules of etiquette, Louis XIII and the cardinal symbolically enforced submissive behavior.[81] What Louis XIV constructed at Versailles was therefore not original; his genius was to emphasize etiquette and ceremony and to perfect them, creating structures of daily life at court that permitted an extraordinary measure of control.

Court society lived by what Norbert Elias has described as a graded scale of prestige. Indeed, he argues that it was a society with a prestige-fetish, a society in which acts had an exactly graded prestige value, that is, they served as indicators or marques of the rank or position of an individual or family. Elias describes etiquette as the 'inexhaustible motor' of court society. And for this motor to function, the king had to provide a constant source of energy, which he did by allowing his nearly every act to be performed in the company of others.[82]

Louis lived therefore in a very public way. From his *levée*, or rising in the morning, to his *couchée*, or retirement at night, his life and daily activities were, with few exceptions, staged for public viewing. To witness the most mundane event in His Majesty's routine became a coveted marque of status at court. Nobles competed for the honor of holding his shirt or the candelabrum. To have access to him in routine contexts was significant, but to be noticed by him, to be acknowledged by the royal gaze, was a tremendous sign of distinction, indeed of merit.[83]

The culture of this court society, so carefully constructed by and around Louis, was one in which behavior was strictly codified according to elaborate rules of etiquette. Drawing upon aristocratic traditions, every act for this hierarchically arranged society was invested with meaning and value. Gestures and comportment reflected rank; the way one conducted oneself in the presence of others, and vice versa, helped to distinguish and place one within the hierarchy. Nor was this a static society. Social mobility, upward or downward, provided the mainspring of court society, driving competition and the desire for closer proximity to the king. For Elias, this is precisely how and why court society developed its prestige-fetish. Louis' thoughtful manipulation of etiquette permitted him to maintain a balance of factions within court society.[84]

We should not, however, place excessive emphasis on court society and Louis' control of its participants. Aristocrats were not required to live at Versailles, and they certainly did not live there year round. Even the great palace had limited capacity, making a system of seasonal quarters necessary. Active service at Versailles took place twice a year for three months, or a total of six months annually. At any given point, there were about 5000 nobles and 5000 commoners in residence. Rotating in and out as they did, about 10 000 nobles resided half of each year at court. These figures represent only a small percentage (5 per cent) of the larger nobility.[85]

As for the other 95 per cent of the nobility, they remained in the provinces, their power base. Here they were not disconnected or cut off from the distribution of favors, as traditional interpretations maintained, but instead functioned as part of the king's greater and more expansive system of patronage. By the use of provincial power-brokers and a carefully directed system of patronage, Louis was able to bring significant elements within the provincial nobility on board. In some ways this policy was not unlike that of Richelieu, who created a ministerial clientele in the provinces, but it was not simply another ministerial clientele. Louis was careful to retain direct control of these ties of dependency, which in and of itself represented a form of innovation. What he constructed was a system of dependency and mutually beneficial relationships that was, as we shall see, very personal in nature.

But what about the other innovations associated with the 'absolutism' of his reign? Here too there is some room for revision and certainly more finely nuanced interpretations. Let us consider, for example, the '30 Tyrants' or the *intendants*. Louis retained the use of the *intendants*, but their role changed substantially. After the Fronde, the *intendant* was put to other uses and redefined to be less objectionable. The crown deployed the *intendants* still to act as watchdogs, but their function became increasingly to supply information, that is, to collect economic and demographic data on the province to which they were assigned. The local interests that *intendants* invariably developed and exhibited served to cast them more as representatives of that province than as agents of the crown. Mettam makes clear that their importance to the process of state-building in the second half of the seventeenth century has therefore been largely overestimated.[86]

And the fate of representative institutions under Louis XIV? In keeping with his traditionalist nature, the king and Colbert chose not to pursue Marillac's reformist course, which would have opposed and eliminated the surviving local estates. Rather, the king opted to continue Richelieu's strategy of working through the estates. By using bribery, threats, and very clever manipulation of their agendas, one way or another Louis got the money that he requested. And in the process, the elites who sat in the estates profited sufficiently themselves. Professor Major has convincingly argued that by the most traditional means Louis and Colbert extracted what they needed from the *pays d'états*. No reformer, Louis relied on the means at hand and his own perceptive understanding of human nature.[87] So convincing is Major's argument that Nicholas Henshall finds it difficult to apply the concept of 'absolutism' to the *pays d'états* where it appears that the local assemblies were actually reborn. As Henshall interprets Major, 'The meticulous preparations made by royal agents before their meetings suggest that co-operation could not be taken for granted. Tactful handling, bribery, bargaining and the avoidance of controversial issues were as responsible for their apparent quiescence as for the *parlements*'.[88]

Louis' posture towards the Parlement of Paris was not much more direct or confrontational than it was towards the estates. Certainly, much has been made of the fact that he denied the parlement the right to remonstrate. But he also avoided issues that would prove a source of contention with the judges. Louis sought to prevent them from meddling in affairs of state and the work of the council by reducing their right to remonstrate royal decrees and by giving decrees of the council supremacy over parlementary decrees, but, by the same token, he limited the right of his councils and the *intendants* to obstruct the work of the parlement. According to Hamscher, he 'made no attempt to dispense with the other equally important procedures the judges had used effectively in the past to oppose royal policies. Plenary sessions, *mercuriales*, the registration of legislation, and the right to issue judicial and administrative decrees remained integral parts of Parlement's privileges and tradition.'[89] Plenary sessions were general sessions which all parlementaires attended. Given their strength in numbers, the parlementaires felt at liberty to discuss and express their opposition to public policy at such meetings. The *mercuriales* were sessions at which the parlementaires examined the courts' internal procedures, but these occasions often led to debates over public policy and relations between the court and the monarchy. Given that both became a venue in which to criticize royal policy, it is obvious that the crown wanted to curtail them. But it was unable to eliminate them altogether.[90] Furthermore, the crown did nothing to abolish the real basis of the parlement's power as a corporate body – the fact that judges owned their offices and could choose their successors. The persistence of the venality and the *paulette* were crucial to the independence and authority of this institution. After the Fronde the crown chose to leave the parlement intact, rather than to bring about permanent institutional change, which meant that Louis' relations with the parlement involved supervision and management and that absolutism as it pertained to the highest court in the realm was of a highly personal nature.[91]

Louis' personal approach to governance is well known and most apparent in his decision to abandon the pattern of his Bourbon predecessors in which they relied heavily on the advice and guidance of a chief minister. After Mazarin's death in 1661 he embarked on a course of personal rule that saw him act as his own chief minister. He also reformed the Council of State by excluding the princes of the blood, the queen mother, and assorted other officials, and instead constituted a smaller council of four. The new council included the superintendant of finances (Fouquet, until his ignominious demise, at which point he was replaced by Colbert), the secretary of state for war (LeTellier), the secretary of state for foreign relations (Lionne), and, of course, Louis himself.[92] These and subsequent ministers constituted the core of a larger circle of advisors that was carefully compiled by Louis to be trustworthy, grateful, and, most of all, a dependable source of good advice. For some time historians wrote about the modest social origins of Louis' advisors, even placing some (Colbert, for example) within bourgeois families. As the older interpretation viewed this circle, it was part of the genius of Louis to exclude the old grandee and sword families and to rely on those, including bourgeois, who would be eminently more trustworthy, talented, and beholden. Obviously, such thinking viewed the old nobility with great suspicion and the middle class as a great pool of talent.

Recent studies have suggested a more complex reading of Louis' advisors. First, few historians would refer to the great ministerial families as bourgeois. Obviously, at some point in their family histories they were connected with the bourgeoisie, but by the seventeenth century they formed part of the robe nobility. Second, few would persist in talking about the exclusion of the grandees and the sword from Louis' government. We know now that Louis still relied on their advice, that he continued to appoint sword families to important offices, and that he arranged for some of them to marry the sons and daughters of his ministers, in this way elevating the social status of the ministerial families. In his study of court society and politics, Mettam argues that senior aristocrats continued to act as close advisors to this king.[93] As he describes it, 'The inner circle of aristocrats, and the ministerial families to whom they were more and more closely tied by marriage, were at the very centre of policy-making under Louis XIV and spearheaded his attempts to make the authority of the crown more effective throughout the kingdom.'[94]

The most important link between the crown and the kingdom was the governor. Traditionally the king chose provincial governors from among the princes of the blood and the dukes and peers of the realm, a policy that could and did prove problematic as they used the governorships for their own independent provincial power bases. Henry IV and Louis XIII opted for governors from less illustrious provincial notables as part of an effort to engender more loyalty and gratitude. But Louis XIV, inclined to observe rank and hierarchy more strictly, once again reserved these posts for aristocrats of ducal rank. In this way, no one could claim that the provincial governor lacked the social background for the office. Where Louis chose to innovate was in his decision to introduce a loyal noble from another family as lieutenant-general, which is to say as *de facto* governor. In this way, he was assured some measure of control over the province, while he managed to keep various grandee families content by his patronage.[95]

In the end, it was his use of patronage and personal ties of dependency that allowed Louis to bring about the control that has subsequently been labelled 'absolutism' by generations of historians. Rather than rely on ministerial *créatures* and clienteles, Louis formed his own networks of dependents that radiated throughout the realm. He relied to a considerable extent, as Richelieu before him, on provincial brokers, and he forged connections with grandee families cautiously and thoughtfully. His manipulation of court society and elite society in the provinces allowed him to bring the institutions in which they were deeply entrenched in line with royal thinking. The key to Louis' reign, as his power fanned out to the provinces, lay not so much in institutional reform, but in the more skillful management of the traditional means of governing: personal ties of obligation and dependency. At this he was the master. Monarchical power in late seventeenth-century France rested not on bureaucratic efficiency but on the relationships that bound man to man and sometimes woman. By these mutually beneficial relationships not only the court but the country was brought into compliance, for the most part, with the policies of the crown. Bringing the country on board was a complex process in which the provincial nobilities were central. As historical agents, they were capable of acting on behalf of themselves, the province, and the crown. In Provence, Dauphiné, and Brittany, the process of constructing these crucial relationships was difficult, prolonged, and particularly revealing in what it tells us about the contours and dynamics of state and society in seventeenth-century France.

The crucial intersection of state and provincial society reveals also the extent to which nationalist sentiment existed in seventeenth-century France. Historians debate the origins, strength, and nature of nationalist sentiment in early modern France, but the trend in recent scholarship is to assert its existence and importance.[96] For Colette Beaune the monarchy played the crucial role in the emergence of French nationalism, and it did so especially during the period of the Hundred Years War as the Valois kings attempted to counter the persistent questions about their legitimacy by the construction of a national propaganda. For Beaune this was part of a longer evolution in which French nationalism took on a messianic character that referred to France's glorious destiny to rule the Western world. Rule by the French dynasty would mark the end of time and would bring the peace and prosperity of which medieval men and women could only dream. In times of crisis, the French were especially drawn to the religious idea that the sacral monarchy/nation would bring about a better time.[97]

The nationalist sentiment that evolved from the late Middle Ages did not observe a neatly linear pattern of development. In fact, historians of early modern nationalism argue that it was in no way linear, that it appeared and receded according to circumstances. During the Wars of Religion nationalist sentiment surged, and at the same time it took on a more complex character. For Catholics, Catholicism and the nation were indissolubly linked. For Protestants, the nation and religion were separate entities, and the St Bartholomew's Day Massacre resulted in a new distinction between the idea of the king and the nation. Henceforth, Protestants identified France as her people, rather than her king, a position that was moderated with the succession of one of their own, Henry IV, and with his effort to defeat the Spanish in the 1590s. The Spanish threat served to bring Catholic and Protestant nationalism closer together by their shared fear of Spanish conquest. Anti-Spanish sentiments, indeed racism, converged from both directions to produce a new national consciousness under the first Bourbon. The rule of Henry IV, a man of obvious valor who governed by Salic right, was for Protestants and many

Catholics, even before his conversion to Catholicism, infinitely prefer-able to a Spanish succession.[98]

Henry IV's reign saw the French nation recreated, but the rhetoric of nationalist sentiment would as a result of these religious conflicts become less religious. The Bourbons took care to direct the development of a national consciousness in a way that tied it to the monarchy. Especially prominent in this effort was a patriotic literature that celebrated French history, and in particular the history of the French monarchy. Following the crisis of the religious wars, writers, including *politiques*, celebrated the survival of the French monarchy and French independence. These authors looked to Henry IV as the king who had saved the nation and given it peace, and in this way the French national consciousness became intensely patriotic, less religious, and focused even more closely on the institution of the monarchy.[99]

Nor was the monarchy the sole source of national consciousness in early modern France; nationalism was not simply part of the state-building process launched from the center towards the periphery. Peter Sahlins maintains that nationalism was a two-way process, a 'dialectic of local and national interests which produced boundaries of national territory'.[100] For Sahlins, national identity was also defined in terms of opposition – 'us' and 'them'. In studying the borderland of Cerdanya in the Pyrenees, Sahlins observed local populations using nationalism to advance their own ends, ultimately to defend their community against outsiders.[101]

In short, national identity had its own autonomous and local sources. It expressed belief in an imagined community with common interests and confronted a common opponent. It was the anthropologist Benedict Anderson who defined nationalism as an imagined political community in which the nation is 'conceived as a deep, horizontal comradeship'.[102] This idea of community held sway over the imaginations of provincial populations, and, in Sahlins's dialectic of local and national interests, definitions of community became a dynamic and variable force. It could set locals in opposition to royal policy, and it could bring them resolutely to the side of the king. The extent to which the king could rely on nation-alism varied according to the imagined communities of provincial societies.

Chapter 3: Provence: The Opportunities of Factionalism

Living at the Mediterranean fringe of the realm, the inhabitants of scenic Provence fought valiantly in the seventeenth century to prevent the encroachment of royal authority and the erosion of provincial liberties. Provence was not like other parts of France. Of course, the same is true to some extent for all the French provinces, but it is particularly true for those that lay at the periphery. Deeply imbedded in the regional identity of Provence was the belief that its residents had their own special rights and privileges, the most important of which was the right of provincial estates to approve, apportion, and collect taxes. In short, Provence was a *pays d'états*, and in the seventeenth century its nobility would instigate and lead popular rebellions protesting the introduction of royal agents and authority. But it was also the same nobility that, in its complicity, would assist the crown finally in establishing greater control over the province. State-building in Provence, and elsewhere in the *pays d'états*, rested on a collaborative relationship forged by the crown and its ministers with the provincial nobility. This relationship between the province and the crown, or, more specifically, between the elites and the crown, bore the character of clientelism, and the construction of royal clienteles proceeded rather differently from one province to the next. In this great effort to infiltrate the outlying provinces, the crown confronted the legendary regional diversity that has become a *sine qua non* for French historians.

Among the traits that distinguished Provence and its elites was the fact of urban nobilities. Provençal nobles tended to live primarily in towns while holding large tracts of land in the countryside, and this pattern of urban residency distinguished the Provençal and southern nobility from

70

that of northern France, which tended instead to be based in their rural *châteaux*. Provençal nobles had lived in town for centuries because the urban way of life was older and more deeply entrenched in the south of France, or the Midi. Dating back to the Roman empire, urbanism left its mark on the entire Mediterranean basin. After the decline of the empire, many Mediterranean populations continued to follow the Roman way of life, a course still possible because not all towns and cities perished during the widespread destruction that accompanied the fall of Rome.[1] Located in towns, the Provençal nobility had access to municipal institutions which they controlled and manipulated to obstruct those policies of the monarchy that they perceived as encroachments on provincial liberties or as detracting from their own power within the region.

The power of the nobility derived in part from their positions as great allodial proprietors. While the nobility of northern France developed out of military necessity along traditional feudal lines, in the south an aristocracy of Gallo-Roman stock predated the appearance of feudalism in the region. By owning large tracts of allodial property, these families formed an elite class. Some families claimed elite status based on their relations to the old senatorial class of the Roman empire, a fact that continued as late as the eleventh century.[2] But land would prove the most enduring basis of the southern aristocracy, and land tenure in the region differed significantly from the way in which land was occupied elsewhere. The territory of Provence and much of the Midi was carved into allods, or land that involved no recognition of overlordship; the owner of an allod could sell or give it away at will because possession was free from service, rent, homage, and fealty. Legal scholars maintain that it was the survival of Roman law in most parts of the south that ensured the preservation of allodial rights. Roman law provided the basis of allodial holdings because it affirmed the rights of the individual and recognized the power of the written contract. It provided for the absolute power of the individual over his or her property, in contrast to the feudal principle of subordination to an overlord. When feudalism did finally trickle down from northern France, where it was indigenous, to infiltrate the Midi, it meant the appearance of fiefs and a relative decline in the amount of property that was owned outright. Nevertheless, since much Provençal land was not held in fief, the allod remained commonplace throughout the seventeenth century.[3]

This is not to suggest that aristocratic and upwardly mobile families did not seek the additional status conferred by the fief. Many southern nobles chose to enter into what were theoretically subordinate relationships by the process of infeudation, that is, by accepting a fief from an overlord and with it all the obligations owed by a vassal. As it evolved in the Midi, however, feudalism appears to have been particularly complex and limited in its intended social effects. Although the ideal feudal pyramid never existed in northern France, one could argue that the northern aristocracy did achieve a considerable degree of rank and subordination among its members. In the Midi, however, feudal ties were often constructed without the desired control, because they bound allodial proprietors of equal wealth, making it impossible to enforce compliance with the obligations of vassalage. These ties appear to have been strong only when they bound a powerful overlord and a lesser noble who, not owning large tracts of allodial property, truly depended on his fief for subsistence. Given the limitations of feudalism in the south, one must conclude that the driving force in infeudation was the distinction that derived from the profession of arms and the judicial privileges accompanying a fief.[4]

The haphazard development of feudalism and the persistence of the allodial regime in Provence and the Midi combined with urban residence to produce a unique aristocracy and society in which sharp distinctions between burgher and knight, town and country, did not exist. Urban society in the south evolved as a freer association of nobles, bourgeois, and the lower orders. This is suggested, for example, by their residential patterns within a town. In Aix-en-Provence, the administrative capital, there was a sizable aristocratic population dispersed through all the *quartiers*. In fact, in Aix their numbers were particularly high (12.75 per cent of the total population) because of the presence of sovereign courts and the professional and social opportunities therein. Traditional or 'sword' nobles, administration or 'robe' nobles, and a very important and large group with characteristics of both all congregated in Aix. There they participated in municipal and royal government, dominated the surrounding countryside, and lived on the rents and revenues of scattered properties, judicial offices, and various other investments. At the same time they figured prominently in expansive networks of alliances with the entire Provençal nobility, and by this means they extended their influence throughout the province and beyond.[5]

Provençal resistance to the expansion of royal authority occurred in three major revolts, in 1630, 1649, and 1659, each centered in Aix because of its political and administrative significance. The residential nobility, including those who lived there simply because of the sovereign courts and those whose families were native to Aix, inevitably played a leading

role in these episodes. But the social contours of this group were important also in determining their involvement. It was not only the simple fact
of urban residence that distinguished the nobility of Aix from provincial
nobilities in northern France; it was also the structure and character of
this nobility, both of which were in turn shaped by the urban milieu. The
city of Aix provided an environment in which assimilation between old
and new families was practically unavoidable, and the consequence of
this was a social structure that was far more fluid than the sword–robe
construct discussed in Chapter 1 would suggest. In Aix families differed
in antiquity and wealth, but rarely in terms of occupation or function.[6]
The nobility of Aix included old native families many of which were not
really sword nobles. Certainly, they owned fiefs, but often they could not
claim chivalric origins. A few families had claims to nobility that were
immemorial, but most of the old families were *anoblis* of the fourteenth
and fifteenth centuries (which was a period of significant upward mobility in Provence, Brittany, and elsewhere).[7] Typically, such families had
started their social progress as attorneys, notaries, or merchants in medieval Provence and had attained noble status before 1500. These *anoblis*
from the period of the Angevin counts may be considered old nobility
because their claims predate the arrival of the sovereign courts, the
venality of office, and the period of wholesale social ascendancy that
created the legendary robe nobility of the sixteenth century. Their origins and early histories determined that the orientation of such families
was urban, administrative, occasionally mercantile, but not traditionally
chivalric or sword. The concept therefore of a sword–robe conflict is
essentially impossible to apply to Aix and much of the south because a
large portion of the older nobility was never a sword nobility.[8]

Conversely, many of the judicial families of Aix did not fit the classic
profile of robe nobles. In 1695 the noble population of Aix included a
total of 596 households, 196 of which belonged to men who held offices
in the courts.[9] It would be impossible to classify all of these 196 households as robe nobility because nearly half of them exhibited some of
the traditional *marques de noblesse* such as owning fiefs, and because
20 per cent of that group held the titles of count, marquis, or baron.
What we find in Aix is that judicial families bore certain sword traits, and
many of the old families came from what might be considered a robe
background.

The native nobility of Aix consisted of approximately 81 extended
families in the seventeenth century; that is, 81 extended families who
lived there and can be classified as Aixois. Among these families, 38 were

old and 43 were new, and a majority (67 families) held at least one office during the century, including positions in the parlement, the Cour des Comptes, the *sénéchaussée* (a judicial unit intermediate in level between the parlement and the seigneurial courts), and the *généralité*. Nearly half, or 31, of these officeholding families came from the old nobility, which means that new families did not dominate officeholding.[10]

How did a Provençal family actually acquire noble status? Most purchased letters of ennoblement. Between 1550 and 1673, 134 new families joined the Provençal aristocracy as a result of purchasing letters to this effect, a process that was both legal and foolproof. Still, there were other means of attaining noble status, and 86 families 'usurped' their positions during the same period. By usurpation we are referring to a less certain strategy that included a certain presumption and the risk of being condemned as *parvenus* or, even worse legally, false nobles. How would a family attempt to usurp noble status? One of the most important means was by purchasing a fief, which in spite of its declining military importance remained a mark of nobility. Exactly half of the 86 families that usurped nobility in this period owned fiefs. As we have already noted, the peculiar nature of the *taille* gave fiefs a special significance in this part of France. Since the *taille réelle* fell on non-feudal or allodial property rather than on people, a southern noble who owned allodial property would have paid the *taille* for that property while being exempt from the tax on his fiefs.[11] The significance of the allod in a discussion of relations between crown and nobility is that it affected the nature of this provincial nobility and its relations with the rest of society by making aristocratic owners of allodial property subject to the *taille réelle* just like commoners who held allodial property.

The fief was therefore the only way in which to acquire one of the most highly valued privileges of the nobility – tax-exempt status – as well as the right to attend assemblies of the provincial estates. In Aix, only 9 of the 43 newly ennobled native families failed to acquire a fief. Moreover, it is clear that new families had invested in fiefs for their social rather than their material benefits, because many of the fiefs acquired were too small to constitute a significant financial investment. In short, new families tended to purchase a token fief so that they could share in the privileges of fiefholding. It enabled them to claim some immunity from the *taille*, and, at the same time, it made these same families subject to the *afflorinement*, a tax levied by the nobility on the nobility (through the Assembly of the Nobility of Provence) and assessed according to fiefholding. What we see here is how noble identity in Provence was paradoxically linked both with immunity from royal taxation and also with the obligation to pay taxes levied locally by their own social kind.[12]

Clearly, offices were important to the process of upward social mobility, and these same families invested heavily in them. But so did old families, the result of which was to inflate the prices of offices through competition. And here too the social rewards of officeholding generally outweighed the financial benefits. Income from offices was actually rather mediocre when compared with the return on commerce, and those Provençal nobles who preferred to put their money in business did so without risking derogation. The salary, or *gages*, for an office in the courts consisted of interest on the sum originally paid for the office, which ranged generally from 1 to 4.5 per cent. These were not spectacular rewards, and furthermore they were not always forthcoming, all of which begs the question of why invest? There seems to be some clue to the answer in the fact that the actual price of offices, the money families had to pay to enter them, soared during the seventeenth century. At the beginning of the period the office of councillor in the parlement sold for between 3000 and 6000 *livres*; the price jumped dramatically in 1626 when one family paid the inflated sum of 54 000 *livres* for the same office. By 1633, the position of councillor went routinely for 50 000 to 60 000 *livres*. Controlling for changes in the value of the *livres-tournois*, Sharon Kettering has shown us that this amounts to a 400 per cent increase in the price of this office over little more than a couple of decades. Furthermore, we know that the inflated prices of offices were not the result of a general inflationary pattern within the economy. We are left to conclude that competition for these offices drove their prices to such extraordinary levels. Specifically, Kettering found that when prices peaked so did the volume of sales.[13] With the numerous ennoblements of the late sixteenth and early seventeenth centuries, the demand for offices raised their costs. Factor in as well demand generated by old-established families who saw in the courts new political opportunities, and the result was that it cost a lot to become a parlementaire. Why do it, other than to enhance a family's social standing? The answer lies in the nature of the southern nobility, and in particular the Aixois: they competed for offices in the courts because of a tradition of service to the community and, of course, to control politics in the region.[14]

The nobility of Aix participated so energetically in their urban community that the town was known in the seventeenth century as a 'ville aristocratique', a description that implies more than numbers. It suggests as well a heritage of civic involvement on the part of its nobility and, in fact, a certain aristocratic hegemony. Their role in the community was elaborate and multifaceted. First and foremost, it included a dominant presence in local government, which was elective with principal power residing in the town council. Nominations for offices were drawn from each of the five *quartiers* of the town. As a result, aristocratic power in local government depended on demographic distribution within the town, and in this respect the nobility were well situated. Although there was some concentration in the southern neighborhoods, noble households were spread throughout the community, a situation that made for a complex mixture of classes by both quarter and street and that enabled them to serve as councillors from each of the *quartiers*. This geographic distribution offered them a broad base of power within Aix.[15]

Even more crucial to their power was the fact that they controlled the consulates. As the highest representatives of communal activity, the three consuls and the assessor commanded great prestige and authority within the town and the province. In addition to their municipal functions, the consuls and assessor served as *procureurs du pays*, the executive committee of the Estates of Provence. Because of the regional component of the offices, the membership of the consulates was not drawn exclusively from Aix, but certainly the Aixois had an advantage in gaining these positions. Custom prescribed that the first consul should belong to the fiefholding nobility of Provence, that the second be a member of the local nobility, and that the third come from 'la bonne bourgeoisie'. The assessor was chosen from among the attorneys in Aix. Custom thus gave nobles an advantage within the consulate of two to one. In reality their advantage often exceeded this because many of the third consuls were also nobles, and by the seventeenth century most of the assessors were nobles trained in law. During the period 1598–1695, nobles held 289, or 77 per cent, of the positions in the consulate, and of these seats 137 belonged to members of the local nobility.[16]

These positions inevitably became the objects of factional competition. Incumbents nominated their successors, which meant that patrons could place their clients as consuls, assessors, and councillors simply by nominating them. Such leverage permitted patrons to annex city government and augment the power that they wielded through the sovereign courts and the *généralité*. Municipal government therefore became a battleground for rival factions, and at no time was this rivalry more visible than during the annual elections, when competing factions contrived to influence the nominations of friends, relatives, and clients.[17] Sides were drawn along clientele lines, but the antiquity of families appears not to have played much of a role. Old and new families participated in local government at almost exactly the same rate, and they did so by signing on with one clientele or another.[18] This factionalism that colored municipal politics and municipal life in Aix was just as important to the political life of the entire province.

The first half of the seventeenth century saw the city of Aix engulfed in a bitter struggle to prevent any further extension of royal authority in Provence, and the period of Cardinal Richelieu and Cardinal Mazarin was one of recurring political crises and rebellion. Specifically, the institutional reforms of the period touched off a series of revolts in which the nobility of Aix played a highly visible role, and on the whole their reactions to reform initiatives were guided by the clienteles to which they belonged, clienteles that had infiltrated all the theaters of political conflict. They included the Estates of Provence, the positions as *procureur du pays*, the Assembly of the Nobility, and the Parlement of Aix. Each of these institutions was dominated by factions of nobles in which the Aixois were particularly well represented; as *procureurs du pays* and as the largest local group in the parlement, the Aixois had the greatest impact on provincial affairs.

A *pays d'états*, Provence traditionally benefitted from the protection of its representative assemblies against royal attacks on provincial privileges. In particular the fiery Provençals treasured the right of their estates to approve, collect, and apportion taxes – a regional prerogative that acted as a check on royal authority. The composition of the Estates of Provence included deputies of the first estate (the clergy), the second estate (all fiefholding noblemen), and the third estate (deputies from the chief town in each *viguerie* of Provence). The nobility, with about 150 members, was the largest of the three orders, and since voting was conducted by head rather than order, the second estate enjoyed a decisive numerical advantage.[19] The provincial governor called annual meetings of the estates to debate and to apportion taxes, the most important of which was the *taille réelle*. After assessment, local responsibility for collection of taxes fell on *viguerie* officials who received monies from taxpayers and transferred them to the provincial treasurer; he in turned channeled these funds to the *trésoriers généraux de France*.[20]

Between sessions of the estates, the *procureurs du pays* tended to all administrative matters. By the late sixteenth century it was customary for the archbishop of Aix, the three consuls of Aix, and the assessor of Aix to hold the positions of *procureurs du pays nés*. In addition, each estate was represented on this committee by two *procureurs joints*. Since the *procureurs* were charged during interim periods with safeguarding provincial interests – often in opposition to the crown – their responsibilities were considerable. They acted as a sort of grievance committee.[21] At the same time the *procureurs* enforced ordinances passed by the estates, a duty that saw their intervention in and supervision over many provincial matters. The *procureurs nés* dealt with daily problems of executing decisions of the estates. Meetings of the *procureurs nés et joints*, however, were called between sessions of the estates to address new issues.[22]

As the executive committee of the estates, the *procureurs* had an important role in tax administration, including the right to examine the books of the provincial treasurers before they were turned over to the Chambre des Comptes for audit. The *procureurs* directed construction and maintenance of all highways and bridges in Provence, and their jurisdiction also included such problems as public health and the billeting of troops. The bulk of the correspondence from Louis XIII and Louis XIV to the *procureurs* concerned, in fact, the costs and logistics of housing and feeding royal troops in the region, as well as the maintenance of local fortifications.[23]

Faced with the growing financial burden of the Wars of Religion, the governors of Provence were forced in the sixteenth century to seek additional taxes to pay the salaries of troops. Because the *procureurs du pays* did not have the authority to impose taxes without the approval of a representative body, and because the estates regularly refused to approve new taxes, the provincial governors sought the alternative of calling deputies from various communities together when the estates was not in session. This Assembly of Communities consisted of the *procureurs nés et joints* and deputies from 19 communities in Provence. The Assembly of Communities and the estates were separate bodies, but their functions were not specifically delineated. Often the assembly was called to deal with the same issues that the estates would have addressed had it been in session.[24]

Within a short span of time royal officials began to display an obvious preference for the Assembly of Communities over the estates. For one reason, the assembly could be convoked more rapidly because preliminary *viguerie* meetings to elect deputies were not necessary. More important, the estates was more costly to hold and frequently impossible to manage. The assembly, whose membership and voting procedure were not weighted in favor of the contentious Provençal nobles, tended to grant most of the taxes requested. By the end of the sixteenth century, royal

government clearly preferred to deal with the Assembly of the Communities, and after 1639 the estates never met again.[25]

Whether working with the estates or the assembly, the offices of
procureurs du pays were central in the administration of the province. And
as the *procureur nés*, the consuls and assessor of Aix were cardinal figures
in the system. Thus, by virtue of their municipal positions, the nobility
of Aix was central to the administration of the province as well.

The nobility of Aix also figured prominently in the separate Assembly
of the Nobility of Provence. This forum debated all matters that pertained to the nobility, particularly the defense of traditional privileges
such as the tax-exempt status of fiefs. Out of self-interest, the assembly
frequently found itself averse to the desires and goals of royal government. In 1639, for example, the war with the Habsburgs forced the crown
to call the *ban* and *arrière-ban* (the feudal levy) in Provence, thereby provoking massive resistance from the Provençal aristocracy, who ultimately
refused to leave Provence for the battlefield. Subsequently, the Assembly
of the Nobility was suspended; it met only three times during the remaining 60 years of the century, having been replaced by a smaller, less fractious
committee of nobles.[26]

During the long intervals that passed between convocations of the
Assembly of Nobility, *syndics* conducted routine business and acted as
spokesmen. Customarily, at least one *syndic* was trained as an attorney
and could deal with litigation involving the assembly. Again, the nobles
of Aix served regularly as *syndics* during the seventeenth century. Between
1598 and 1700, the Assembly of the Nobility had a total of 133 *syndics*, 37
(or 28 per cent) of whom were native to Aix, suggesting the extent to
which the Aixois were involved in the affairs of the provincial nobility.
Furthermore, Aixois routinely served as *commissaires* of the nobility, who
were nobles elected by the assembly to guard and control membership
by investigating the social background of those who joined. Over the
course of the century, 36 of 83 *commissaires* were Aixois.[27]

It was through these various positions and institutions that the noble
residents of Aix positioned themselves to act as the major protagonists
in disputes with royal agents, and it was through these institutions that
elite society engaged in factional politics. In addition to the problem of
factional politics and the issue of provincial rights, the crown had to
confront in Provence the fact that provincial governors eluded their
control. This was the problem of the provincial governors – they created
their own independent power bases, which placed them beyond the
control of central government, because on the frontier such support was

essential for the governor to function in his official capacity. The result was a governor who had made so many appointments, with the recipients obligated directly to him, that he could function independently of central government. Richelieu's refusal to tolerate such independence stemmed from the fact that it allowed governors to pursue personal policies that ran contrary to those of the crown. The conflicts that erupted in Provence began over the *élus* and popular conceptions of provincial rights, but they were propelled even more by factional politics and the problem of the provincial governor. The crown's strategy for quelling resistance and raising additional revenue would be two-pronged – its goals were first to bring the parlement and certain provincial institutions on board with royal policies and second to control the provincial governor. As we shall see, the interests of the parlement and those of the governor were often in direct opposition, but the crown's approach to each was the same and, in fact, overlapping. By the construction of ministerial and royal clienteles within provincial institutions, the crown could not only control these institutions but could isolate the provincial governor.

The Revolt of Cascaveoux

The first great episode of resistance to royal policy took place in 1630 and is known as the Revolt of Cascaveoux. It began as a response to the creation of *élections* in Provence. In 1629 a royal edict called for the establishment of ten *élections* and 350 positions of *élus* to assess and collect the *taille*, a responsibility traditionally claimed by the Estates of Provence. To make matters worse, Richelieu also raised the *gabelle* (salt tax), the *taillon* (a tax supplemental to the *taille* and generally raised to meet military emergencies), and the *don gratuit* (a 'contribution' to the crown levied in the south on the province as a whole). The Provençaux correctly regarded these actions, together with the proposed *élus*, as infringements on their traditional rights and as a deliberate effort to supplant their estates. The fact that Richelieu had also increased troop movements in the area to support his campaign against the Protestants in neighboring Languedoc and to assist with the war in Italy only served to create more ill will and distrust towards central government. To add insult to injury, the cardinal demanded of the local populations that they provide 700 mules and muleteers, a request that placed a great financial strain on the resources of several communities. And even worse, in order that it be available to provide for his troops, Richelieu forbade the export of grain from the province. Faced with the *élus*, with tax increases, with increased expenses for the war effort, and with the unpleasantness of troops billeted upon them, the Estates of Provence, perhaps naively, demanded that the king revoke all the edicts in question. The crown's response was entirely predictable – their demands were denied.[28] The situation was therefore one of widespread discontent and even hostility towards the crown when, in June 1629, the plague appeared, igniting this volatile atmosphere. Predictably, the plague arrived on the heels of a major subsistence crisis in Provence, one that was exacerbated by the destruction done by Richelieu's troops and the demand placed on a declining supply of wheat, oats, and other grains. The price of wheat climbed steadily from 1625 to 1630, and the cost of bread placed it beyond the reach of greater and greater numbers.[29] This was an early modern formula for violence: scarcity, high prices, plague, hostility over new taxes, and anxieties over the intrusions of outsiders. It explains how the indignation that was earlier expressed through common political discourse in the market, taverns, and *quartiers* escalated into violent acts of retribution. Emotions had smoldered to such a point that only a single incident was needed to cause an explosion of violence.[30]

The plague not only contributed to the heightened tensions in Aix, but was also the cause of the fateful decision to divide the parlement. To escape the epidemic, the parlement voted to leave Aix and to adjourn in two separate groups to the uninfected towns of Salon and Pertuis, as there was no single uncontaminated town in Provence large enough to support the entire court. The group of parlementaires that arrived in Salon was under the leadership of First President Vincent-Anne de Forbin-Maynier d'Oppède, a client of Richelieu; the other magistrates followed Laurent de Coriolis, second president and Baron de Corbières, to the town of Pertuis. This separation of the parlementaires worsened factional rivalry and created a major power struggle within the court. After an initial period of cooperation and free communication between the two chambers, relations deteriorated rapidly. There were complaints about the speed of communication, willingness to consult, and the amount of money that was being spent. Tensions were mounting when on 20 March 1630 Coriolis entered the chamber at Pertuis wearing the vestments of the first president, an act that symbolized the sovereignty and ambitions of this chamber. Oppède and his followers in Salon responded to this provocative act by obtaining orders from Paris to reunite the two courts. Coriolis and company held out until September, at which time both courts were rejoined in Aix.[31]

Although the two groups of magistrates were now seated together, the division between them persisted, and disputes regularly interrupted proceedings. In some ways, Oppède and Coriolis seemed destined to oppose each other. Oppède belonged to one of the most prominent and powerful houses in Provence, a family that traditionally supported the interests of the monarchy. Coriolis also belonged to a powerful family, but one that had been ennobled more recently, in the fifteenth century, and that had sided with Henry of Navarre and the opposition to the Catholic League. His father had established the family's tradition of insurgency during the Wars of Religion, when he directed the secession of a group of parlementaires from the pro-League parlement in Aix and established a rival court at Manosque. This rebel parlement upheld Salic law and supported Henry IV's claims to the throne, for which Coriolis became something of a provincial hero. In the tradition of his father, Laurent de Coriolis would oppose Oppède and the central government in the name of Provençal liberties.[32]

Supported by a host of clients and sympathizers, Coriolis demanded the position of first president as compensation for the poor treatment suffered by the parlementaires in Pertuis, and to this end he and his clients used the arrival of the *intendant*, Dreux d'Aubray, as an excuse to set off a popular revolt in late September. Aubray had traveled to Aix for the purpose of registering the royal edict that would establish the *élus* in Provence. This was the spark needed to set off a round of popular violence. Aubray took his lodging at the *hôtel* of the governor, Guise, who was away on campaign. At noon, just as the tocsin rang, groups of agitated and armed young men gathered and marched towards the Guise residence. They had been waiting for Aubray's arrival and they were ready for him. As they moved through the city, they shouted: 'Long live the king! Down with tax officials and thieves!'[33] Their street rhetoric is significant in what it reveals about popular perceptions and fears. It tells us, first, that it was tax collectors whom they believed to be committing crimes against them, and, second, that in their minds the king was untainted. As was so often true in early modern Europe, blame was directed towards the king's agents and not the king. The king himself commanded great respect in Provence, and in their attachment to him the Provençaux revealed an early modern sense of nationalism. For the Provençaux, 'les Français' referred to the king's subjects, including themselves. They were not separatists; they were loyal subjects of the king. But they did not view themselves in the same way as they viewed the rest of the king's subjects. The Provençal language and culture were alive and well in the seventeenth century, and the Provençaux viewed provincial rights and liberties as something to be jealously guarded. As Pillorget writes, 'the moral integration of Provence into France had not yet been completely realized'. There still existed a profound cultural and political sense of their own community as defined separately from the outsiders like Aubray.[34] In their attachment to the king, the provincial population was part of the nation. In their opposition to Aubray, they were defending their imagined community.

Aubray was the target because he was the 'outsider' whom they believed to be responsible for the *élus*. Someone had to be blamed and punished, a sentiment that was part of what Beik calls the culture of retribution, and predictably the culprit and his possessions would be the objects of violence. Crowds felt they could act in this way because of their traditional, unwritten authority to right the wrongs of their superiors.[35] Aubray had to flee the crowd by slipping out across the roof to a neighboring house. Having failed to lay their hands on him, the crowd engaged in a common ritual of rebellion by burning his luggage and coach in the Place des Prêcheurs. If they could not bring retribution directly to Aubray, they could do so symbolically. The Place itself became the locus of political activity since the rebels continued to hold public meetings there at night. It was there, in fact, that the movement acquired its name and emblem, a small bell hung from leather straps or white ribbons and known as the *cascaveoux*. The bell represented that worn by cats to warn their prey, and it involved a specific reference to the classical fable by the nobleman Paul de Joannis, a nephew and supporter of Coriolis. The bell was an emblem of their imagined community, which they were defending against external intrusions. With bells, placards, pamphlets, and effigies the crowd continued for weeks to express their anger and the reasons they felt violated by the outsiders who would try to impose the *élus* upon them.

But it was not only outsiders that had touched off this episode. The parlementaires themselves were to blame. Coriolis and his supporters wanted revenge for the treatment they had suffered, and they wanted Coriolis appointed first president. To these ends they manipulated the crowd and aligned themselves with the cause of opposing the *élus*. Oppède had been forced to leave Aix after a mob attacked his *hôtel*, which meant that Coriolis was left in control of the parlement. On 18 October, the parlement refused to register the royal edict and forbade citizens to accept positions as *élus*. The night before, a small crowd had attacked the home of councillor Louis de Paule, who managed to escape, but some of his possessions were burned in the Place des Prêcheurs. According to Kettering, it was Coriolis who instigated the attack on Paule to serve as punishment for the role that he had played in thwarting the ambitions of Coriolis and his chamber at Pertuis.

Coriolis's political use of the crowd came back later to haunt him, because as things became more and more unstable an opposition movement formed and the seemingly united front against Oppède and the royal government began to disintegrate in early November. Specifically, on 3 and 4 November circumstances became uncontrollable and the residents of Aix experienced a night of rioting and terror as marauding peasants pillaged the Place des Prêcheurs. These events resulted in the formation of an opposition party, the 'Blue Ribbon'. Headed by the first consul, the baron de Bras, they denounced and condemned Coriolis's machinations and his self-serving use of the crowd of Aix. René Pillorget describes the events that ensued as a factional struggle for control of Aix, instigated at least in part by a fear of the populace. Many of the notables of Aix had been frightened by Coriolis's success in mobilizing their social inferiors; threatened by these unconstrained popular forces, they began to resist the Cascaveoux.[36] This opposing faction, however, still posed as defenders of provincial liberties, while at the same time expressing their loyalty to the king. By the end of November, what had begun as a defense of provincial liberties and a power struggle within the parlement had become a major factional struggle, complete with a component of social or class conflict, for control of the city.

In early December, Baron de Bras successfully engineered Coriolis's expulsion from the city along with his supporters, and the movement's strength appeared to be rapidly eroding.[37] But the continuing threat of violence from Coriolis's proletarian supporters and dismay at the treatment served someone of Coriolis's rank and stature induced the parlement to recall him to Aix and to permit him to continue as a president. Moreover, the first consul had meanwhile discredited himself by provoking a brawl between his men and a captain of a *quartier* who refused to execute one of his orders. At first, the parlement attempted to mediate this dispute, but in the end it resorted to assisting the first consul and some supporters in getting safely out of town.[38] This retreat appeared to leave the Cascaveoux in control of Aix once again.

Coriolis, however, did not stop there. His partisans produced a polemic, entitled 'Laophile', that portrayed him as 'the father of the people', and the Blue Ribbon as 'seditious enemies of the king'. It also maintained that the Coriolis machine enjoyed the support of Marie de Médici, which, since the Day of the Dupes, was of absolutely no consequence. As soon as the duke of Guise informed Aix of the fateful episode that confirmed the ascendancy of Richelieu over Marie and Marillac, it was apparent that Coriolis could not count on her or her agents. Furthermore, Richelieu had dispatched the prince of Condé and 5000 troops, along with two *intendants*, to restore order in Provence. He intended to abandon Marillac's absolutist policies for the more pragmatic course of appeasement.[39]

With appeasement, order, and fiscal urgency in mind, Condé convoked the provincial estates on 7 March at the town of Tarascon. Here he negotiated a compromise by which the edict on *élections* would be revoked and the estates would in return consent to 1.5 million *livres* in taxes to be paid over a period of four years. Having addressed the king's fiscal problems, Condé and his troops then moved on to the city of Aix to re-establish order and to punish the rebels. Overall, Condé, given his earlier conduct at other besieged towns, acted magnanimously towards the Aixois. Residents temporarily lost their right to elect consuls, and *intendants* made the obligatory example of a few rabble-rousers by sentencing one to death and the others to the galleys. Coriolis and company fled to Les Baux, where they linked up with the duke of Orléans and participated in the famous Montmorency rebellion. Eventually, though only after a prolonged period of self-imposed exile in Spain, Coriolis's luck ran out. In 1640 he returned to the province and was apprehended in Avignon. There he was imprisoned and spent his last remaining days.[40]

During the Cascaveoux revolt the parlement had made little effort to control the violence, a fact that did not escape the attention of Richelieu. At times it actually contributed to the insurrection by sending remonstrances against the *élus* to Paris. More important, the court's failure to take repressive measures resulted largely from the fact that the Coriolis network of clients controlled its deliberations. In the absence of Oppède, who fled to Paris after the attack on his residence, Coriolis himself presided over sessions of the court, and unusually high rates of absenteeism left him with very little opposition. Thus Coriolis and his supporters could successfully manipulate the parlement to remonstrate against the *élus* and to remain silent while his men fomented rebellion among the populace. His clients numbered 15 members of the parlement, and he claimed the support of at least five others. The heart of the Revolt of the Cascaveoux was this network of Coriolis's clients and relatives organized in defense of their provincial rights and seeking retribution for their treatment at Pertuis. Pillorget argues that this insurrection rapidly became a feud among rival factions to control the city and the parlement. Coriolis's opposition played on fears of a popular movement to alienate notables from the movement and thereby to undermine his aristocratic base of support. Divisions among notables contributed mightily to the failure of the revolt. Combined with the highly localized nature of the rebellion, this lack of unity permitted the king to extinguish the revolt militarily, and rather easily.[41] But that did not mean the end of the opposition to the fiscal policies of the crown, nor did it mean the end of factional strife within the city.

What it did mean was that Richelieu would use his own powers of patronage to complete the construction of a loyal Provençal clientele. To do so he sought clients who held positions in the important provincial institutions, and these were often individuals who had clients of their own and could in turn act as brokers by directing his patronage to nobles of lesser rank and wealth. In this way his influence and largesse could infiltrate the province and reach nobles who otherwise would never have been privileged by connections to the cardinal. He used his clients 'to undermine, intimidate, and contain hostile or disobedient governors, and whenever possible he suborned great noble clienteles by seducing away their members into his own networks'.[42]

His first goal in Provence was to encircle and to isolate the unreliable and often hostile provincial governor, the duke of Guise. Kettering has shown us exactly how he went about doing this. He began his strategy by first placing his brother in the very important position of archbishop of Aix, which also made him one of the *procureur du pays*. Next, he placed one of his own men in the position of lieutenant-governor of the province and as governor of the citadel at Sisteron. Then he set about recruiting from the provincial nobility. First, he focused on two of the most important clients of the duke of Guise – Oppède, the first president of the parlement, and Cosme de Valbelle, who controlled the municipal government of Marseille. By enticing them away from the governor, Richelieu had gone a long way towards isolating Guise. Then, he secured the service of the bailli de Forbin and made him lieutenant-general of the galleys. He made Henri de Séguiran a naval lieutenant-general; Séguiran already held the position of first president of the Cour des Comptes, and during the Cascaveoux he had been forced to flee Aix along with Oppède because he had tried to assist Aubray in registering the dreaded edict. To reinforce his control over naval defenses in Provence, Richelieu placed his *créature*, Henri d'Escoubleau de Sourdis, as naval commander-in-chief, and Sourdis proceeded in turn to recruit his own clients from among the provincial nobility, thereby placing them under the control of the cardinal. Among those whom Sourdis enlisted were the bishop of Marseille, a first president in the parlement, the governor of Château d'If in Marseille harbor, and a couple of galley captains. In the end, to secure his control of the province, Richelieu enhanced his clientele by sending 15 provincial, naval, and army *intendants* to Provence, half of whom were his own clients.[43]

Having carefully composed this network of supporters, Richelieu used them to govern Provence directly. Oppède and Séguiran had after all tried, though without success, to see that the *élus* came to Provence. Other initiatives would be more successful. There was, for example, the problem of the governor, the duke of Guise. His independence and power in Provence derived from his position as a great court noble and from his wealth. Guise belonged to the house of Lorraine, one of the great families of France whose members had led the Catholic League in the Wars of Religion. Once installed as governor, he had the money and influence to construct his own extensive network of clients in Provence. Guise's refusal or failure to put down the revolt certainly did not ingratiate him with the minister. Indeed, he had ignored requests from the municipal government of Aix and the parlement asking him to intervene. His failure to fulfill the responsibilities of his office appears to have been Guise's way of taking revenge on the parlement, with whom he had engaged in a longstanding feud over his own attempts to transform the governorship into a hereditary sinecure for the Guise family. This certainly earned him no points with Richelieu; the fact that Guise was probably one of the queen mother's partisans meant that his days as governor were numbered. Guise interpreted, and rightly so, Condé's arrival with troops in Aix as a sign of his own demise and opted for voluntary exile.[44]

Guise's successor would be Nicolas de L'Hopital, marquis de Vitry, former captain of the royal guard, a man whose background was not nearly so illustrious as that of Guise and who could acquire a position traditionally reserved for the great nobility only because he had managed to win the gratitude of Richelieu by killing the despised Concini. The governorship of Provence was Vitry's reward for having eliminated a political rival. Vitry was therefore Richelieu's *créature*, and he was a poor choice at that. His quarrelsome and even brutal nature made him totally unsuitable to work with the various institutions and individuals that he would have to consult as governor. 'After four years in office, Vitry had alienated the Parlement, intendant of justice, provincial lieutenant general, the Estates and General Assemblies, procureurs du pays, archbishop of Aix, and municipal government.'[45] Richelieu tried to solve the problem by appointing as lieutenant-governor the marquis de Saint Chamond. A man of diplomatic skill and discretion, he was probably chosen as an antidote to Vitry – someone who could handle Vitry and replace him if necessary. Vitry, however, managed to provoke Saint Chamond to drastic action, and at one point the province was on the verge of a civil war in which the lieutenant-governor, the parlement, and the provincial nobility, or those who responded to the call to arms, opposed Vitry. It seemed to Richelieu that Saint Chamond had acted rashly, especially given the impending Spanish invasion, and the cardinal recalled him as part of an effort to make peace. The root problem, Vitry himself, remained, a situation that was becoming intolerable. His belligerent nature resulted in incident after incident, so that Richelieu's *créature* lacked completely any *crédit* with which to control the province. Having recognized him as a political liability, Richelieu recalled and imprisoned Vitry (on charges of undermining coastal defenses).[46] Here we see the advantage of choosing a provincial governor by reaching down the social ladder. Richelieu made him, and Richelieu could unmake him.

But the provincial governors were only part of the problem confronting central government. Nine years after the Revolt of the Cascaveoux, royal agents demanded an additional 400 000 *livres* annually to support troops stationed in the region until the end of the war with the Habsburgs. The king convoked the Estates of Provence to approve the request. But the estates opposed the tax increase, forcing him to turn to the Assembly of Communities, which complied with most of his wishes. Louis XIII also called the *ban* and *arrière-ban*, but the Assembly of Nobility chose to ignore the crown's appeal for military and financial assistance. The year 1639 saw the final session of the estates, and the Assembly of the Nobility met only three times after this date.[47]

In addition to unpopular fiscal measures, the crown attempted to find an immediate remedy to budgetary problems by the creation and sale of numerous new judicial offices. This ensured the survival of an opposition party within the parlement during the 1640s. The 'opposition' parlementaires vigorously protested the establishment of the Chambre des Requêtes, offices which would raise 370 000 *livres* for the crown, because they feared that the proliferation of judicial offices would deflate the value of their own sinecures. The crown had also initiated measures that would result in declining revenue from their offices, thereby insuring opposition. There were important links between this opposition party and the old Cascaveoux movement; several members had participated in the earlier revolt, and as before, they continued to pursue their own interests in a growing antagonism between the parlement on the one hand and the crown and provincial governor on the other.[48]

In the absence of the estates and the Assembly of the Nobility, elements within the Provençal nobility attempted to obstruct royal policy through the parlement and the offices of *procureurs du pays*. The concessions sought by the opposition parlementaires – a party maintained by a network of kinship, clientage, and friendship – reveal a determination to defy unpopular royal edicts. For one, the parlementaires requested the abolition of the Semester, a disciplinary and revenue-producing device with the purpose of controlling the unruly parlement by first dividing it and then packing it with judges loyal to the crown. This royal contrivance had been instituted by the provincial governor the previous year with no local assent. The Semester was abolished in return for 200 000 *livres* of compensation, and the Chambre des Requêtes for 300 000 *livres*. The parlementaires also protested the presence of 3500 soldiers billeted in Aix without the approval of the *procureurs* (the troops were subsequently removed) and objected vigorously to royal interference with free municipal elections, particularly to the presence of the governor's appointees in elective offices (a royal edict later reconfirmed the elective nature of municipal government in Provençal towns). Altogether the parlementaires presented 15 grievances to the crown during the course of the revolt, most of which had nothing to do with provincial privileges but instead addressed the threat of new judicial offices and served to protect the parlementaires' vested interests as part of a privileged elite. Faced with insurrection, Mazarin agreed to make several changes, though none proved to be permanent. After 1650 and this preliminary revolt, the opposition party as such came to an end, but some of its members, the so-called Sabreurs, reassembled on the side of the princes for the civil war that took place in Provence from 1650 to 1653. Others supported Mazarin during the Fronde.

The Fronde in Provence

The story of the Fronde in Provence is predictably complex and extends well beyond the parlement in Aix. A revolt against the very unpopular provincial governor, the count of Alais, in 1649 actually ushered in the Fronde. Here again we see the intersection of the conflict between the crown's problems with the parlement and with an autonomous provincial governor. Alais was Vitry's replacement, and by his appointment in 1637 Richelieu had reverted to the tradition of appointing great nobles. He was a cousin of the royal family, and like Guise before him he possessed a personal fortune that would enable him to construct his own clientele. Included in his network were the *intendant*, a first president in the parlement, a president in the Chambre des Comptes, the first consul in Marseille, and the general of the royal galleys in Marseille, to list a few. Alais's supporters ranged far and wide within the province, and he relied in particular on his access to military patronage in trying to construct the kind of independence that Guise had enjoyed for so long. In the end, however, his ambitions were blunted by the strategies of Mazarin who successfully built his own ministerial clientele to balance and to encircle Alais's men within the administration and defense of the province.[49]

From the perspective of the local elites, Alais was a villain because he had forced the parlement to register the edict that established the controversial Chambres des Requêtes. He had also expanded the military presence, and hence his opportunities for military patronage, at great cost to the Provençal communities. But it was his relations with the parlement that would cause the political atmosphere to deteriorate into open revolt. Through Alais and the *intendant* Champigny, the crown tried to bribe and intimidate the court into accepting its various revenue-generating initiatives. The 1640s saw a prolonged struggle between the opposition parlementaires on the one hand and the governor and royal government on the other. Parlementaires who indicated some willingness to cooperate were given titles, pensions, exemptions from taxes, and military commissions. Royal government also used these favors to lure some of the leaders of the opposition to its side. Still, it was necessary for the crown to resort to intimidation by such means as *lettres de cachet* (warrants) and threats to increase the amount of the *paulette*. The issue that finally produced open conflict between the opposition parlementaires and the royal government was the creation of the Semester in the parlement.

The Semester was in essence a separate court which would sit for the first six months of the year, while the old parlement would sit for the second six. It offered the crown the opportunity to sell 95 offices and to split the existing parlement into two courts. By adding a group of judges that were loyal to the crown and dividing their opponents, the crown hoped to control and to discipline the parlementaires. The opposition

responded in predictable ways, and the situation intensified when Philippe Gueidon, one of the first to buy an office in the Semester, arrived
from Marseille, only to be murdered by several masked assailants. Alais
conducted an inquiry, which resulted in an arrest and two attempts at a
trial. The whole affair became the focal point of conflict, because Alais
and the *intendant* used it as a pretext for exiling 17 parlementaires for
their opposition to the Semester. The exiled parlementaires would lead
the revolt which began ten months later.

The opposition parlementaires prepared for the impending conflict
by recruiting troops in Provence. Upon learning about their activities
and about the Day of the Barricades (26–28 August) in Paris, Alais
responded by bringing troops into Aix, where they were billeted. He
then suspended municipal elections. These reactionary responses did
nothing to help his cause. Alais was not a popular figure among the
masses, and now he was even less so. The fact that he refused to negotiate with the parlementaires, combined with his military preparations,
made it appear that he was planning for a bloody conflict. Cardinal
Mazarin had come to realize that Alais was a political liability, and, much
to the governor's objection, he sent a royal commissioner down to negotiate with the judges. Eventually relations between Mazarin and Alais
deteriorated to a point that saw Alais side with his cousin Condé and the
princes in the Fronde. Once again, we see how the independence of a
provincial governor not only detracted from the effectiveness of royal
policy but actually became a major obstacle. It created a struggle
between the parlement and the governor, and became the dominant
theme of the Fronde as it played out in Aix and the major towns of
Provence.[50]

The Fronde actually started just after the beginning of 1649. The
festivities and procession for Saint Sebastian's Day (20 January) offered
the occasion. The violence that broke out that day was the beginning of a
revolt orchestrated by the opposition parlementaires who hoped to rid
themselves of Alais and to force Mazarin into serious negotiations and
concessions. The revolt of 1649 was not like that of 1630. The popular
element was not as prominent in this episode, perhaps because the
economic context in which it took place was significantly better than in
1630. This time the parlementaires were not able to draw on extensive
popular support, largely because their goals were entirely self-serving.
This was not a conflict over provincial rights and liberties; this was
a struggle over the Semester and over a provincial governor whom
they despised. Their specific demands amounted to 15, most of which

addressed their privileges as parlementaires. As Kettering has noted, the actual enemy was the governor and his accomplice, the *intendant*, rather than the king. 'By refusing to attack the monarchy and its absolute policies directly, the Aix parlementaires vitiated the impact of their demands for change. They evaded the main issues.'[51] For Pillorget, the parlementaires were fighting to preserve their investments and the social distinction that offices conferred on their families. In the course of their struggle to preserve their privileged status, the parlementaires drew on the support of the peasants who worked on their various lands and seigneuries scattered through the Provençal countryside.[52] The vertical ties that organized elite society by linking greater to lesser noble also bound noble to peasant. In this way nobles mobilized peasant support for their own aims.

For Alais's part, the revolt was made all the worse by the Bichi Treaty, which he had been compelled to sign in March 1649, while a prisoner. By signing the treaty, Alais and the royal government agreed to most of the opposition's demands, though Mazarin would ultimately, when in a position to do so, repudiate these concessions.[53] This would not happen for some time, as the 1649 revolt evolved into the Fronde in Provence. Alais's policies were crucial. His recalcitrance most certainly led to the Fronde. Once free, he was determined to take revenge, and he had no intention of observing the treaty. He formed his own party and army to fight the parlementaires, thereby causing the conflict to escalate into civil war. Alais succeeded in recruiting an expansive military presence throughout the province. To this end, he used provincial regiments and the patronage he could offer Provençal nobles. The nucleus of his party consisted of some of the oldest and most illustrious houses in Provence. The provincial nobility split between those who sought opportunity with Alais and those who sought to preserve the status and value of their offices.[54]

Not all of the opposition parlementaires participated in the Fronde; after an outbreak of plague in 1650, many officers retired to their country estates. The rump that remained, joined by three officers from the Cour des Comptes, would become known as the Sabreurs, the local party supporting the princes. They were headed by the baron of Saint Marc and the baron of Oppède (son of the earlier baron), and their first agenda was to rid Provence of Alais. To assist them in achieving this, they enlisted the support of Condé, who was by this point estranged from Alais. The Sabreurs included 11 magistrates in the parlement and the Cour des Comptes, a figure that represented only a tiny minority of the officers in both courts. This group was young and volatile, and their fellow magistrates viewed them as such and criticized them for pursuing their personal political interests.[55]

Within the parlement a party of Mazarinistes emerged, headed by Président Régusse. Along with Oppède, Régusse had acted as a leader of the parlementaires in the 1649 revolt. A client of Mazarin's brother, the archbishop of Aix, he was staking his political future on the cardinal. By attacking Alais (who at that point was in league with Condé and Mazarin's enemies), he hoped to score points with Mazarin. For his loyalty, Régusse was confident that he would receive the office of first president. When forced to occupy this office alternately, each week, with Oppède, he was not happy, and a rivalry developed between the two men that widened even more the divisions within the parlement. Further complicating the situation was the fact that Alais could claim the support of the Semesters, a group of former members of the Semester court, whose goal was to re-establish the court and to preserve the governors. Their numbers were extremely limited.[56]

The rivalry between Oppède and Régusse served to shape the elaborate contours of a three-way struggle in Provence. By 1651 Régusse was at the helm of a parlementaire party that sided with Mazarin and whose position was strengthened later as the cardinal's own situation improved. Oppède and the Sabreurs were expelled from Aix in 1651 and forced to conduct their operations outside the provincial capital. Meanwhile, the object of their resentment, Governor Alais, had been called to court in 1650. Mazarin contrived ways of preventing his return to Provence, but Alais managed to continue his campaign through his clients and supporters and through the support he received from the city of Toulon. For most of the period of the Fronde, Alais retained the position of governor, but Mazarin tried to control the province through a lieutenant-governor, Aiguebonne, and through his clients. Specifically, Antoine de Valbelle in Marseille, Archbishop Grignan in Arles, and Président Régusse in Aix succeeded in maintaining the loyalty of their respective cities.[57]

In April 1652, the duke of Mercoeur was named acting governor, a choice that led to significant factional realignments. He massed sufficient troops to enable him to negotiate from a position of strength. In the summer of 1652, Oppède and Saint Marc crossed over to join him as clients, and with this shift in alliances peace was at hand.[58] Mercoeur came to Provence as Mazarin's *créature*. He had entered the cardinal's network by marrying Mazarin's niece. As the son of César de Bourbon, duke of Vendôme, the legitimized son of Henry IV, he had rank and wealth; Mazarin gave him access to power. In return, Mercoeur was expected to act as a broker for Mazarin. His first major success in this regard was to pull off what Kettering has described as 'one of the most spectacular switches in Provençal politics'. Specifically, Mercoeur recruited Oppède to join him and to abandon the cause of the Sabreurs, which started a 'stampede among provincial notables to join the winning side' and ended the Fronde in Provence. Oppède was rewarded for his switch with the position of first president; Mercoeur was named permanent governor.[59] By successfully recruiting Oppède, Mercoeur had defused an opposition which was based overwhelming on the self-serving use of provincial politics.

This is not to suggest that with the end of the Fronde all was settled in Provençal political circles. The marquis de Régusse was left empty-handed, and he too had wanted to be named first president. After all, he had led the cause of the Mazarinistes during the Fronde, and had kept the majority of parlementaires, as well as the city of Aix, loyal to Mazarin. Why would Mazarin turn his back on this loyal supporter and promote the ambitions of a man who had opposed him? Oppède was simply more successful in demonstrating the extent of his influence and his clientele, his *crédit*, in Provence. If there were any doubt of the relative *crédit* of the two rivals, the 1653 municipal elections in Aix offered plenty of evidence to support Oppède's claims. They resulted in the elimination of Régusse's men and the introduction of Oppède's agents as consuls and assessors. Oppède made his resources and political utility even more plain to Mazarin by spending an extended period at court, something that Régusse was unwilling to do. Moreover, Oppède was not reluctant to put up a good deal of his personal fortune for the office. He paid 15 000 *livres* more than Régusse bid for the office; he also made loans to Mazarin. In fact, it appears that he actually went into debt because of his relationship with the cardinal. In the end, however, he managed not only to procure the office of first president, but to act as Mazarin's broker in Provence.[60]

As Mazarin's *créature*, there was plenty of work for Oppède to do in Provence. The position of first president, in fact, became secondary to him because he devoted much of his energies to financial and military matters in the region. He came to assume the responsibilities of an *intendant*; he directed the provisioning of troops, and at some personal expense. He maintained a close watch on the political atmosphere and activities of the province, and he did not hesitate to report to Mazarin on the conduct of individuals. And, most important, he did his utmost to procure from locals the funding that the central government so desperately needed, to the extent that he became ruthless with the Assembly of Communities, meeting in Tarascon in 1658–9, by resorting to a royal ultimatum – either Provence pay up or the returning troops from Italy that were currently quartered in Dauphiné would be moved south to Provence. Needless to say, Oppède had come to be regarded as the foremost local representative of central government, a position that brought with it a great deal of resentment and animosity.[61]

Moreover, the conflict and competition between Régusse and Oppède did not end with Oppède's appointment as first president. They would persist and escalate to the extent that they served to provoke the last Provençal revolt in 1659. The specific context of this revolt was that Mazarin had raised taxes and moved troops into Provence to support renewed fighting in Italy. In January 1658, Governor Mercoeur demanded of locals both quarters and money for his troops. The *procureurs du pays* refused. The governor and the *intendant* responded with *lettres de cachet* for the first consul of Aix, Forbin de la Barbin. Still the *procureurs* refused to acquiesce. In May 1658, the *intendant* for the army, de Chouppes, and Lieutenant-General de Marsilly presented *lettres de cachet* for payment and quarters to the provincial treasurer, Gaillard, and to the first president of the Cours des Comptes, Séguiran, but both were adamant about the necessity for approval by the *procureurs*. Meanwhile, unpaid soldiers streamed into Aix, where they provoked confrontations with crowds that had assembled to protest the arrest of the first consul and the imposition of the proposed tax. At the same time, Oppède, who was by then acting *intendant* and whom Kettering describes as 'the new instrument of centralization in Provence', announced that the *intendant* would have the authority to raise the additional levies without the consent of the *procureurs*. The *procureurs* naturally condemned this as an attack on provincial privilege, and the parlement responded by annulling Oppède's ordinance.[62]

Resentment towards Oppède had been mounting steadily, even among some parlementaires who had sided with him as Sabreurs during the Fronde. Now many saw him as betraying the interests of the parlement and usurping more and more power within provincial administration. Anxious to disqualify his major rival, Régusse was behind much of the opposition and popular protest against the military tax. Oppède did not ignore the rivalry either; he did his utmost to poison Mazarin's impressions of Régusse, and eventually succeeded. The opposition to Oppède consisted of a small group of men who had struggled against the crown for the past three decades; some of them had earlier been friends of Oppède, but they had become highly suspicious of his political ambition. His most powerful enemies were not parlementaires, however; they included Jérôme de Grimaldi, archbishop of Aix, and François de Simiane, marquis de Gordes, who was lieutenant-general of Provence. Grimaldi and Oppède had struggled over conflicts in authority, and the archbishop, as the first *procureur du pays*, had obstructed Oppède's effort to introduce the new tax. Similar conflicts shaped the rivalry between Oppède and Simiane de Gordes.[63]

As sides were drawn for the impending conflict, clientage and kinship determined the line-ups. The Oppède clientele included an extensive list of parlementaires and officeholders in the other courts. Oppède also enjoyed the support of Governor Mercoeur, and at times he controlled the offices of *procureurs du pays* (consuls of Aix). Until his death in 1656 Jean de Pontevès, the provincial lieutenant-general, had also been an important political ally. Oppède's clientele was not, however, limited to provincial government and the courts; his men were scattered throughout the Provençal towns and countryside.[64] He was particularly well situated to serve as Mazarin's broker.

The Régusse machine also included parlementaires, but it failed to extend to the other courts. Instead, it was linked to the Valbelle faction in Marseille, a connection of great importance. The Valbelle network was large and deeply entrenched in Marseille; Richelieu had used the Valbelle machine to keep the city loyal during the Revolt of the Cascaveoux. Later, as enemies of the unpopular governor, Alais, the Valbelles were able to become the clients of Mazarin. In his service, they managed once again to keep Marseille loyal during the Fronde. The rift between Mazarin and the Valbelles occurred later over taxation. Oppède and Mercoeur persuaded Mazarin that Marseille must assume a greater share of provincial taxes, and to do this they ran up against the Valbelle machine which controlled municipal government in Marseille. Oppède advised Mazarin to reform the electoral process in the city with the specific purpose of eliminating the Valbelle monopoly. By reinstating an older process, Mazarin and Oppède made sure that Valbelle opponents were elected to the city council. In 1658 these anti-Valbelle policies resulted in their engineering a popular protest. Mazarin and some of the city moderates took decisive action, and eventually destroyed the Valbelle clientele. But in 1659 they still formed a powerful component in the Régusse machine.[65]

This uneasy situation exploded on Saint Valentine's Day 1659, when a shooting incident began several days of violence in Aix instigated by armed noblemen demanding the arrest of Oppède, whom they believed was responsible. Oppède took refuge in the archbishop's private apartments. There he was held captive for ten days while Aix once again became a battleground for two feuding factions. On 27 February Governor Mercoeur, Oppède's ally, entered Aix with troops to quell the revolt. He arrived with 2000 infantry, 200 cavalry, 80 nobles, and 15 companies of provincial infantry. His expedition had been anticipated by the rebels, particularly after he called the *ban* and *arrière-ban*, and he entered the city without resistance: Oppède's enemies had fled. In the end, a total of 17 nobles were prosecuted and punished for their roles in the uprising.[66]

The Provençal nobility justified the insurrections of 1630, 1649, and 1659 as opposition to the centralization of royal authority for infringements on traditional regional privileges. In reality, they were violently pursuing their own narrow political interests. Assisted by the structure of provincial government and its concentration in Aix, the nobility of Aix dominated regional politics and figured prominently in all three insurrections. Their efforts were colored by factionalism that limited their effectiveness and ultimately contributed to their defeat. By its careful manipulation of factionalism, royal government was eventually able to obtain control of provincial institutions. It is not that the interests of the crown and the nobility never coincided; rather, royal ministers successfully sought out provincial clients and brokers who were willing to abandon their earlier causes in order to promote their own ambitions and careers.

Oppède would be one such broker. Through his connections first Mazarin and then Colbert would be able to control provincial government. Kettering has reconstructed the Oppède clientele, at the center of which was his family. 'Kinship with the prolific Forbins gave Oppède an extensive, ready-made noble clientele in Provence, while the Mayniers d'Oppède, who had held office in the parlement for over a century, allied him to the major robe families of Aix and to noble families in the Comtat Venaissin where their barony was located.'[67] His men were well placed in provincial government. Through his own influence, 15 of Oppède's relatives and clients served as consuls and assessors of Aix, which meant that they also acted as *procureurs du pays*. A cousin served as *syndic* of the nobility from 1661 to 1667. In 1666 a client was chosen as one of the two noble *procureurs* to the Assembly of Communities, and both of the *procureurs* from the clergy were also Oppède men. (The positions within the assembly were particularly useful in that they allowed Oppède to control debates.) And this was only part of his clientele; he had many other supporters, in the assembly and elsewhere – for example, in the parlement and in the Cour des Comptes, the latter including the first president, Reynaud de Séguiran. Furthermore, Oppède's influence extended to the municipal governments of Marseille, Toulon, Draguignan, and Carpentras. Finally, he profited from ties to Governor Mercoeur, who had originally recruited him, and to the lieutenant-general Jean de Pontevès.[68]

Pontevès was the count of Carces, and his was an old and distinguished Provençal family. During the rebellion of 1649, Pontevès recruited 300 of his own clients to fight with the parlementaires. Relations with individuals like Pontevès allowed Oppède's influence and power to fan throughout the province. The social origins of the nobles who fell in line behind him were mixed. Himself a president and later a first president in the parlement, Oppède drew many of his supporters from the ranks of recently ennobled officeholding families; however, as a major power-broker, he was also able to attract the older families of Aix and Provence at large, including the houses of Forbin and its various branches, Laurens, Puget, Castellanes, and Pontevès. Kettering regards the Oppède machine as 'an example of a geographic administrative clientele: province wide, cross-institutional, mixed noble in composition, attracted by the political power of its patron, and used as a political machine in helping him govern'.[69]

After the insurrection of 1659, it was this Oppède machine that enabled first Mazarin, and then Colbert, to govern the province. Exactly what were the mechanics of brokerage? What were the routine ways in which a provincial bigwig acted on behalf of his ministerial patron? How did Oppède's career serve to tie this frontier province closer to the center of the realm? First and foremost, Oppède worked through the Assemblies of Provençal Communities to gain approval for the taxes that royal government demanded. The assembly had replaced the Estates of Provence, and it consisted of the deputies of the third estate and *procureurs* from the nobility and the clergy. In 1664, the assembly voted to comply with the crown's demands. Oppède had assured Colbert that the assembly would comply because he knew much of the assembly to be composed of his men. It was important too that Oppède's protégé, cousin, and successor, Toussaint Janson-Forbin, became senior *procureur* of the clergy, a position he used to chair and direct the debates of the deputies. By placing his own relations or friends as *procureurs* of the clergy, nobility, and *pays*, Oppède insured that his own hand would control the debate and outcome of these meetings. His success in persuading the assembly was also based on the fact that he represented Provençal interests. By approving the taxes demanded by the crown, the assembly guaranteed that at least part of them would be spent in Provence.[70]

At Oppède's death Janson-Forbin assumed leadership of the Forbin network and shifted into the role of Colbert's client and broker. Specifically, he acted in the crown's interest by presiding over the debates of the General Assembly as senior *procureur* of the clergy. His *crédit* was extensive, and his clients included the *procureurs du pays* to name just a few. Later royal government, recognizing his talents in negotiating, deployed him on a series of diplomatic missions that climaxed with his being named bishop of Beauvais and being called to court for a career as an ambassador.[71]

Janson-Forbin's good fortune cleared the way for the ascent of his rival, the count of Grignan, who to the modern reader is better known as the son-in-law of the famous epistolary writer Madame de Sévigné. A member of a very old and distinguished Provençal family with tremendous *crédit* and resources, the count took over the job of managing the General Assembly. Grignan's family and network included an uncle who was the archbishop of Arles, a client of Mazarin, and the head of a machine that dominated Arles. When the archbishop died, he was replaced in this position by Grignan's brother who became also the senior *procureur* for the clergy. The rest of his family was similarly placed in high-ranking ecclesiastical, military, or political positions, making Grignan and his family the perfect provincial brokers for royal government. Grignan himself was lieutenant-general and acting governor, positions that he sometimes used to intimidate the deputies of the General Assembly into cooperating with the crown. In 1675, he managed to end Forbin control of the consulate in Aix and to install his own clients in these crucial municipal and provincial positions. Specifically, his clients and relatives permitted him to manage and direct the debates of the General Assembly, so that this institution, associated with provincial privilege, granted the monarchy the money it requested.[72]

The process of integrating Provence more completely into the realm was, as we have seen, a long and violent one. The nobility of Provence, and especially the families of Aix, played a dualistic role in this process. On the one hand, they were obstructionists, mobilizing popular forces and their imagined community in the name of provincial liberties and rights to oppose the introduction of royal agents and new taxes. On the other hand, they were the crucial, indeed singular, agents of integration; it was the provincial nobility who made it happen. Not all of them served the interests of the monarchy; some, like Alais, sabotaged royal designs so as to promote their own independent power bases. But others made up for it in their eagerness to become the clients and brokers of Mazarin, Colbert, and the crown. Acting on behalf of their ministerial and royal patrons, Oppède, Janson-Forbin, and Grignan enabled the central government to control this frontier province by using the most traditional of means – the vertical ties that bound one man to another.

Chapter 4: *Dauphiné: The Potential in Class Conflict*

Dauphiné was another *pays d'états* where the issue of provincial rights and privileges produced a series of conflicts in the late sixteenth and early seventeenth centuries. Here the crown by its efforts to increase taxation and revenue ignited a great contest between the nobility and the crown on the one hand, and the nobility and the third estate on the other. In contrast to Provence where the cleavages were essentially vertical and factional in nature, in Dauphiné efforts to raise taxes revealed deep divisions between the estates. In protecting its own interests, the third estate questioned the traditional privileges of nobility to the extent that the very notion of nobility came under attack. But this social conflict was much more complex than a simple dichotomy of noble vs. *roturier*. Over time it revealed fissures within the second and third estates. In challenging the rights of the nobility and in guarding their own interests, urban elites were placed in opposition to the peasantry and to urban artisans. As it played out, the conflict in Dauphiné encompassed a series of contests: noble vs. commoner, town vs. country, professionals vs. artisans, and bourgeois elites vs. *anoblis*. It brought into focus the growing divisions and subdivisions in provincial society. And the crown, in responding to the crisis over taxation, hardened the layers of horizontal solidarities, capitalized on an emerging national conscience, and succeeded in bringing about its desired tax reforms.

Dauphiné was an important frontier province with a unique institutional history, particularly in matters of taxation, as a result of the terms of its transfer to the French crown in 1349. Dauphiné became part of France as a result of the bankruptcy of its dauphin, Humbert II, who sold it to the Valois. In the transfer of the province, the French government had confirmed its traditional liberties and its special status. This meant that Dauphiné would retain its traditional institutions, including its very active representative assemblies, and that the province would continue to be exempted from direct taxation. These special privileges, however, were not always upheld by later French monarchs who seized opportunities to reduce the independence of institutions and to encroach on the privileges of the province. As the French crown experienced the fiscal realities of dynastic and later religious wars, it set about raising more money in Dauphiné by imposing direct taxes.[1]

At the crossroads of conflict, Dauphiné figured prominently in the military campaigns of the early sixteenth century. The French armies that were deployed to Italy marched via Dauphiné, and it was incumbent upon provincials to feed these troops. Moreover, the crown began to insist that it was the responsibility of the local population to provide the funds for garrisons along the frontiers. In this way, the monarchy laid claims to more than the occasional *don gratuit* or 'free gift'; by its regular demands for contributions, the crown was in essence imposing the *taille*.[2] Much of this money would be spent in Dauphiné for the defense of the province, but the fact of regular impositions raised the issue of the traditional provincial exemption, and this in turn raised the issue of personal exemptions.

Actually it was as early as 1484 that the estates of Dauphiné agreed to pay the *taille*, but only at a very low rate. The wars of the sixteenth century forced the French government to increase the size of this levy by various means. These increases ultimately set off the great taxation controversy known as the *procès des tailles*, which dominated provincial politics for decades to come. At the heart of the issue was the way in which the *taille* was assessed. Dauphiné was a bifurcated province in which part of the territory, the lowlands, drew upon Germanic customary traditions, and part of the province, the more mountainous regions, had been shaped by Roman law. This distinction determined separate ways of assessing the *taille*. In the lowlands the *taille* was *personnelle*, which meant it was assessed only against non-noble individuals; in the more mountainous areas it was *réelle*, which meant it was assessed against non-noble property, including the allodial property of nobles and clergy. By its efforts to increase the *taille* in Dauphiné, the crown set off a prolonged debate and conflict over the nature of the *taille* and the privileges of the first two estates.[3]

The issue of social privilege in turn raised questions about the social status of many who claimed the traditional tax exemptions of nobility. As elsewhere in France, Dauphiné had seen a growing number of families engaged in the process of upward social mobility. Their claims to nobility and therefore to tax exemptions became a hotly debated issue as the *taille* controversy unfolded. When a noble, no matter how recently ennobled, purchased *roturier* property, that property was exempted from assessment, thereby decreasing the available taxable land and increasing the burden on the rest of the village, which was still responsible for producing the full amount. But ennoblement was not the only path to tax evasion. The impoverishment of the peasantry saw more and more townspeople, whether *anoblis* or not, invest in the countryside, and the net effect of their rural investments was still to increase the burden of taxation on the village. By claiming that they had listed their rural holdings with the municipal assessors, townspeople could avoid disclosing to the rural assessor. And, if indeed they had disclosed their rural holdings to the municipality, the town gained the advantage of a larger tax base while the village lost out. Whatever the scenario, the purchase of land by nobles and urban elites worked to the disadvantage of the peasantry.[4]

The resentment rural populations began to express was made worse by the fact that some towns claimed to be tax exempt, and towns in general used the advantages they held in the provincial estates to shift much of the burden for supporting troops to the countryside. Representation within the third estate was disproportionately weighted in favor of townspeople, a fact that did not escape the attention of the crown. Henry II became involved in this growing dispute when he asked for more funds to support his campaigns in Italy. In 1548 he acted without consulting provincial institutions and issued an edict that would make townspeople pay taxes on all rural property acquired in the past 30 years. Two years later he followed this by recommending that the villages be given greater representation in the form of a *commis* or representative from each bailliage. The *commis* sat on a standing committee of the provincial estates which met when the assembly was not in session and conducted the crucial accounting functions that followed meetings of the estates. For these reforms, the villages came to view Henry II as their protector.[5]

The crown's intervention alerted the towns to the problems inherent for them in a declining tax base and rising taxes. More important, it resulted in their recognition that the problems confronted now by townspeople were like those confronting villagers, that these were shared problems of the third estate. In time, the tensions between town and country began to fade as their common interests became apparent and set the third estate in clear opposition to the two privileged orders.[6] Over the course of several troubled decades, the third estate challenged the privileges of the nobility and the clergy, and their attorneys advanced a lengthy and sophisticated argument for the uniform implementation of the *taille réelle* throughout the province.

Upon close examination, the major effect of the 1548 edict was to propel town elites, those most affected, into the forefront as leaders of the movement for tax reform. For Daniel Hickey, whose work on the *procès des tailles* and absolutism in Dauphiné is now the standard, their participation was fundamental to the events of the following decades. Not only did they take up the cause, but 'the new role of town leaders as opponents of the traditional fiscal structure upset the social harmony that had previously existed within the institutions of Dauphiné'. The political consequences of rising social tensions left provincial institutions dysfunctional and provided the crown with ample opportunity to intervene.[7]

Conflict in Romans

The reforms and resulting social tensions that radicalized town elites did not instantly create third estate solidarity. Deep-seated resentment of bourgeois power did not vanish overnight, if ever, from the consciousness of villagers and artisans. Indeed, in the town of Romans it found expression in what became one of the most notorious episodes associated with the *procès des tailles*. Romans was the scene of a year-long contest that occurred squarely within the context of rising taxes and the discussion of reform.

The summer of 1578 saw the formation of a 'league' among the lowlanders of Dauphiné. They were responding to the heavy taxes imposed that year and to marauding bands of brigands whose presence, like the heavier taxes, was the result of the Wars of Religion. It has been argued that the lowlanders may have been emboldened by the fact that the government had recently approved for the villagers a permanent representative or *commis* on the executive committee (the concession made in 1550 was for that year only), and that opposition to taxation played a major role in the alliance. By imposing additional or interim *tailles* royal government helped to radicalize the league, and in 1579 it actually took up arms. Specifically, the leaguers of Romans liberated the fortress of Châteaudouble, which had been seized by Protestant troops who used it to terrorize the surrounding countryside. Jean Serve, known as 'Captain' Paumier (or Pommier), successfully led 4000 Leaguers against the fortress. Paumier was a draper and merchant whose origins were not bourgeois, since years earlier he had migrated to Romans from a nearby village. Eventually he became a master craftsman and acquired some status within that community. He was also known for his contributions to the citizen militia, and after the assault on Châteaudouble he rose to prominence as a popular hero.[8]

With popular support, Paumier and the Leaguers dominated Romans for the rest of the year. Among their objectives was to acquire a share of political power. By their insistence the city council was enlarged to include 20 extraordinary councillors who came largely from the ranks of the Leaguers. According to Scott van Doren, the fundamental issue at play in the enlargement of the council was the social conflict that resulted when 'new men' like Paumier felt shut out of the arenas of power despite their economic and social importance to the municipality. Their response was to use popular discontent and to direct it against the patriciate that dominated local government. Once in power, they proceeded with their radical program.[9]

May 1579 saw the arrival in the province of the queen mother, Catherine de Medici. The purpose of her visit was to settle the *taille* dispute at the meeting of the provincial estates and to solidify peace with the Protestants. Her ruling on the *taille* amounted to a defeat for the third estate, and she made no real concessions to them. Her resolution would be viewed as no resolution and the struggle continued. The delegates of the third estate would not give up their reform initiative, and the Leaguers were frustrated by the failed efforts of the delegates. Van Doren argues that this situation was compounded by the fact that the enemies of the third estate found in Catherine's actions reason to believe that the central government was on their side and that she would approve their use of force to maintain order. In short, the queen mother's involvement failed miserably, and circumstances became steadily more volatile until finally things exploded in the town of Romans.[10]

The occasion for violence was the annual festivities and ceremonies surrounding the celebration of St Blaise and the pre-Lenten carnival. Feelings ran high throughout the carnival period, fed by several earlier incidents. But it was at a masked ball that violence erupted to engulf the town. The arrival of some of Paumier's Leaguers set off a bloody conflict in which Paumier himself was murdered. Only after three days of mayhem were the 'worthy men' of Romans able to restore order. Why had

carnival gone so wrong? Contemporaries present rather different interpretations of that evening, but historians generally find the account presented by Eustache Piémond to be most compelling. For Piémond it was
clear that Paumier had been set up, that the elites had planned to seize
the occasion 'to exterminate the most factious'. By 'factious' Piémond
was referring to the fact that Paumier's men had pronounced publicly
during the various activities of carnival that Romans' elite had become
rich on the backs of the poor.[11] A different interpretation was presented
by Judge Guérin, a city father who played a primary role in putting
down the revolt, who attempted to portray the actions of the elites as
strictly honorable and as a matter of self-defense.[12]

Such divergent perspectives point to fundamental social cleavages
within the town of Romans and beyond. By demanding a more representative municipal government, Paumier and the Leaguers had
challenged the political monopoly held by Guérin and men like him,
that is, lawyers, professionals, and prosperous merchants. Although
there is some question about the social composition of the League, it
seems reasonably certain that most of its members were artisans. For
Emmanuel Le Roy Ladurie, the symbolism of the carnival makes this
plain. The drapers and artisans chose as their emblems the sheep, the
bear, the hare, the donkey, and the capon, all animals of poor men. The
capon was particularly important as a symbol because it had been both
domesticated and castrated. On the other hand, the symbols of the
patriciate – the rooster, the eagle, and the partridge – were airborne and,
in the case of the rooster, decidedly sexed. What Le Roy Ladurie reads
in their choices of symbols is class conflict.[13]

The frustration and hostility that was expressed when artisans at
Romans chose to represent themselves as capons and hares was directed
at the elites of the third estate. Viewed from below, the elites had failed
to make a convincing case for the reform of taxation in Dauphiné, and at
worst they had been complicitous in the exploitation of the lower orders
by assessing, collecting, and embezzling taxes. In the 1570s, this conflict
occurred largely within the third estate. In the 1580s the leaders of the
third estate would regain credibility and control. And as the struggle for
tax reform continued, the leaders of the third estate, the urban elites of
Dauphiné, argued much more effectively on behalf of all non-nobles the
case for an end to aristocratic exemption from taxation.[14]

In 1583 representatives of the towns and villages met in an assembly at
Romans and reached a major agreement that would reunite the third
estate under the leadership of town elites. The agreement, approved the

next year by the provincial estates, determined that townspeople of *roturier* status would pay the village taxes on property that they had acquired since 1518. This represented a major concession on the part of the towns to the villages, and in political terms it restored order to the third estate. For Hickey, order does not mean that it eliminated social divisions within the estate, simply that it allowed more moderate voices to assume leadership in pursuing common goals.[15]

In 1591 and 1592 the three estates met to discuss rising levels of taxation within the province. This led to discussions about the reduction of *taillable* land, a trend that continued to occur as nobles purchased *roturier* lands, and it was in this context that an earlier and short-lived spirit of cooperation among the estates began to dissipate. In subsequent meetings of the provincial estates, relations among the three orders became confrontational, the third estate arguing that the rural acquisitions of nobles and *anoblis* had caused the impoverishment of the people by shifting more and more of the tax burden onto them. Between 1592 and 1595, the provincial estates became a battleground in which the third estate refused to vote taxes if the other two estates did not agree to assume a fair share of the burden.[16]

During his visit to nearby Lyons in 1595, Henry IV agreed to hear the case of the third estate. This was not the first time that they had sought the intervention of the king; recently the third estate had sent a series of ambassadors to court to obtain royal support. They chose Ennemond Marchier to make their case before the king. His remarks focused on the exemption of the nobility, and his line of argument maintained that they had never actually been exempted from the extraordinary taxes that accompany war. He continued to the effect that the nobility's acquisition of *roturier* lands constituted an abuse of their privileged status, and that it placed a heavier burden on commoners, particularly since the numbers of officials and others who claimed exemption by ennoblement were growing steadily. By the end, he had painted a tragic picture in which the people suffered enormously as a result of taxation and the cruelty and indifference of the nobility.[17]

The nobility did not sit idly by and allow the third estate to proceed without interference. They sent two lawyers, Jean Aquin and Julien Dufos, to present their position to the king. During the course of their remarks, Aquin and Dufos relied on historical arguments in favor of a privileged elite, that the nobility was the basis of stable societies. Moreover, they attempted to undermine Marchier's argument by pointing out the similarities between his remarks and the rhetoric and ideas of the

1579 revolt. In short, they argued that historically stable societies rested on the nobility and that attacks on their privileges resulted in disorder.[18]

In consideration of these preliminary testimonies, the king's council agreed to hear the case. The council also stated that there were to be no new taxes levied in Dauphiné without Henry's permission. This concession was in response to the fact that Alphonse d'Ornano, lieutenant-general in Dauphiné, and François de Bonne, seigneur of Lesdiguières and the Protestant whom Henry had appointed lieutenant-governor, had been levying taxes without the king's permission. Together the concessions represented a minor victory for the third estate.[19]

The Case of the Third Estate

As the third estate prepared its legal case, it became clear that the group which bore the greatest interest was the third estate elite. Hickey has argued convincingly that urban elites were the element of the third estate most affected by taxation and the reduction in *taillable* land. By working with the *taille* rolls for Grenoble, Valence, and Romans, he has demonstrated that the bourgeois elite of these towns was the most heavily taxed social element. In Grenoble, the legal professionals represented 14 per cent of those taxed, and their share amounted to 23 per cent of the taxes paid. Merchants (5 per cent of the taxable population) paid 11 per cent of the taxes, and bourgeois investors (also 5 per cent of the taxable population) paid 12 per cent of the taxes. It was the bourgeois elite who were the most affected by the tax structure as it currently existed. 'They saw their tax payments rising and their future investments compromised due to the fiscal structures of the province.'[20]

To make matters worse, the social and professional worlds of this bourgeois elite were essentially the same as those occupied by recently ennobled families whose exemption from the tax rolls had just increased the burden on everyone else. They lived in the same *quartiers*; they worked in many of the same professions; their lifestyles were entirely similar. As Hickey has pointed out, very little separated the two groups except the fact that one paid the *taille* and the other did not. The resulting rivalry and resentment between the two elite groups became a major factor in the *procès des tailles*. In particular, the bourgeois elite used its advantage within municipal governments to force town councils to examine closely each new tax exemption and claim to nobility.[21]

The institutional basis of bourgeois power was their position of dominance in the governments of the towns in which they resided. Despite the fact of municipal elections, most town governments were essentially self-perpetuating oligarchies in which sitting consuls nominated or co-opted their successors. The bourgeois elite used their positions as consuls to oppose the existing tax structure and to question the noble status of families whose lives and livelihoods were remarkably similar to their own. As the *procès des tailles* progressed, the principal cities of Dauphiné and their bourgeois elites turned increasingly to the Assembly of the Ten Cities to make their case for reform. And by the 1590s it had become apparent that the provincial estates and the parlement, institutions that by their very composition were disposed towards the interests of the nobility and the clergy, would never effect change. For tax reform to take place, they were forced to find an alternative forum, and the Assembly of Ten Cities became 'the pivotal element of the new offensive'. Each of the ten principal cities of the province could send its first and second consuls as delegates, which meant that bourgeois representation was a significant element in the composition of the assembly and that bourgeois interests were well represented on the assembly's agenda.[22]

Between 1595 and 1602, the two sides prepared their cases for presentation before the king's council. They constructed legal and historical arguments and did their utmost to create an atmosphere of public opinion that was favorable to their respective causes. The result is a paper trail of pamphlets and legal documents that permit the historian not only to understand the details of the case as it was presented to the Conseil d'état but also to probe the systems of values and the social identities associated with each side. Each side constructed arguments that its attorneys felt were most likely to win a favorable decision. At the same time each side constructed a social identity for itself that sprang from the identities of the attorneys who argued its case. It has been argued that, given the prominent role that lawyers played in the very litigious society of early modern France and in the culture of Renaissance Europe, they were uniquely well situated to 'give expression to society's changing perceptions'.[23] Perhaps more than any other group the lawyers of France had their finger on the pulse of the society in which they lived, and their world-view reflected with incredible sensitivity the fundamental changes in outlook that engulfed their lives and the lives of those around them.

In the case of the nobility, the attorneys came from recently ennobled families, whose financial and social progress had resulted in the ultimate confirmation of their families' inherent virtue, noble status. In the case of the third estate, the attorneys were drawn from the bourgeois elite who, despite great material and professional success and mobility, did not seek or had not yet attained the status of nobility but relished their achieved status as hardworking, talented, and successful individuals.[24] Ultimately, both sides would construct identities that relied on achievement; both arguments referred to acquired characteristics and talked in terms of self-fashioning. Even the nobility, which relied so heavily on the idea of virtue through inheritance, would write about acquired characteristics and virtues, a kind of self-conscious construction of virtue or *honnêteté*. Aristocratic culture valued ambition and the idea of professional success. Indeed, Dewald argues that by the seventeenth century the ambition and success of the nobleman had become paramount in defining his personal identity and contributing to his sense of self-worth.[25] Achieved status was a cultural concept that held sway over early modern imaginations because they lived in a society, albeit a society of orders, in which social mobility as a result of achievement was more than a mere possibility.

The case for the third estate was made by several attorneys, among them Claude Delagrange. His pamphlet *La juste plainte et remonstrance* appeared in 1597, and it was the prototype for the sort of cases mounted by these attorneys. A meticuously argued and documented brief, it constructed a legal and historical case by surveying the history of the *taille* in Dauphiné. Using documents from the fourteenth, fifteenth and early sixteenth centuries, he attempted to show that originally the nobility of Dauphiné had been subject, like everyone else, to the *taille*. He went on to maintain that the nobility was undeserving of the exemptions they had claimed in more recent times because their military contributions to the province and the realm had been minimal and highly exaggerated by their defenders. Turning from the legal and historical to contemporary problems associated with tax exemption, Delagrange described the financial crisis of the village which resulted from the acquisition of property by nobles and townspeople.[26]

These themes were reiterated in the works of Antoine Rambaud and Jean Vincent, but they, as Hickey notes, 'went further than Delagrange in describing the damage done to the economic stability of the villages by the continuing acquisitions of the *anoblis*, the children of officials, the bastard sons of nobles, and the self-proclaimed nobles'. They raised questions about the virtue of a nobility that could engage in such behavior with utter indifference to the suffering of the people, and they raised questions about the actual nobility of nobles' illegitimate children and the children of tax-exempt officials.[27]

In composing their case, the lawyers for the third estate wrote in political terms that were decidedly different from those used by the nobility. Central to their rhetoric were two related ideas: the notion of the public good (*le bien public*) and the concept of *la patrie*. They invoked the ideas of devotion to the public and the good of the state, and they charged that the nobility's claims to immunity from the *taille* ran contrary to the welfare of the state.[28] In contrast with the nobility, which acted with total disregard for the nation, their attorneys argued that the third estate possessed a sense of the greater good that surpassed their own group interests.

What appears in the rhetoric of the third estate is a sense of nation or nationalism. How deeply imbued this feeling was remains to be determined. It is, however, significant that those writing on behalf of the third estate made very effective use of a nationalist and patriotic vocabulary with all its ideological weight and attendant emotions. If, as Sahlins argues, this imagined community was conceived in conflict and opposition, then the third estate of Dauphiné had come perhaps to think of itself as a community with shared interests, as the nation with a common foe. Their attorneys argued that the nobility were not motivated by the good of the nation, thus placing the nobility in the role of 'them' and the third estate in that of 'us' or the nation. Their sense of national identity and patriotism took shape in the midst of social and political conflicts that placed the third estate in clear opposition to the nobility, in this way causing the third estate's self-image to crystallize as the community of the nation. By advancing the cause of *la patrie*, the third estate offered the monarchy another weapon that it might use against provincial nobles – the interest of the nation, a concept that was not imposed from the center on the periphery, but rather sprang from the social conflicts of the periphery among its local populations.

The third estate of Dauphiné clearly identified its interests with that of the nation. Jean Vincent expressed the belief that everyone had what he referred to as a natural obligation to *la patrie* and to the king. But he went further, identifying the interest of the people with the interest of the king; they were one and the same. And to exploit or place undue burden on the people was for Vincent to violate the majesty of the king.[29] By refusing to pay their share, the nobility had shirked their natural obligation to the state and shifted a disproportionate share of responsibility onto the third estate. They had thereby detracted from the majesty of the king.[30] The people and the king were one community, the nation, the nobility its opponents. The nobility were motivated by self-interest rather than the good of the nation.[31] As such, they were not part of the nation.

In responding to the nobility, who based much of their case on the idea that they worked or sacrificed for the public, the third estate's authors charged hyprocrisy and self-interest. They accused the nobility of enriching themselves at the expense of the public. Antoine Rambaud argued so vociferously that the nobility contributed nothing to the public as to speculate that the world would be a happier place without them.[32] He wrote that only the greater nobility, the *seigneurs de marque*, actually fulfilled the obligation that entitled them to exemption from the *taille*, indeed, that they never missed an occasion to do good. It was the rest of the nobility, the majority, who shamelessly never wanted to leave their homes.[33] Here Rambaud used the culture of nobility and the arguments launched by the attorneys for the nobility as a weapon against them. Much of the nobility's case was based on the idea that military service and sacrifice for the community exempted them from taxation, and yet Rambaud argued that many of them never served and never left home. Why then the tax exemption?

By making a distinction between the greater nobility and the majority of those claiming noble exemption, Rambaud drew upon the contempt with which the urban elite regarded those families who had only recently been recognized as noble. It was this group whose exemptions had increased the burden on the third estate, and it was this group about which he had the most disparaging things to say. He referred to the fact that their numbers were great and that they stayed at home and never served. By the fact that they lived in town and owned rural property, they placed a surcharge or extra burden on the rural community that was devastating and ultimately forced many to abandon their property. He argued that most of these *anoblis* engaged in 'secret traffic and illicit negotiations', which did more harm to an area than a company of soldiers. Moreover, he pointed out that, in addition to bringing about the ruin of the rural communities by their purchase and speculation in land, they never committed a sou for the public good.[34]

Rambaud had offered harsh words about the *anoblis* whom he knew so well. Hickey has shown that Rambaud, Vincent, and Delagrange (the three principal attorneys for the third estate) came from families that were painfully familiar with the way in which ennoblement had shifted an additional tax burden onto the urban elite. As part of this tax-paying urban elite, the three attorneys 'reflected this new social group's jealousy of the privileged orders, whose new acquisitions were not weighed down by *taille* assessments'.[35] By singling out the recently ennobled and reserving praise for the older and greater nobility, Rambaud's pamphlet brings the nature of this social conflict into clearer focus. Only in the most superficial way was the *procès des tailles* a conflict between noble and commoner. Fundamentally it was a competition between those who had recently succeeded in claiming nobility and its attendant honors and those who had not yet managed to do the same. Nor was this conflict simply a matter of envy; it was true that the advantages gained by the recently ennobled added to the tax burden suffered by those who had not managed to make their way in. One's success made the other's failure more significant. And each group's familiarity with the other inspired the greatest contempt. In the case of the attorneys arguing for the nobility, this familiarity resulted in a great discussion of virtue; their disgust with the *anoblis* produced a nationalistic/patriotic rhetoric that established the third estate as the nation, and the *anoblis* as their enemy and a threat to the public good.

Among those claiming exemptions, the *avocats consistoriaux* were a particular point of contention for the attorneys of the third estate. These *avocats* were senior lawyers within the parlement of Grenoble. Traditionally these positions had elevated the holders to noble status and therefore exempted them from taxation. According to the third estate, the number of individuals who could actually claim to be *avocats consistoriaux* had been greatly inflated. The response of the *avocats* and their spokesmen was to emphasize the obvious virtues of this group, to portray them in terms of their achieved identity as noble scholars and guardians of the public good. Their partisans referred to their *honnête* and industrious nature. They described them as men of eminence based on their profound understanding of the law, and they celebrated their mental dexterity and sagacity, all of which involved the language of achievement, ambition, and self-construction.[36]

The illegitimate children of nobles and the children of officeholding *anoblis* also bore the full force of the third estate's contempt and hostility. In writing about the bastard sons of noble fathers, their attorneys relied on a language of unforgiving moral superiority. They depicted the fathers of these children in the most abject terms and referred to their routine lack of self-control as evidenced by their bawdy and even incestuous conduct.[37] As for the children of officeholders, they too were held in contempt for having usurped their privileged immunities and increased the tax burden on the third estate. Their claims to immunity, it was argued, defied reason, the law, and custom.[38]

The Nobility's Response

How did the nobility respond? Their attorneys, among them Claude Expilly, took the position that the third estate's proposals were radical and would lead to great instability by disturbing the ancient order and customs of the realm. Expilly argued that the nobility had at no point been subject to taxes in Dauphiné and that Dauphiné had never been subject to the *taille réelle*. He painted a nobility who had suffered enormously during the Wars of Religion, and he blamed the bourgeois elite for the suffering that both noble and peasant had experienced. Ultimately, Expilly argued that the political activities of the third estate constituted an attempt at insurrection, which would result in the degradation of the nobility and the ruin of the monarchy. To support his claims, Expilly invoked the idea of what Jouanna has called the 'myth of race'. By their natural and inherited qualities, the nobility, he argued, were the purest blood within the body of the state.[39]

In an anonymous pamphlet, a spokesman for the nobility took this attack against the bourgeois elite even further. The author wrote about emulation and envy of the nobility as the cause of the *procès*. With undisguised contempt, he described how the bourgeois elite enriched itself at the misfortune of the nobility. By the purchase of alienated aristocratic lands, they sought to set themselves up as nobility, and yet all the while they continued to enjoy the benefits of commerce, a source of income that was denied the nobility.[40]

Another pamphlet author pursued a similar argument against the accusations of the third estate by lamenting the hardships faced by the nobility. He wrote about nobles who were ruined in the service of the king and contrasted their sacrifices with the opulence enjoyed by the third estate, suggesting that the third estate profited from aristocratic misfortune. But the third estate to which this author really refers is the bourgeois elite, for he goes on to express sympathy for the poor laborers and peasants who cannot protect themselves against the subtle ways of the bourgeois and townspeople. There were repeated attempts to contrast the wealth of the bourgeois elite with the poverty of the nobility. Such efforts contrasted the honorable noble who had sacrificed his material well-being while at war for the king with the rapacious merchant who continued to gain at others' expense. Or, noble apologists offered the image of the public servant who labored and sacrificed his life of wealth and opulence so that he might serve the public. They portrayed themselves in the most altruistic terms, and they villainized the bourgeois elite. Indeed, they too invoked the idea of *le public*.[41]

In making these comparisons, it is clear that the attorneys of the second estate found virtue in achievement. They talk about valor in battle and about service to the state through officeholding, and they acknowledge the practical benefits of ennoblement. Audeyer addressed the problem of extinction and the diminishing number of older families and argued that it was essential to replenish their depleted ranks with individuals of ambition and courage.[42] Those who replenished these ranks, according to one author, had earned what older families possessed by nature; by loyal service to the crown and the public they had achieved the character and status of nobility.[43] For the defenders of the second estate, achievement and contribution to the public sphere held more importance than inheritance. Their language was that of ambition, and they defined themselves and justified their privileges in terms of their public life.[44]

What seems to have evolved in the polemical literature associated with tax reform is a kind of class conflict in which the focus of both sides was directed at two closely related segments of elite society. Through the prism of tax reform Dauphinois society was separated into its constituent parts, and by its respective horizontal solidarities made visible. For the third estate, those who had recently made it into the nobility were the enemy; for the nobility, the bourgeois elite represented the biggest problem. And it was from these two closely related groups that the attorneys for each estate came. It is their world-view, their values, and their respective senses of self that resonate through the legal and historical cases they mounted on behalf of their larger constituencies.

Both sides used the language of achievement and ambition. Their attorneys were, after all, spokesmen for a growing culture of ambition and achievement. They belonged to families that through their own efforts at self-construction had pursued upward social mobility, some with greater success than others, but success defined both groups. And, indeed, envy and emulation were basic to the whole affair, as they constituted emotive forces in the social world of self-construction.

In the end, however, it was the attorneys for the third estate who depicted themselves and their order in a way that proved most desirable to the monarchy. Each side had talked about its achievements and contributions to the public, but the third estate was more successful in defining the public. Its attorneys made clear and unambiguous the inseparable relationship between the king, the nation, and the community to which they belonged. It was their construction of *la patrie* that enabled the bourgeois elite to present the crown with a definition that it could not refuse.

The Crown's Decisions

In 1602, however, it was not apparent that this was the case, for the crown's decision that year seemed to be a victory for the nobility. The decision was conservative and recognized the nobility's immunity from taxation. But it did bring changes: the bastard sons of nobles could no longer enjoy exemptions; future *avocats consistoriaux* would only be ennobled by the king, and not by the nomination of the parlement (in other words, ennoblement would no longer be *pro forma*); and the children of the *avocats* could no longer claim exemption (only children of the holders of major offices in the parlement or the Chambre des Comptes could do so). It is also significant that the decision mandated that all families claiming ennoblement in the previous 40 years should provide the parlement with specific justification and proof for these claims. These concessions to the third estate show that the 1602 decision was not a judgment in favor of the nobility only, and certainly the third estate did not perceive it as such.[45]

That the king and his council arrived at a decision that was immediately favorable to the nobility was in part due to the intervention of François de Bonne, the duke of Lesdiguières, and his role in the *procès* makes clear the political uses of patronage and clientage in Dauphiné. The duke enjoyed a close relationship with Henry IV that dated to the Wars of Religion. Born to a minor noble family, Lesdiguières's life itself reads as a classic tale of self-construction and ambition. Through service to Henry he managed to ingratiate himself and to promote his career. A man of talent, both as a soldier and an administrator, he was elected head of the Protestant party in Dauphiné in 1577 at the age of 34. Upon the succession of Henry IV, Lesdiguières formed an alliance with the Catholic lieutenant-general of the province, Alphonse d'Ornano, and together they re-established order on behalf of the first Bourbon monarch. His success in managing the struggles in Dauphiné brought rewards. At the beginning of the religious wars, Lesdiguières had an annual income of only a few hundred *livres*; by the end of Henry's reign he was reaping the financial benefits of loyal service, and he brought in 121 699 *livres* annually.[46]

Lesdiguières used some of his political capital to promote the case of the nobility. He wrote to Chancellor Bellièvre to ask that the privileges of the nobility be maintained, and to make clear that the third estate was the obstacle in the way of a settlement. He believed that the nobility had made concessions to the third estate, and that the third estate had failed to respond. The 1602 decision was a partial victory for the duke, but it jeopardized the privileged status of many of his own recently ennobled supporters and clients. He went quickly to work lobbying on their behalf. He wrote numerous communications to Bellièvre requesting letters of nobility and arguing the merits of a particular family.[47] Lesdiguières's efforts on behalf of his clients included tending to the career of Expilly. Thanks to the duke's *crédit* and Expilly's loyal service, the attorney advanced from *procureur général* in the Chambre des Comptes to *avocat général* in the parlement, and in 1616 he became president of the court.[48]

As Lesdiguières used his connection with Henry IV to advance the cause of the nobility in general and his clients in particular, a new figure emerged to challenge the privileged orders on behalf of the third estate. This phase of the *procès* saw Claude Brosse take center stage. Brosse was chosen as *commis* of the villages, and he worked aggressively for his constituents. His background is not completely documented, though it appears that he was the *chatelain* to an important noble family. At times he is referred to as seigneur of Serizin and it appears that he may have represented himself as noble or had aspirations in that direction. It is clear that Brosse was born into the third estate, and it was their cause that he took up. He was a man of great ability and achievement, and someone who had much in common with the bourgeois elites of the towns. He entered the fray as a spokesman for the villages, but soon he was speaking for all of the aggrieved third estate.[49]

Brosse won a significant victory in 1606 when the crown agreed to the creation of a commission for the purpose of reducing village debts. As rural creditors, the nobility and bourgeoisie stood to lose as a result of this intervention.[50] Another measure that posed a problem for the nobility was the crown's decision to use indirect taxes paid by all as a means of alleviating some of the burden of the *taille* on the rural populations. The nobility argued that to use indirect taxes to reduce the *taille* on the third estate was in essence asking them to contribute, when, in fact, they had already done so through the *arrière-ban*. This issue was taken up by the estates, and the debate there made manifest the horizontal solidarities and social cleavages that would characterize the remainder of the *procès*. The bourgeois elite was drawn back into a close alliance with its third estate compatriots, while the second estate remained steadfast in its claims to exemptions and privileged status.[51]

As the contest continued, the nobility relied increasingly on the connections to the crown that Lesdiguières provided. The lieutenant-general played an essential role in the pacification of the province, and his presence assured the tranquility of the Protestants and the compliance of the nobility.[52] At one point the king wrote to Lesdiguières, who was about to embark on a trip beyond the province: 'Return to Dauphiné quickly, because I am at rest when you are there and I am always worried when you are absent.'[53] But there may have been an important subtext in the king's remark. Henry was not always certain that he could count on Lesdiguières's fidelity and probably preferred to have him on the job in Dauphiné rather than plotting against him elsewhere. For a time there was serious doubt about the duke's loyalty, largely on the part of Sully who never shared the king's fondness for the Protestant grandee. Lesdiguières had been so fantastically successful in accumulating money, troops, fortifications, and clients that it aroused the suspicions of Sully and others. His ties to powerful Swiss and German families were also the cause of some anxiety.[54] This was the problem with the patron–client relationship. It was an informal arrangement that had to be constantly evaluated and negotiated, and loyalty had to be regularly demonstrated.[55]

Over time Lesdiguières persuaded Henry IV that he was indeed his devoted servant, and he proved indispensable to the king's foreign policy by looking after French interests in the Alps. The duke not only alleviated the king's anxieties, but he also managed to levy and collect taxes without the estates' consent. Most of these taxes were spent in Dauphiné, making them a little less onerous to local populations, but the fact remains that Lesdiguières produced the taxes essential to the defense of the province and the realm.[56]

The favor Lesdiguières had carefully cultivated with Henry IV allowed him in turn to influence the crown's role and intervention in the province. In 1606, thanks in part to the duke's influence, the king agreed to allow the estates to debate a tax on imported wine; his underlying objective was to provide an opportunity for them to reach a compromise. Henry hoped that the meeting would allow them to reconcile their differences, as his goal was not to divide provincial society in order to pacify it. He simply wanted to put an end to all the social conflict that was generated by the *procès*. This meeting, however, was a failure, and the wine tax remained the most immediate source of controversy and debate within Dauphiné. In 1609 the king tried once again to bring the three estates together for the purpose of reconciliation. Lesdiguères's son-in-law, the duke of Créqui, presided over this meeting of the provincial estates and exerted pressure on the nobility to reach some kind of agreement. After months of deliberation the nobility reluctantly agreed to allow revenues from the salt tax to be used over a period of five years for the alleviation of rural debts. The nobility agreed to this compromise in 1611 only after Lesdiguères himself had intervened.[57] Though Henry IV did not live to see it, his reliance on a client/broker with ample *crédit* produced the desired results.

Still there remained the larger issue of the nobility's claims to immunity and the crown's desire to produce additional revenues from Dauphiné. In the early reign of Louis XIII the conflicts with the Huguenots and the grandees created financial exigencies that made the issue of taxation in Dauphiné even more pressing. The third estate continued to propose indirect taxes as a way of meeting these financial demands, and the nobility was steadfast in its opposition. In 1616 the third estate proposed using the salt tax to support troops. Again, for the nobility the use of indirect taxes, except to alleviate village indebtedness, amounted to shifting the burden of the *taille* onto the privileged orders. Loyal servant that he proved to be, Lesdiguères continued to act on behalf of the crown in the hope that he could persuade the nobility to act likewise. By their opposition and obstruction over the next few years, the nobility succeeded in alienating both Lesdiguères and the crown. Louis XIII responded in 1622 by ordering that the tax on salt be increased. The privileged orders protested the king's intervention at a meeting of the provincial estates, and they argued that the new taxes violated the 1602 edict in which Henry IV had recognized their immunity from taxation. In the following years, the nobility became more deeply entrenched, and their reactionary posture widened the breach with Lesdiguères and therefore with the crown.[58]

The provincial estates was not convened from the fall of 1623 until the spring of 1627. During the interim the Assemblée du Pays continued to meet and acted as a *de facto* estates, a situation that suited the monarchy because the assembly was a considerably easier group with which to work. The meeting of the estates in 1627 was called to address the same issues, the salt tax and the support of troops in the region, but it proved

to be more interesting when a member of the third estate proposed that
the king revoke all ennoblements within the past 60 years. This was an
undisguised attempt to separate the older nobility from more recently
ennobled families and to forge horizontal alliances that would weaken
the nobility. It failed miserably as the old nobility stood firm in their
commitment to all members of the order, and the order stood firm in its
opposition to the tax reform.[59]

At this point the crown began to take decisive steps that would climax
in victory for the third estate. First, it issued an edict in 1628 that created
ten *élections* in Dauphiné. This would permit the king to collect the *taille*
without consulting the estates. A few months later the crown decided to
insure provincial compliance by suspending the provincial estates and
replacing them with a barebones version of the Assemblée du Pays.
These moves constituted a direct assault on provincial liberties, and
the sovereign courts, in which noble interests were deeply embedded,
responded accordingly. The crown had acted with such decisiveness
because rebellions and external conflicts created a situation of fiscal
urgency. Moreover, the duke of Lesdiguières had died in 1626. For 37
years he had been in control of the province and had acted as the king's
intermediary and broker. As a result of Lesdiguière's death, the crown
was compelled to intervene directly and decisively. After his death, no
one emerged to replace Lesdiguières as the provincial power-broker.[60]

The parlement registered the offending edicts, but not exactly as they
were issued. It reduced the power of the *élus* and insisted that royal
government, and not the province, pay the salaries and expenses of
these new and unwelcome officials. Louis insisted that the parlement
register his decree in its original form, but it was not until 1630 that he
was successful. In the meantime, the *élus* had arrived and set about their
work. What followed was a series of delaying and disrupting tactics on
the part of the parlement.[61]

In obstructing and diluting these royal edicts, the parlementaires
were struggling to shelter themselves from taxation. The *élus* were an
omen. Clearly, their introduction took place because of the crown's
desire to produce more revenue, a fact which meant that tax reform
could not be far behind. If the third estate won their case, most of the
parlementaires would be adversely affected. At the end of the sixteenth
century, the Parlement of Dauphiné was a court populated by a mixed
group. In 1596, about 57 per cent of the parlementaires were nobles,
and 43 per cent were members of the third estate. By 1635, however, the
nobility had gained an advantage within the court, and almost 67 per cent

of its members were nobles, and another 19 per cent were individuals whose families were striving to attain that status (*noblesse commencée*). This meant that only 14 per cent of the officers in the parlement were clearly identified as third estate.[62]

Particularly relevant to the *procès* was the number of individuals who were in the process of claiming nobility and its most coveted privilege. According to Maurice Virieux, who has studied the social composition of the parlement, between 1596 and 1635, 26 per cent of the officers were attempting to claim nobility but remained on unstable ground.[63] Approximately 10 per cent of its members had only established nobility as recently as the late sixteenth century.[64] In the province as a whole, 107 households were ennobled during the period 1587–1634. The amount of potentially taxable property held by these families was enormous. *Cadastres* indicate that the revenue from their holdings that would have been subject to the *taille réelle* varied from 450 000 *livres* to 10 000 *livres*, and that the potentially taxable holdings of 45 households generated revenues of over 100 000 livres.[65] It was these *anoblis* who were most vulnerable, because the third estate in its various appeals and pamphlets had focused particularly on families that had been recently ennobled and families that were in the process of claiming nobility. To the third estate, they constituted the real enemy. The villains of their polemics, these were the families with whom the third estate elite shared quarters and lifestyles, the families that inspired particular contempt within those individuals spearheading the third estate effort. They were also sure to be the first families affected by the crown's decisions on reform, and their presence had an obvious impact on the politics of the parlement.

Despite these factional interests, the parlement's actions were not merely self-serving; it acted also on behalf of the province as a whole, which was suffering terribly under the strain of providing for the troops that were deployed to deal with Protestant rebellions and the Valtelline crisis. This crisis involved a series of conflicts between France and the Spanish Habsburgs over a passage running from northern Italy to the Alpine passes. It was crucial for French interests in Italy to keep it free from Spanish control, while for Spain it offered a means of moving troops from Italy to the Low Countries.[66]

Domestically, Dauphiné's involvement in the problem of Huguenot rebellion and resistance caused provincial strife. With the death of Henry IV, the Huguenots found themselves in a substantially less secure position. Fearful about the future of the Edict of Nantes under the regency, the Huguenots chose as their political and military leader a militant member of their movement, the duke of Rohan. With time it became clear that the crown intended to dismantle the edict completely, and in 1620 Louis XIII conducted a military campaign in southwestern France in which he tried to 'root out those few Huguenot militants who might be able to rouse significant opposition to the crown'.[67] Lesdiguières, having recently abjured the reformed faith and been rewarded with the new title of constable of France, was placed in the position of combating his former co-religionists. In 1622 he took Huguenot fortresses at Pouzin and Baix-sur-Baix. Fighting resumed in 1625, forcing the constable to take more decisive military action against the Protestants, which in turn meant more troop movements. In short, the 1620s were miserable years for Dauphiné, and the parlement felt that the introduction of the *élus* merely imposed an additional burden on the beleaguered population.[68]

Despite the parlement's efforts to undermine the work of the *élus*, the crown was ultimately successful and its new officials siphoned from Dauphiné ever greater revenues. More important, the introduction of the *élus* to Dauphiné was a prelude to the crown's decision in 1634 to declare the province a *pays de taille réelle*. Both the parlement and the *intendant* made it plain to Louis XIII and Richelieu that Dauphiné suffered enormously under the weight of troop movements and increased taxation. Moreover, Louis and Richelieu had first-hand knowledge of the suffering, as they had both visited the province in 1632. This may explain why they seemed particularly receptive to the *intendant* Talon's report, a document that exhibited a clear third estate bias. Their decision also reflects the influence of Claude Brosse, who argued persuasively that the 1602 decision had never been respected or observed by the second estate. The objective in 1602 had been to reduce the debts of the villages, but, according to Brosse, the situation had actually deteriorated as tax-exempt families had purchased even more rural property since then.[69]

The 1634 edict established the *taille réelle* throughout Dauphiné. All non-noble or *roturier* lands were to be assessed for purposes of taxation, which meant, of course, that a great deal of property in the hands of the nobility would now be subject to taxation. The crown was not totally indifferent to noble arguments, and it exempted the property of nobles whose status dated to before 1539. Also, all those families whose claims to nobility before 1602 had been confirmed would enjoy immunity from taxation, but only for the property that they had held prior to that date. The most direct assault on the *anoblis* came in the provision that revoked all ennoblements since 1602. According to Hickey, fiscal imperatives moved the crown to take such action. Its agenda was financial rather than political, though the wording of the edict explicitly refers to the problem of rural indebtedness and the suffering of the people. Still, sympathy for the people stemmed from the practical realization that the second estate had seriously eroded the provincial tax base.[70]

The nobility responded predictably. In 1635 they held a meeting in Grenoble to prepare a response with counter-proposals. This assembly was dominated by officeholders, and they selected four very recently ennobled attorneys to represent them between sessions. In other words, they chose four attorneys who personally had most at stake. What followed over the next few years was a decided deterioration in relations between crown and nobility. The crown and its representative, Talon, were adamant that the tax reform must go through, and more than once Louis forbade the nobility of Dauphiné to assemble and accused them of fomenting rebellion. Having identified the parlement as the center of resistance, the king's council diluted its power by setting up a competing presidial court (*siège présidial*) at Valence and a Court of Aids in Vienne.[71]

The second estate persisted in their resistance, even resorting to personal attacks against Talon, and eventually secured a series of important revisions. In 1639 the central government agreed to recognize the nobility of those who had claimed noble status since 1602, but they were not permitted to claim tax immunity. As for other *anoblis*, they would be able to claim the same exemptions as the old nobility, but only if they had completed at least ten years of military service. The standard of exemption for old and new nobility was property acquired before 1628.[72]

These concessions on the part of the king climaxed in October 1639 with the promulgation of the final word on the *procès des tailles*. In recognizing Dauphiné as a province of the *taille réelle*, the edict moved the marker from 1628 to 1635. All those enobled before 1602 would not be taxed for property acquired before 1635. The same right was extended to officeholders in the parlement and the Chambre des Comptes, as well as for the *trésoriers de France*, if they had held their positions before 1602. But those who had acquired office since 1602 were left empty-handed except for a modest concession of an annual indemnity of one-fourth their assessment.[73] Hickey regards these revisions as a defeat for the most recently ennobled. By their radical opposition they had convinced Talon that it would be possible and opportune to drive a wedge between the very recently ennobled and more established noble families by making concessions to the latter.[74]

The concessions negotiated by the second estate between 1634 and 1639 represent a significant victory for a portion of that group. As the crown retreated from the provisions of its earlier edict, the older nobility carved for themselves an immunity not extended to those ennobled after 1602. For recent *anoblis*, victory had been redefined to mean simply retaining their status as nobility, and in this sense the revisions constituted an important concession to them as well. Tax exemption was not the only privilege of nobility; there remained juridical privileges and the honor conferred on noble families in a society where social privilege was determined by the esteem society attached to rank. Certainly, immunity from taxes was not the sole incentive driving the process of upward social mobility.

Yet the *procès des tailles* is largely viewed as a third estate victory, because in the end their goal was met in the establishment of the *taille réelle*. But the fact that older families, and even families ennobled in the sixteenth century, were still permitted to claim exemptions on their *roturier* lands meant that this third estate victory would be delayed in producing most of the desired results. It would be a victory for future generations, but those who had fought for it so energetically and vociferously would not live to see its full benefits.

As for the crown, it had, in fact, driven a wedge between old and new noble families by providing cause for horizontal alliances that separated the larger nobility into two parts. But these were not equal parts – the crown had divided the nobility into a large group consisting of old families and families ennobled in the sixteenth century and a considerably smaller group of early seventeenth-century *anoblis* who had scrambled to get in before the door shut. By its policies, the crown had energized the scramble, and by the dates of demarcation in the 1639 decision Louis XIII had grandfathered in the majority of noble families. For them, the only thing that had changed was that future *roturier* acquisitions would be subject to the *taille*. As relations between crown and nobility deteriorated in the final stages of the controversy, the central government settled on concessions that suited most of the nobility. It had created an arrangement that was mutually satisfactory.

In so doing, the central government had extended its fiscal reach over a crucial frontier province without alienating permanently the local nobility who were so vital to the defense of the region. It has been argued that representative government, on the surface a casualty of the monarchy's attempts to get tough, was not eliminated by the suspension of the provincial estates in 1628. The three orders continued to meet in the Assemblée du Pays, which René Favier describes as a sort of mini-estates carrying similar authority as the voice of the province. For Favier, the fact that the assembly continued to meet and to be heard for 30 years confirms the gradual, rather than abrupt, way in which the state effected centralization.[75] And in the face of so-called centralization, the parlement managed to preserve a measure of political autonomy by exercising political as well as juridical powers within the local context. This it was able to do in the interest of the public order and strictly through its prescribed role. But from mid-century the decisions rendered by this court allowed it to fulfill a political and administrative role that had previously belonged to the provincial governor. As the actual powers of the provincial governors eroded or were dismantled, the parlement acted more and more in their capacity. In this way the parlement reconstructed a sort of autonomous local government dominated by the provincial nobility.[76]

Over the course of the *procès* it appeared that the crown's posture *vis-à-vis* the provincial nobility evolved from conciliatory to adversarial. Early on in the conflict, Henry IV's government rendered decisions in favor of the nobility, but as the conflict ground on in the reign of Louis XIII central government sided more and more against the nobility, especially the newest elements within it. Such a change in attitude suggests a shift in royal strategy from a more subtle reliance on the vertical ties of patronage to the overt use of social divisions and rivalries to create horizontal bonds that would allow the crown to divide and control the province.

But the control that Louis XIII and Richelieu sought did not require the emasculation of the provincial nobility. Indeed, the crown relied on clientage networks to minimize conflict. It was only after the death of its broker Lesdiguières that the crown began to act in a way that seemed to favor the third estate. Even then its decisions targeted the most recently ennobled families, those who had raced to get in before it was too late to gain a tax advantage, rather than the older families who dominated the second estate. In 1638 the crown appeared to side with the third estate, and yet it had instituted a law that benefitted most of the existing noble families. In fact, the monarchy had struggled to find the middle way, to pursue a course that would respond to the grievances of the third estate while preserving good relations with the nobility. This had been a difficult course to navigate, but it yielded the desired results. Royal policy had broadened the tax base in Dauphiné, answered the complaints of the third estate, and placated the nobility in this crucial frontier province.

Chapter 5: Brittany: The Limits of Elite Solidarity

Far removed from Provence and Dauphiné lay Brittany, the last of the three *pays d'états* and a fiercely independent province. Unlike the others, however, Brittany and its provincial estates were not objects of tax reform under Louis XIII. Cardinal Richelieu did not attempt to introduce the *élus* and *élections* to the province, and thereby avoided the confrontations that such initiatives provoked elsewhere. Indeed, the Bretons only fell subject to the scrutiny of an *intendant* in 1634, and the *intendant* only became a permanent fixture in 1689. Thanks to the minister's special interest in Brittany and to the cooperation of its elites, the province was spared most of the changes, reforms, and attendant conflicts that defined the histories of Provence and Dauphiné in the early seventeenth century. It was only after Richelieu was gone and under Colbert that relations between the province and the crown deteriorated to the point of violence. The expenditures of Louis XIV's reign induced the crown to make demands sufficient to threaten the financial interests of the Breton landed elite. The resulting breakdown of cooperation between king and provincial nobles contributed to the rebellion of 1675. In resorting to hard-hitting tactics, Louis and his agents exposed the self-interests of the parlementaires and revealed the extent to which horizontal ties had formed in this provincial society and the challenges that they posed for central government. In the end, the Breton rebellion of 1675 suggests the delicate balance that 'absolutism' had to maintain – a juggling act in which crown struggled to manipulate clientage, and sometimes class interest, without allowing one or the other to escape its control.

Brittany came into the realm later than the other two provinces, and the circumstances of reunion revolved around female inheritance and royal marriages. Anne of Brittany inherited the duchy from her father, Duke Francis II, in 1488. Her marriage to King Charles VIII in 1491 was the first stage in bringing Brittany under royal control. When Charles died in 1498, Louis XII (before becoming king) proceeded to negotiate a marriage (1499) with Anne which would insure future control over Brittany. By the terms of their marriage contract, Brittany was to devolve to the second son of this union, or, in the absence of children, to Anne's family. When Anne died, the duchy, in fact, went to her daughter Claude, who was the wife of Francis I. Claude then designated her son, the *dauphin*, as heir, and upon his majority in 1532 Brittany became part of France. Along the way, the terms negotiated as part of this union had insured the traditional rights of the province; specifically, the French kings had promised not to levy taxes without the consent of the provincial estates.[1]

The main direct tax in Brittany was the *fouage*, a hearth tax that fell overwhelmingly on rural areas, because most towns had long since secured exemptions in consideration of the indirect or sales taxes they were required to pay. The *fouage* was ambiguously both a real tax on property and a personal tax on the individual according to social status. Over the years, the Breton dukes had sold exemptions, some to the nobility as nobles and some for their noble properties. Other important taxes were the indirect taxes on the sale of wine and import–export duties that were highly lucrative in this maritime province.[2]

Under the Valois, the tax structure of Brittany was left untouched, and until 1542 the kings asked the provincial estates to approve a standard and not particularly controversial amount of money based on traditional assessment rates. It was Francis I who tried to raise this figure significantly by increasing the rate at which the *fouage* was assessed. After some compromise, the estates agreed to raise the *fouage* slightly, but their agreement was that it would remain fixed. A fundamental consequence of this compromise, according to James Collins, was that the estates would now approve the *fouage* only in a ceremonial sense, and the king would be forced to seek other means of increasing revenue in Brittany. Henry II attempted to collect more money from Brittany by the sale of offices and the creation of new taxes, and the estates responded by choosing the actual form of taxation. Their choices involved the use of indirect taxes rather than direct taxes, and in this way they protected the revenues from their rural holdings.[3]

During the Wars of Religion, the monarchy resorted to a variety of expedients to raise additional revenues in Brittany. It sold *rentes* on the *fouage* as well as exemptions. In addition, the crown levied military taxes on the Breton countryside in order to pay for the war that took place in its midst. According to Collins, the burden of military taxes on landed revenues explains in part why the estates would see little alternative to choosing indirect taxes over direct taxes. Rural areas were being heavily taxed by military officials. By the 1580s, direct taxes supplied only 35 per cent of total revenue from Brittany.[4]

The 1590s and the reign of Henry IV further complicated fiscal arrangements in Brittany and added substantially to the burden of taxation. The costs incurred by Bretons resulted from the resistance that Leaguers and a good portion of the Breton nobility, led by the royal governor, the duke of Mercoeur, mounted to this Bourbon regime. Both sides used every means of collection at their disposal, and the resulting costs were enormous. Beyond the usual levels of taxation, there were demands for special grants and surtaxes, surtaxes even on the *fouage*, and direct taxes even on previously exempted urban areas. For Collins, this period and the financial demands it placed on Brittany were enormously important to politics in the province. It left the estates in debt, both to the wealthy individuals from whom they had borrowed money to make their payments to the royal government and to the king himself. Noble families and towns were left similarly in debt. In fact, the estates often assumed the debts of noble families struggling to make their ransom payments. The debts of towns provided the estates with political opportunity because they were able to claim the right to approve all new and renewed urban taxes.[5]

To meet their own debts, the estates voted to tax wine. This would become their regular pattern. In particular, they did so to meet their commitments to the king, to whom they had offered a great deal of money if he would enter Brittany with an army and subdue the Catholic League and its allies, the Spanish. The estates, however, did not pay the king at the rate originally promised, a fact that Henry was not in a position to complain about because of his own insolvency. After failed attempts to make the estates pay the balance of what they had promised, the king shifted his approach in .1602. At this meeting of the estates, the king's agents asked the assembly to buy back the royal domain in Brittany that had been mortgaged or alienated during hard times. The request failed, but they did agree to pay some of the funds voted the king in 1598.[6]

The issue of the royal domain dominated relations between king and estates until 1605, when the estates agreed to a wine tax that would be used to repurchase lands. Strings were attached to this agreement, including the fact that the estates, rather than royal officials, would have administrative control over the tax. For Russell Major, this was the basis of Breton power – the fact that the estates controlled the farming of indirect taxes.[7]

In 1608 Henry IV greatly desired to induce the estates to approve farming the wine tax for a set period of the next nine years. Had the estates agreed to this arrangement, it would have meant losing annual opportunities to give their approval (on a one-year basis) and to demand concessions in return. Such power they were not willing to abrogate. For the estates it was not so much the issue of redeeming the royal domain; rather, it was the control of indirect taxes that they intended to maintain.[8]

The control that the estates wielded over the forms of taxation reflected the desire of the Breton nobility to direct taxation away from their rural holdings. Major attributes their success in resisting royal demands (especially Sully's absolutist objectives) to the fact that provincial privileges had been clearly laid out in the contract by which Brittany joined the realm. Furthermore, he argues that the Breton estates and the sovereign courts cooperated (in contrast to Dauphiné) to preserve those privileges.[9] Through the estates and the parlement, Breton nobles watched over the province in general and took care of their own needs in particular.

Sword and Robe

One of the most striking characteristics about the Breton nobility was the preponderance of sword families. In his massive study of the eighteenth-century Breton nobility, Jean Meyer acknowledges the primacy of warfare in shaping this provincial elite. To describe the background of noble families, Meyer divides them by antiquity and origin into three large groups. The oldest group, those ennobled by the early fifteenth century, constituted 28 per cent (577 families). This group included 410 families whose origins were chivalric but whose antiquity could not be precisely dated. What is certain is that they presented at the first reformations of nobility in the early fifteenth century and emerged with their status upheld. They ranged from the very ancient to a larger group ennobled in the fourteenth century just prior to the Breton civil war. Together with the 167 families that were able to date their antiquity precisely, these were the oldest sword families.[10]

The second group consisted of more recently ennobled sword families, dating at least to the first half of the sixteenth century and described by Meyer as 'écuyers d'extraction'. They constituted 55 per cent of the provincial nobility.[11] Their numbers, particularly those ennobled by 1500, may be explained in part by a renewal of the sword during the fourteenth and fifteenth centuries, a period when a number of families rapidly entered the nobility by virtue of the abundant opportunities for military service and by the acquisition of a fief.[12] In addition, Brittany saw the birth of a fifteenth-century ducal robe nobility that exhibited sword characteristics and that was sometimes related to the older provincial aristocracy. These were the ducal secretaries, some of whom belonged to very old noble families and were the progenitors of the local robe nobility.[13] The Rogier family, for example, met the qualifications to be certified as 'nobles d'ancienne extraction de chevalerie' by the Chambre de Réformation in 1668, and they had been actively involved in judicial politics at least since the fifteenth century. We know that Jean Rogier, sieur du Cleyo, served as counselor to the duke of Brittany in the fifteenth century, and after the creation of the royal parlement in 1553 several Rogiers occupied offices in the court.[14] Similarly, the Kerméno family extended back to the fourteenth century and served the dukes of Brittany in a variety of capacities. In the late 1400s Guillaume was *procureur général* for Brittany, a position that was later held by his son Nicholas. Under the French kings two members of the family became counselors in the Breton parlement.[15]

The third component in the provincial nobility consisted of families ennobled by office or letter after 1550. This group, which corresponded most closely to the traditional definition of a robe nobility, constituted 17 per cent of the nobility. Their weak representation and the extraordinary number of sword families is certainly peculiar to Brittany. For Meyer this can be explained by the duchy's unique circumstances, which spared the Breton nobility the most tragic effects of the late Middle Ages. Although affected by the first part of the Hundred Years War and the Breton civil war, this region did not endure the widespread destruction and loss of life that occurred in other French provinces. The relative peace of the fifteenth century and the prosperity of the sixteenth preserved a robust sword nobility. The Breton nobility also avoided adversity by virtue of their geographical isolation within the kingdom and the fact that urban development in the province was limited. Isolation may have shielded their families from the menacing economic and political developments of the fifteenth and sixteenth centuries discussed in Chapter 1.[16]

One result of having such a large sword nobility was their involvement in all aspects of provincial government, including judicial politics. The sword's numerical presence in the Parlement of Brittany was almost precisely that of the robe, and almost equal numbers of sword and robe families occupied positions as parlementaires during the seventeenth century. The more recently ennobled robe families tended to precede the older families in obtaining these offices, but by the 1630s their numbers were approximately the same and the sword had clearly shifted into robe activities.[17] Sons of families like the house of Budes, who had for generations been warriors, now became magistrates as well. Christophe de Budes entered the parlement as a counselor in 1624. Previously he had pursued a military career, as had his father and relations before him. Meanwhile, two of his brothers carried on the family's military tradition, as did two of his sons. Another branch of the family followed a similar pattern. After a chain of military careers dating to the early fourteenth century, in 1554 Jacques Budes became *procureur général* in the parlement. His son opted not to enter the court, but instead fought for Henry IV during the 1590s. It was Jacques's grandson, Charles, who resumed the family's involvement in the parlement.[18] We see with this family just how easily noble houses shifted between sword and robe.

How do we explain the extent of this sword participation in a judicial body? In part the answer lies with the sword's participation in the old ducal parlement and in the estates during the Middle Ages. The histories of these two institutions are intertwined to the extent that they are virtually indistinguishable during the fourteenth and fifteenth centuries. In Brittany, the estates emerged from the ducal parlement. For a period, the parlement consented to taxation, thereby acquiring the function of the estates, and assumed the judicial functions of the *curia ducis*. The terms 'parlement', *parlement général*, and 'estates' appear to have been used interchangeably and without distinction as to the agenda and content of individual meetings. The bourgeoisie entered this assembly only in the fourteenth century, and failed to play an effective role for some time, so that this parlement/estates remained a distinctly feudal institution for most of the Middle Ages. Its feudal nature was guaranteed by the fact that the third estate was not included in its sessions until rather late in the assembly's evolution. It was this experience of the ducal parlement/estates that conditioned sword families to enter the royal parlement and made them comfortable in the capacity of magistrates.[19] Even the dukes' financial administration was staffed by families already established among the nobility. In the late fourteenth and fifteenth centuries, one in two financial officers belonged to a noble family.[20]

Henry II created a sovereign parlement for Brittany in 1553. Concerned that this action might encourage independence in a province accustomed to considerable autonomy and localism, the king was determined to prevent the court from being dominated by the Breton nobility. He restricted Breton officeholding to only half of the councillors (*originaires*), and the remaining councillors (*non-originaires*) were to come from other provinces.[21] In reality, however, this fifty-fifty rule was never observed. When *originaire* positions were unavailable, native families managed to enter the court by taking positions reserved for non-natives. One such case involved René de Beauce, who became a councillor in 1609. His office had been designated *non-originaire* and its former occupant, who had recently died, was a non-Breton. There was no question that Beauce was a local – his family dated back to the thirteenth century in Brittany. Not only did Beauce purchase an office that was technically off-limits to him, but he ensured that his family would continue to occupy this *non-originaire* slot by resigning it in favor of his son in 1638. And when the son, Joachim, died in 1653, another Breton family scrambled to claim the same office. These positions reserved for outsiders were so coveted by Breton families that wives were sometimes sent beyond the province in order to deliver their babies so that sons would technically qualify to occupy such openings.[22] Over the course of the seventeenth century, old, native, and largely sword families of Brittany had 228 members occupying offices, 47 of which were supposed to be reserved for outsiders, showing the value they attached to judicial offices and suggesting the power they would be able to wield through the institution.[23]

The other institutional voice of the nobility was the estates, long since defined separately from the parlement. Noble participation in the estates was usually very limited (to about 16 or so) in the sixteenth century, but the number in attendance rose dramatically during the Wars of Religion and then again during the reign of Henry IV. At the meeting in 1607 there were only 59 nobles present, but in 1608 that figure jumped to 146. And it is during this time that the estates of Brittany became more powerful, because by voting large sums to pay off debts and to redeem the royal domain they were able to claim the right of determining the form that taxation would take. For Collins, this power was crucial because it enabled the nobility to protect their own interests and at the same time to preserve order in the province.[24]

Henry IV's drive to redeem the royal domain provided the occasion for the estates, and within it the nobility, to consolidate political power. Moreover, representation of the third estate had declined relative to that of the nobility. Although the number of delegates from towns increased over the same period, it did not begin to keep pace with the rate at which noble representation increased. By the early seventeenth century, it was possible for any nobleman to sit in meetings of the estates (parlementaires were an exception to this custom after 1625, when they were excluded from the estates). From the urban perspective, the result of growing aristocratic domination was negative. It meant higher taxes on wine and urban consumers rather than higher taxes on grain and rural profits. Exacerbating their weaker numerical status within the estates was the fact that the third estate delegates were drawn not only from merchants' quarters but from landlords who were part of the legal profession and whose interests were much akin to those of the delegates of the nobility.[25]

After the death of Henry IV, relations between the Breton estates and the crown entered a period of greater uncertainty. By meeting the financial requests of their governor, the duke of Vendôme (the illegitimate son of Henry IV), they had provided him the means to build a personal guard of 100 men. In so doing, they had unwittingly helped to finance his failed rebellion in 1614, a fact that left the estates at something of a disadvantage in terms of their future financial negotiations with the royal government. Embarrassed at the turn of events and alienated by the duke, the delegates to the estates chose to express their loyalty to the king in the form of a *don gratuit*. Their relationship with the crown, however, remained unclear for a period, largely because they were not convoked in 1615. Instead, Brittany was asked to pay the customary taxes without being given the opportunity to consent. Louis XIII attributed his failure to call the estates to the urgent situation created by Condé's rebellion, a cause with which Vendôme eventually sided. When the estates did finally convene in 1616 Louis presented them with a demand for nearly 1.2 million *livres* above their regular taxes. They agreed to the usual levies, but they drastically reduced the amount and opted again to raise it from a tax on wine. The remainder of the decade saw them complete their commitments to domain redemption, and also establish the pattern of renewing the *don gratuit*. Given that the *don gratuit* was still to be negotiated each year and that in the end it was the only new component introduced by the crown to the Breton burden of taxation, Major believes that the estates of Brittany came out on top.[26]

During the period 1620–4, just prior to Richelieu's entry into the king's council, central government stepped up the pressure on Brittany to contribute financially. It threatened the creation of a Bureau of Finances, a royal intrusion that undoubtedly foreshadowed the introduction of the *élus*. The estates managed to persuade Louis to revoke the edict, but it cost them an additional 450 000 *livres*.[27] Brittany narrowly escaped the introduction of these royal officials by essentially paying the crown to remove the threat.

Richelieu and Brittany

With the rise of Cardinal Richelieu, Brittany's relations with central government entered a new phase. Royal demands for money increased, and Brittany was forced to contribute more, but the province did not experience the sort of administrative reforms that took place in the other *pays d'états* until significantly later. Instead, they enjoyed a special relationship with central government based on the cardinal's personal ties to the province. Brittany was a crucial component in the cardinal's own power base, and Richelieu took pains to construct carefully a provincial clientele that would mediate his policies.

Richelieu's special relationship to Brittany derived first from his energetic policy of maritime development. Determined to promote France as a sea power and a maritime economy, the cardinal moved to develop its navy and to reorganize and expand its coastal fortifications. Driving these policies was not only the cardinal's interest in economic development but also the problem of the Huguenots and the English at La Rochelle, and Brittany figured prominently in royal efforts to end the independent power of that port. From the Breton perspective, the menace at La Rochelle was not Protestantism or the Protestants' relations with the English – it was the Rochelais piracy that threatened to erode profits from the Breton wine trade. As Richelieu took greater and greater interest in the Breton seaports, he began to gather offices into his own hands. In 1626 he was named *grand maître et surintendant général du commerce*, a position whose jurisdiction he expanded to include navigation. That same year Louis named him governor of Le Havre. By 1631 the cardinal had acquired in one way or another the authorities and jurisdiction that gave him control over admiralty affairs. In the process he also acquired the governorship of Brittany. The Bretons wanted a governor who exercised admiralty rights, and by 1630 Richelieu was admiral of France and Brittany. It seemed a perfect match.[28]

Brittany had not always been enthusiastic about the cardinal's plans for naval reorganization, and the estates' decision to offer the governorship to Richelieu was largely a pragmatic one. Admiralty issues were crucial to the province, and Richelieu controlled the admiralty. The decision was also influenced by the ample presence of the cardinal's clients within the estates. Richelieu systematically constructed a clientele among the Breton nobility that proved indispensable in his relations with the province. By 1630 this Breton clientele was already sizable, and a number of his clients were delegates to the estates. Their presence undoubtedly served to influence debate in the cardinal's favor.[29]

As in Provence and, to a lesser extent, Dauphiné, Richelieu's clientele would be the foundation of his provincial policies. His governorship provided even more opportunities to establish personal connections with Breton nobles and to place them in important positions. Among his clients in Brittany was his cousin Charles de La Porte, duke of La Meilleraye, who acted as lieutenant-general of the province. In addition, La Meilleraye represented Richelieu within the estates, keeping the cardinal informed about its activities, assisting with financial negotiations, and reporting to him about potential clients within the assembly. His rewards for faithful service were substantial and varied, and, in addition to money, La Meilleraye was given the position of grand master of the artillery. This is not to suggest that La Meilleraye was the perfect client. His temper and shortcomings in interpersonal skills created problems for Richelieu which sometimes neutralized the benefits of his successes.[30]

More successful was another cousin, Charles de Cambout, baron of Pontchâteau. He proved a crucial agent within the estates, because he had plenty of clients whom he could direct to vote as the cardinal wanted. Richelieu also relied on the *crédit* and influence of the duke of La Trémoille, who from the late 1620s into the early 1640s headed the second estate. Of all his clients within the estates, however, the most useful was Jean de Bruc, sieur de la Grée, who was the *procureur syndic* for the estates.[31]

Richelieu also desired to establish similar ties to high-ranking members of the sovereign courts. Claude de Marbeuf, first president in the parlement, was the cardinal's most important client in the court, and one of the very few. Richelieu was not very successful in establishing a network within the court, and it acted at times as a hostile body.[32]

Overall, the cardinal's clientele included a wide assortment of individuals, ranging from the lieutenant-general to bishops, to officers in the estates, and to judges in the sovereign courts. His more powerful clients in turn put their own agents at his disposal, thereby creating an expansive network that enabled him to pursue within the province the projects and *dons gratuits* that contributed to the cardinal's larger plans.[33]

What were the cardinal's goals in Brittany? For what purposes did he deploy his clientele? First, he wanted to raise more revenue, but he wanted to do so in a way that would not harm the welfare of a province so central to his maritime policies. Under Richelieu the amount of money voted by the Breton estates increased substantially, and Brittany was taxed at a much higher rate than it had been during the reign of Henry IV. In 1626 the estates voted the king 850 000 *livres* to be paid over two years. In 1642, shortly before the cardinal's death, the estates voted 2.9 million *livres* to be paid over only one year.[34]

The number of individuals receiving pensions from the estates increased significantly because Richelieu made sure that many of his clients were placed on the list. Why were the estates so cooperative in voting greater taxes and in funding the clients of the cardinal? As Collins puts it, they sought protection, and Richelieu was beautifully situated to provide it. The most important benefit they derived from their cooperation and their special relationship with the chief minister was that Brittany was spared the *élections* during this period. While Richelieu imposed them on other provinces, he left Brittany alone.[35]

But Breton nobles benefitted in other ways as well. Most of the money levied was spent in Brittany, often to maintain troops in the region, and their presence opened opportunities for military positions sought by nobles and, specifically, by deputies to the second estate. Or, conversely, the nobility used their influence to direct the movement of troops out of the province or away from their own areas of interest, because the garrisoning and provisioning of troops could prove disastrous for the local economy.[36]

By their generous support of the monarchy, the estates were also in a better position to negotiate reforms that would benefit commerce. Over the years they requested a variety of changes to promote trade within the region and beyond. Their requests reflected a concern for freedom of trade, a position which often brought them up against the crown over prohibitions on grain exports but which also placed them in line with the merchants of Brittany. Though the merchants were not well represented within the estates, many of the assembly's requests and policies favored them because of the overlap in noble–merchant financial interests.[37]

The Reign of Louis XIV in Brittany

This mutually beneficial relationship between the elites (and the province overall, to some extent) and central government came to an end with the deaths of Cardinal Richelieu and Louis XIII in 1642 and 1643 respectively. Anne of Austria's regency saw the queen mother and Mazarin step up demands on the estates. For example, Anne demanded that the estates advance some money by borrowing it themselves and pay the interest on the loan with their share of the duty receipts. There was precedent for such a request; Richelieu had also obtained advances, but he had paid the interest himself. The interest made heavy inroads into the estates' share of receipts. Even more important was the fact that in the 1640s the receipts from the wine tax began to decline precipitously. As less wine was sold, so the duty rate per unit of wine rose in order to raise the necessary sums. In 1643 the estates, recognizing that they could not raise the wine tax again, voted to create a *fouage extraordinaire*, a desperate act that raised direct taxes and forced landlords' tenants to pay more. Collins reports that this extreme measure did not provide a permanent solution to the estates' financial problems, because as the taxes went up so did the demands on the estates, to the extent that the 1640s and 1650s constituted a fiscal crisis for the province.[38]

Brittany's crisis was not a direct result of the Fronde, though certainly the Fronde and the crisis of the monarchy affected the province and its estates. In 1651 the local nobility divided over the leadership of the second estate; the conflict soon extended to include the parlement, and the monarchy supported the estates over the parlement. The disagreement centered on the duke of Rohan and the duke of la Trémoille, each of whom claimed the right to preside over the second estate. Both had support among the deputies, and Rohan enjoyed the support of the parlement as well. When Mazarin interfered, the situation developed into open confrontation between the estates and the parlement, and the monarchy, in need of money, lent its support to the estates. By 1653, sufficient enmity remained between the two bodies that the estates demanded that the king enforce regulations on the books concerning kinship and minimum age requirements for judges. Such enforcement would have unraveled many networks of judges holding positions in the court. The estates even asked to have the magistrates exempted from the *paulette*, a request that amounted to a frontal assault on the carefully constructed dynasties of the parlementaires.[39]

The strife between the estates and the parlement abated with the restoration of order after the Fronde, because both bodies recognized the advantage of cooperation for the interests of Brittany and, of course, for their own interests. What followed in the ensuing decades was increased pressure from royal government to make Brittany contribute more. Compared to his predecessors, Louis XIV dealt with the Breton estates in what can best be described as a more emphatic manner. He usually asked for exactly what he wanted and threatened to appear in person if his requests were not forthcoming. Indeed, he did travel to Brittany in 1661, and the estates promptly responded as the young king had hoped by voting him the requested sum. With this firm and direct approach, Louis XIV succeeded in his collection efforts.[40]

But the king's controlled approach to handling the Breton estates does not alone explain their cooperation. An additional factor was the agency of two well-placed clients, the duke of Chaulnes, who was made governor, and the duke of Rohan, who had been enticed to side with the king and who had placed plenty of clients in the estates. Colbert came to rely on Rohan and his clientele within the assembly, and, in fact, designated a specific sum to be used as rewards for deputies who promoted his goals.[41] Family ties further solidified the relationships between Colbert, Rohan, and Chaulnes. Chaulnes was the nephew of Marie de Rohan, and Chaulnes's nephew in turn married the daughter of Colbert. Malo II of Coëtquen, who held the position of lieutenant-general in Brittany, also married into the Rohan family.[42]

The effect of these connections made it easier for central government to obtain what it requested from Brittany, and for a period the estates became significantly more cooperative. But this spirit of cooperation proved ephemeral as Colbert's impatience led him to turn up the pressure on Breton elites. Among the tactics employed was an edict that established a Chamber of Justice, the purpose of which was to punish individuals who had usurped seigneurial justices, and which was strictly conceived to intimidate the nobility. There were also efforts to obstruct cooperation between the parlement and the estates, including an edict that prevented the parlement from informing the estates when it received royal acts for registration.[43] Then, in 1673, came a series of attacks on Breton privileges, including taxes on pewter, tobacco, and stamped paper. The estates that convened that year responded by paying the government sufficiently (with a *don gratuit* of 2.6 million *livres* and another 2.6 million *livres* expressly for the revocation) to end the offending edicts, and made other financial concessions to the king. Such concessions were not made freely. The delegates agitated and protested this use of authority; it took the duke of Chaulnes's intervention to calm the assembly and secure the requisite votes.[44]

To raise the money, the estates agreed to special taxes on nobles, clerks, and lawyers, in addition to a variety of other measures including an increase in the *fouage extraordinaire*. The problem with this approach was that the nobility refused to pay, and, in fact, the peasantry's increased contributions were largely not forthcoming.[45] In 1674–5 the crown again introduced the edicts creating taxes on pewter, tobacco, and stamped paper, this time touching off a ferocious popular rebellion.

The parlementaires' hostile position was not simply the result of new taxes. For almost a decade the parlement had watched Colbert, in his struggle to reform the French judiciary and jurisprudence, encroach systematically on their authority. At the same time, his policies threatened to devalue their offices. In particular, he objected to the venal nature of judicial offices and to the *épices*, or fees, which judges charged for hearing civil cases and which were one of a judge's most important sources of income. Colbert also hoped to reform civil and criminal procedure within the courts and took specific action to do so. Beginning in 1667, a series of new legal codes appeared which altered local custom in the courts. By edicts in 1667 and 1673 royal government attempted to reduce the power of the courts by eliminating their power to remonstrate, or to object to a royal ordinance. Ordinances had to be registered within seven days, and the king could accept or reject any remonstrance. These edicts substantially eroded the power of the courts, which explains in part the adversarial role that the Parlement of Rennes took in the rebellion of 1675.[46]

In the 1660s Colbert made a significant effort to control the prices of offices and their transmission in the future. The government announced in 1665 that the *paulette* was to be extended by three years rather than the customary nine years. It also took the drastic step of setting limits on the prices of judicial offices and establishing a minimum age for the occupant. The parlementaires in Rennes responded with outrage; they regarded the reforms as a direct assault on their privileged community. By the price limits, the monarchy was challenging their right to make a profit on these offices. By establishing 27 as the minimum age for officeholding, the monarchy was jeopardizing the parlementaires' right to transmit this office from father to son. These edicts were followed in the early 1670s by others that were similarly threatening to the judicial nobility – namely, the edict on the usurpation of seigneurial justice discussed earlier, and an edict creating several minor offices that would fall strictly under the control of the crown. Again, the parlement protested what they perceived as an effort to undermine their authority.[47]

The Revolt of 1675

The institutional background against which the revolt of 1675 took place was therefore one of rapidly deteriorating relations between the crown and the parlement, and weaker relations between the estates and the parlement. For this reason historians have traditionally assigned responsibility to the parlement for the revolt in the city of Rennes. Its stated hostility to royal policies and its weaker relations with the estates, combined with the parlement's failure to stop the revolt, all seem to implicate its members. How did the actions of the parlementaires contribute to this great violent episode of popular resistance? What was the role of the Breton elites?

The urban phase of the revolt began in Rennes, home of the parlement. The new taxes had already provoked a major eruption in Bordeaux, and when news of that violence arrived in Brittany it found a receptive audience. On 18 April violence broke out in Rennes, as a mob came together and proceeded to move about the city destroying property. The particular targets of their aggression were the offices associated with the offending tax edicts; they smashed windows, destroyed furnishings, burned documents, and appropriated any wine, cider, and tobacco located on the premises.[48] Clearly, the mob felt it had the moral authority to behave in this way – the taxes were wrong, and it set out to eliminate them for the good of the community. Additionally, the mob may have felt it held the political or even legal authority to proceed as it had. As the son of René de Coëtlogon, governor of the city, recounted later, local shopkeepers had gone to the first president of the parlement, Argouges, to ask if they could save their businesses from financial ruin and mob destruction by selling tobacco again (sales had been suspended when the parlement had earlier suspended the tax edicts) at the untaxed prices. The first president allegedly responded by telling them to wait until violence broke out, at which point they would be forced to sell tobacco as a way of appeasing the mob. By asking the shopkeepers to wait for violence before resuming sales, Argouges, the highest magistrate in the court, arguably gave them tacit permission to instigate the violence. Certainly, the shopkeepers and the mob appear to have interpreted his instructions in this way.[49]

The opening round of violence ended when Coëtlogon moved troops into town and fired on the crowd, killing several people. His action ended the protest for a week, but on 25 April violence broke out again, this time in a Protestant suburb of Rennes. In the belief that some of the tobacco and stamp tax agents were Protestant, an angry crowd set fire to and burned to the ground a Huguenot temple in Cleuné. According to Beik, this religious component was rarely a factor in tax revolts. It appears that the mob desecrated the tombs of Protestants in ways that recalled forms of violence commonplace during the Wars of Religion. For Beik the connection of 'new enemies to old prejudices had revived an earlier mode of behavior linked to religious fervor'.[50] It seems that, in addition to moral and political authority, the crowd's actions may also have derived from a sense of religious authority.

On 2 May the duke of Chaulnes, who had been with Colbert in Paris, arrived in Rennes to take matters in hand. Beik points out that his reception was not typical for a governor who entered a city in revolt. The Rennais were hoping to win the provincial governor to their side, and their conduct was at first conciliatory, if not celebratory. He stayed at the archbishop's residence where that evening he received a delegation of parlementaires which included the first president of the parlement as well as President Marboeuf, six councillors, and others. On 4 May the governor went to the parlement to direct a parlementary act announcing that the tax offices would be reopened and the tax edicts would be enforced. As Chaulnes left the palace he found that his military escort had dwindled to about a dozen noblemen, whereas he had arrived with nearly 300. In response to his complaints, his surviving entourage pointed out that the edicts were just as ruinous for the nobility as for the peasantry.[51]

Confronted with the resumption of violence, Chaulnes marshaled his forces. Rennes was not the only hotspot in Brittany; violence had already broken out in Saint Malo and Nantes, and the crown recognized the need for a substantial commitment of troops. Chaulnes responded to the crisis by convincing the elites of Rennes that he would prevent the arrival of his full forces if the city would remain loyal. In early June he introduced a smaller force to the city for its symbolic and psychological effects, and deployed the rest elsewhere. He proceeded in the hope that this plan would work, but everything worked against it. The situation in Rennes was simply too tense for the populace to accept the arrival of three companies of the king's soldiers, and their presence was considered provocative.[52]

The citizen militia was already on duty in Rennes, and Chaulnes hoped he could rely on the militiamen if necessary. After an episode of rock-throwing on 8 June, citizens from the *faubourgs* marched into the city with the stated intention of assisting the militia stationed in the town. Having imbibed wine or cider, this group was predictably excitable. They heaped abuse on the soldiers and headed off to the residence where the governor was staying in order to hurl insults at him. The evening proved a nerve-racking one for the governor, because he was pelted with rocks each time he tried to step outside. Even worse, by daybreak it was apparent that Chaulnes could not count on the loyalty of all the militia units. In fact, there appeared to be a separation between more loyal units from the town and renegade units from beyond the town walls. For the rest of the month there were minor incidents, and Chaulnes was unable to control the militia. On 17 July, violence erupted again when a crowd stormed into the building that housed the parlement and the stamp tax office.[53]

Meanwhile, the rebellion also manifested itself in the Breton countryside, where various tax bureaux and their agents served as targets of resentment. The violence of the countryside, however, was not just confined to tax collectors, nor was it merely an expression of outrage over new taxes. Instead, this movement soon broadened in meaning and purpose to express deep-seated resentment towards the entire seigneurial regime. In Lower Brittany the peasants wanted an end not to rents, but to the traditional seigneurial obligations. The traditional labor dues, the *corvée*, as well as the hunting restrictions were considered most onerous. They also demanded lower court costs and greater access to the courts. Finally, they took this opportunity to express their hostility towards both the new taxes and the old wine taxes. Peasants objected less to direct taxes because the elites had to some extent sheltered peasants from direct taxes and their economic consequences for landlords. More than taxes, it was the seigneurial regime that prompted peasants to take up arms; what distinguished the rural movement from the urban revolts was the fact that the peasantry broadened its purpose by moving against the landed elite. The marquis de Lavardin wrote to Colbert that they vented more anger towards the nobility than towards the authority of the king.[54] The revolt in 1675 gave peasants the opportunity to express their hostility to the class of landlords that exploited them.

There was no ambiguity or subtlety in the acts of the Breton peasants. They burned tax records, ransacked and destroyed *châteaux*, broke open barrels of wine and partook of their contents until intoxicated with alcohol and power, and assaulted and killed a number of their oppressors.[55] They sought retribution for grievances that are easily discerned by their violent patterns of protest. When the end came, it was abrupt and violent. In the fall of 1675 Chaulnes and the central government acted decisively against the movements. Colbert sent 6000 troops to Brittany. After restoring order in the countryside, the governor ruthlessly punished the instigators and used the troops to terrorize sympathetic and supportive village populations.[56]

In Rennes the government acted with the same determination to punish those responsible and prevent future incidents. Chaulnes entered the city in October with several thousand soldiers. To punish the most unruly *quartier*, the faubourg de la rue Haute, he forced the inhabitants to evacuate and announced his intention of razing the entire neighborhood. In the end, most of it was spared, and the governor's policy focused retribution on those considered ringleaders. Jean Rivé from la rue Haute was one such individual. Executed publicly, his head was then mounted on the end of a pike and placed near the bridge of Saint-Martin with a warning and an inscription that identified him as the leader of the seditious.[57]

In the wake of this clean-up, Chaulnes blamed the parlement for what he perceived as their complicity in the revolt. He was convinced that parlementaires had been actively involved in directing the June violence. Others argued that by their failure to respond properly the parlementaires had contributed to the movement, that they had enabled it to take place.[58] Whatever the nature of their perceived role, it is clear that the crown held the parlement responsible, because it responded by exiling the judges to the small town of Vannes, where the court remained for the next 15 years.

By putting distance between the parlementaires and the Rennais, the crown obviously hoped to avoid similar eruptions in the future. For Colbert this was the last of the parlement's independent political and legislative authority. But was such stringent action really necessary? In actuality, the crown had earlier dealt the parlement its most severe blow when it had succeeded in driving a permanent wedge between the court and the estates. By putting to an end once and for all the cooperation that had normally existed between the two assemblies, Colbert had undermined the power of both. John Hurt argues that the working relationship between the two institutions had been a powerful coalition against the demands of government. Since the period of the Wars of Religion, the estates had claimed the right of addressing and opposing all legislation sent to the parlement that ran contrary to provincial privilege. In 1579 Henry III had formally recognized this tradition, indeed this institutional prerogative, and had brought the full force of both assemblies to bear. The parlement could refuse to register an offending edict; the estates could force the amendment or modification of an offending edict by refusing to approve a requested sum of money. The combination of the power of remonstrance and the power of the purse had presented the crown with effective opposition.[59]

This relationship had its origins in the Middle Ages, when the parlement and the estates evolved from the same ducal institution. As noted earlier, the two bodies were still indistinguishable as late as the fifteenth century. The estates emerged from the ducal parlement, and for much of the period the parlement consented to taxation. It is impossible to discern a clear difference in function in these late medieval assemblies or meetings. When Henry II created a sovereign court in Brittany in 1553, the new court defined its role in association with the estates.

Through most of the seventeenth century, the parlement and the estates worked in close order to guard provincial privileges and to protect elite interests. The seigneurial elite, who dominated the estates, and the judicial nobility shared the same economic interests and landed wealth. For this reason, Collins argues that Breton elites acted in class-based ways, especially when it came to matters of taxation. He is careful to point out that these landlords came in two forms: the seigneurs who held feudal rights over their land and peasants, and the sieurs who were merely landlords. Despite this distinction, their economic interests almost always coincided and caused them to act in concert. The positions they took within the estates and the parlement were consistent in choosing a form of taxation that would not erode the income from landed wealth.[60]

In his important study of the Breton parlement during the period 1661–75, Hurt documents step by step how the crown, after Mazarin, worked to eliminate collaboration between the parlement and the estates, thereby undermining the political power of each institution. In the 1660s Colbert instituted a series of policies that were unpopular with the parlement, and in 1669 he began to act significantly more aggressively to curb the court's political authority. The government introduced a series of controversial edicts on a variety of topics, including one that proscribed the sale of judicial offices, and before the parlement could remonstrate or send the edicts to the estates for debate, the central government acted to interrupt the court's traditional patterns of operation. By sending its agent, Chamillart, to Rennes with instructions to register the edicts without further discussion (*lettres de jussion*), the crown acted decisively and with the intention of cutting off its deliberations with the estates.[61]

During the period 1671–3 the monarchy effectively eliminated the independent authority of the court. This process began in 1671 when, as was customary, the parlement referred several fiscal edicts which it felt threatened traditional Breton privileges to the estates for debate. Typically, the nobility denounced all the offending edicts, including one that set a limit on the price of parlementary offices. They offered the crown a *don gratuit* of 2.5 million *livres* if it would annul the edicts. The provincial governor, Chaulnes, refused the offer. In response, the delegates discussed taking more strident action by refusing any *don gratuit* at all, but Chaulnes persuaded them away from this reactionary and ill-considered position. Instead, he managed to coax from the estates a *don gratuit* of 2.2 million *livres* with no strings attached. Hurt notes that this was the first instance in which the estates approved money but failed to ask for conditions.[62] It was Chaulnes's ability to mobilize his clientele within the estates that enabled him to secure this unprecedented decision.

Despite the capitulation of the estates, the parlement did not abandon its struggle. Determined to remonstrate and to invoke the political leverage of the *don gratuit*, the court prepared a legal argument which maintained the authority of the estates to pronounce on these issues. The basis of their argument derived from a 1614 contract between the estates and the king. The contract held in part that indeed all royal acts were to undergo the examination and approval of both the provincial estates and the sovereign courts before they became law in Brittany. This legal tactic did not play well with Colbert, and the Conseil d'Etat replied that such remonstrances violated the civil ordinance of 1667 which required provincial parlements to register royal edicts immediately and allowed remonstrance only within six weeks of having received them. The Conseil concluded that the legal argument advanced by the parlement constituted a challenge to royal authority, thereby confirming its illegal nature. It demanded that the edicts be registered and that the parlementaires responsible for this spurious legal argument and assault on the authority of the king report to Paris to explain themselves. The parlement acquiesced.[63]

Shortly thereafter, to consolidate its victory over the court and the estates, the Conseil forbade the parlement to send royal acts to the estates. A subsequent *arrêt* forbade the court to receive opinions from the estates. In effect, central government had separated the two institutions and left each alone to address the king.[64] This destroyed the real basis of the court's independent political power. Now that the court's working relationship with the estates had been severed, royal acts could no longer be held hostage to the funding process.

Between the time of this confrontation with the crown and the revolt of 1675, Colbert tested his authority and the extent of his success with a series of edicts that were onerous and offensive to various social groups, but especially to officeholders. Knowing that their actions would be inflammatory, the parlement still resisted by remonstrating against the edicts. This time the legal basis of their argument involved the theory that, because parlements were created by kings, they were *ipso facto* part of the monarchy and therefore duty bound to inform the king when his acts endangered the well-being of the kingdom. To do otherwise, they argued, would be to turn their backs on duty to the king, the people, and God.[65] In short, they advanced the idea of mixed monarchy. By invoking the idea of duty and the name of God, the court tried to construct a moral authority that would explain its resistance in loftier terms than apparent self-interest.

Unimpressed and undeterred, Colbert proceeded in 1673 with an array of edicts designed to fund the war with the Dutch. This was also when he instituted the Chamber of Justice to investigate the usurpation of seigneurial judicial rights and presented the edict to limit the amount that parlementaires could charge for legal services. The estates intervened, as noted earlier, by voting an additional 2.6 million *livres* (on top of an original allocation of 2.6 million), in the naive hope that the offending edicts would be suspended. Their delegates seriously misjudged, as central government made off with the money and the edicts remained intact. Colbert and Louis XIV had made their point in unambiguous terms – there would be no further negotiations or compromises. In striking against the parlement, they had succeeded in permanently eroding the independent political authority of the estates as well.[66]

In contrast to the crown's actions in Provence and Dauphiné, Louis XIV and Colbert opted not to suspend the estates of Brittany. Their decision was based on the fact that they had successfully transformed the assembly into an instrument of royal policy. They had succeeded in establishing control over the institution by bringing to an end its traditional collaboration with the parlement and by skillful manipulation of the ties of patronage. The sheer size of the noble delegation to the estates prohibited the distribution of pensions and favors to every person (as had been the policy with the estates of Languedoc), but they relied on the duke of Rohan to place his own clients within the assembly and to maintain the necessary ties of dependency that would bind these delegates to the royal will.[67] Collins has demonstrated that the interests of the king and the interests of the estates were not mutually exclusive. As long as royal government proposed taxes that were assessed against something other than land, the two could see eye to eye. The *modus operandi* of the estates was to divert taxation away from land, the economic base of aristocratic power.[68]

The introduction of the stamp tax in 1675 did not threaten the economic interests of the estates or the seigneurs who dominated it. Rather, it threatened to diminish the income of the judicial nobility in the parlement by taxing legal documents, and, whatever the parlement's degree of complicity in 1675, the perception was that the court had been a force in the revolt. The estates proceeded to distance itself from the court, and it sent a delegation to Louis to apologize for the episode. Meeting in November 1675, the estates voted the king a *don gratuit* of 3 million *livres* and dispatched a committee, including Rohan, for the purpose of apologizing and redirecting blame. There were no conditions attached to the *don gratuit*, and the delegation attributed the disturbances to people of no means whose purpose was to pillage more than to protest royal policy.[69]

This aristocratic delegation revealed their fears and concerns about the underclass when they described in horrific terms the destruction carried out by the poor. The revolt of 1675 revealed, and then magnified, the ruptures appearing in Breton society. In taxing legal documents, tobacco, and pewter, Colbert and Louis XIV exposed the class-based interests of the various social groups in Brittany. Collins has persuasively argued that Breton society functioned simultaneously as two hierarchies, one based on orders and the other on classes. The policies of the 1670s drove an institutional wedge between the estates and the parlement, thereby undermining the independent political authority of both. The stamp tax drove a social and economic wedge between the two parts of the Breton elite, the seigneurs and the sieurs, and contributed further to the widening gulf between the estates and the parlement. The seigneurs dominated the estates and the sieurs comprised most of the judicial elite. Both drew income from land and both the estates and the parlement had traditionally cooperated in avoiding the taxation of land, but the judicial elite had also invested its wealth in offices and drew income from the practice of law. It stood to lose financially by the taxation of legal documents, while the families seated in the estates remained virtually unaffected. The policies and taxes of the 1670s widened and exploited ruptures within the elite as well as the gap between the elite and the poor. This permitted the monarchy to gain the upper hand.[70]

But was this institutional rift inevitable? Was the membership of one so different from that of the other that their alliance could be undermined by a tax that threatened the income of one and not the other? Was the second order within the estates comprised strictly of old seigneurial families, while the parlement consisted of nothing but new families owning land without seigneurial rights? This was not the case. The composition of each institution was significantly more complex and less homogeneous than events of the 1670s might suggest. As noted earlier, the parlement was particularly complex, because over the seventeenth century nearly equal numbers of sword and robe families held office. But not all old families were seigneurs – an important distinction – and no parlementaires sat in the estates – a crucial distinction.

Over the course of the seventeenth century, 542 noblemen occupied positions in the parlement. Of these, 260 came from families ennobled in the sixteenth or seventeenth centuries, a group that corresponded most closely to the classical definition of a robe nobility. Even more, 282 office-holders came from old families, that is, from families whose nobility dated to at least the fifteenth century and before the existence of the royal court. It is this second group whose composition was most complex and perhaps most important in influencing the behavior of the court. As mentioned earlier, Brittany had a disproportionately large sword nobility, and many of these families invested heavily in the parlement. In fact, more magistrates came from old families than from new families. These old families held ties by marriage and clientage to the seigneurial nobility; indeed, a portion were seigneurs themselves. Upon closer examination, however, we find that the number of seigneurs was rather limited. Only 65 of the parlementaires were titled nobles, in contrast to the 226 men who were from older families but held no titles. These 226 parlementaires were known merely as 'seigneur' or 'sieur', and it is certain that many of them were shut out from seigneurial rights over the peasants. In many cases, the extended families, or their older brothers, may have had seigneurial claims, but their relations in the parlement did not. Their family backgrounds placed them within the sword tradition, and yet many had no claim to seigneurial rights. While technically part of the older, sword, nobility, 226 parlementaires depended on sources of income that had more in common with the robe families than with the seigneurs who dominated the estates.[71]

What then was the relationship between social composition, wealth, and the behavior of each institution? In the case of the parlement, members with seigneurial rights were a minority with a voice not strong enough to direct or influence the court's behavior in 1675. This is not to suggest that new judicial families constituted a larger presence within the court, but to say that most parlementaires, whether from old or new families, drew income as simple landlords with no seigneurial rights. Legal fees and documents were an important and alternate source of revenue for these households. In contrast, the estates were traditionally dominated by seigneurial families, and no parlementaires sat with the second estate, a highly relevant fact. In 1625, officeholding nobles had been specifically excluded from the delegates of the nobility.[72] They had no actual voice in the proceedings of the second estate, and the second estate thoroughly dominated the assembly.

We are left with an image of the estates as an assembly monopolized by sword nobles and seigneurs of varying antiquity. They were the focus of peasant hostility towards the seigneurial regime, and this left them unsympathetic to the rebellion and to the parlement. Consider also the fact that the estates were easily manipulated by the clients of the duke of Rohan and Colbert, and it is not difficult to explain how the estates not only failed to support the parlement but actually moved to distance themselves from the court. These sword families stood to reap rewards in the many military positions generated by the foreign policy of Louis XIV.

In 1675 Brittany rose up unsuccessfully against royal government and the seigneurial regime. For Collins the failure of this revolt resulted from the fact that the class-based interests of the seigneurial regime coincided most closely with those of the monarchy. More to the point, their class-based interests diverged from the class-based interests of the parlementaires. Without the support of the estates and in light of Colbert's judicial reforms, the parlementaires had no significant political recourse at their disposal except to exploit popular resentment towards the new taxes, a strategy doomed to fail.

The policies of Louis XIV and Colbert in Brittany were not unlike those of Louis XIII and Richelieu in Dauphiné. By exposing the horizontal ties and nascent class conflicts of provincial society, they created and exploited a political opportunity. With unrelenting pressure, they subdued one class, the judicial elite. By skillful manipulation of the vertical ties of patronage, they brought another class, the seigneurial and sword nobility, into a royal alliance.

Conclusion

In examining the relationship between the crown and the provincial nobilities of three great *pays d'états*, this book has sought to convey several interpretations and perspectives. First, it maintains that the nobility, revived, enlarged, and more modern, claimed social and political power within the locality that made them the major force with which the monarchy had to contend in order to increase revenue from the remote parts of the realm. Nobles dominated life in the provinces; they dominated provincial political institutions and they dominated provincial society. Although the institutional context varied somewhat from one province to the next, nobles maintained control through the local estates and as a result of venal officeholding. As magistrates and seigneurs, the political arena was theirs to control and they presented a determined obstacle to the expansion of royal authority.

Second, influenced by Beik, Collins, Mettam, and others, this book argues that the crown was not 'absolute', at least not as traditionally defined. It portrays a government driven not by reformist and centralizing impulses, but largely by the simple desire to collect, by whatever means at hand, more taxes from provinces that had historically paid less. In all three provinces, the crown's policies and strategies involved traditional means, including the use of patronage, either that of a chief minister or the king himself, to secure the compliance and assistance of crucial elements within the provincial nobility. By its reliance on personal relationships, brokers, clients, and vertical ties, the crown revealed the limits of its institutional authority. Specifically, it revealed the personal nature of monarchical power. Even when central government attempted to introduce its agents to new terrain, such reformist initiatives usually produced sufficient resistance to cause the crown to retreat to some extent or, in the case of the *intendants*, to dilute the agent's mission and authority. Belying absolutism was the fact that royal policy was successful when it was based on mutually beneficial arrangements negotiated or arranged by the crown's brokers and clients. What Louis XIV constructed was a larger, grander, and, in its ability to tax, more successful version of a Renaissance state.

The strategies and expedients employed by the crown varied from province to province; conceived on an individual basis, they bear the signs of *ad hoc* responses rather than a grandiose plan to centralize. Driven by the fiscal urgencies of Bourbon foreign policy, there was little attempt to standardize or systematize tax collection and governance from one province to the next. *Intendants* are the obvious exception, but their powers diminished during the reign of Louis XIV so that they ceased to be the institutional weapon they had been earlier under Louis XIII and Richelieu. Instead, central government responded to the institutional and social context peculiar to one province or the other, and therefore no two provincial stories are the same.

This is not to suggest that no single part of the story is repeated from one province to the next. Indeed, there were recurring themes and there was some commonality of experience among the three provinces examined. The crown's reliance on patronage is, of course, the most important example. To some degree or another, central government used patronage and provincial brokers to control provincial institutions and to direct local politics in ways that conformed to the crown's interests. Nowhere is this more evident than in the case of Provence. The crown's conflicts with the Provençal nobility were ultimately put to rest by manipulating vertical ties and by playing one faction off against another. Patronage and factionalism enabled the crown to bring to an end the tradition of independent and unruly provincial governors, and they enabled it to establish control over the parlement which had resisted reform so vociferously. So riddled by factions was Provence that it has reminded historians of an Italian Renaissance city-state; feuding factions offered a golden opportunity to prevail by simply relying on the dynamic forces of the political status quo. By its sensitivity to Provençal political culture and its patient and thoughtful manipulation of factions, the crown succeeded in establishing its control over the single most recalcitrant institution – the Parlement of Provence – and over the provincial governorship.

Patronage and clientage also proved instrumental in the crown's relations with Dauphiné and Brittany, though they were more important in the case of the latter. It was through ministerial and royal clienteles that central government controlled the Breton estates, separated them from the provincial parlement, and induced them to vote the amounts of revenue needed to sustain Louis XIV's wars. In Dauphiné the crown relied on the assistance of its *créature* and broker, Lesdiguières, but in the end it was horizontal divisions and solidarities that enabled it to adjudicate the *procès des tailles* to its best advantage.

By a complicated and legalistic settlement, the crown sided with the third estate, which had advanced the most compelling legal arguments and had mounted an irresistible and emotional plea. At the same time, however, royal government shrewdly avoided taking a position that would disadvantage the local nobility, or most of them. In fact, the lines of demarcation for paying the *taille réelle* were conceived explicitly to placate the more established and powerful noble families and their clients. Here we see the results of vertical ties. Having alienated only a minority within the nobility – those most recently ennobled, less well connected, and therefore most vulnerable – the crown emerged from the decades of debate and appeal with the money it wanted and most still on its side.

The intervention of the crown had catalytic effects which for brief instances exposed clearly the class outlines developing within provincial society. In all three provinces, class conflict reared its head at some point or another, providing the crown with windows of opportunity. In Provence, the nobility had manipulated and incited the populace to rebel, and popular participation grew easily and predictably beyond aristocratic control, thereby inspiring elite fears of the underclass and leading to moments of horizontal solidarity. In Brittany, the rebellion in 1675, as it moved to the countryside, became an even more significant and classic movement of peasants against a particularly harsh seigneurial regime.

It was in Dauphiné, however, that class conflict constituted a more prominent and consistent part of the story. Here the king reaped the benefits of horizontal alignments and conflicts. By asking for more money, the crown had provoked the decades-long debate over the nature of the *taille*, a debate that had at its heart the very meaning and nature of social orders and that forced provincial society to line up in horizontal formations. More subtle and more complex than the simple dichotomy of noble vs. commoner, this prolonged episode focused increasingly on the newest of the *anoblis* and the most successful professionals of the third estate, two social groups that shared income levels, education, and neighborhoods. What separated them into opposing and even hostile elites was social mobility – one group had made it across the finishing line of noble status and one had not. The successes of one imposed a greater tax burden on the other. Indeed, the successes of one led to greater exploitation of the other, and therein lay for royal government the potential for class conflict. The *procès* became a contest between two closely juxtaposed and competing layers of provincial society.

In Brittany, conflict between horizontal layers of elite society also presented itself when the crown exposed the limits of elite solidarity by forging a permanent gulf between the families represented in the estates and the families represented in the parlement. Traditionally these institutions acted in concert, but Colbert and Louis XIV separated them by legal reforms and by patronage. Their shared class-based interests had traditionally seen both institutions cooperate to direct taxation in ways that were least harmful to their rural investments. Under Louis XIV, government exposed the limits of such class-based interests. By taxing legal documents and cultivating personal ties with the estates, the crown separated the Breton elite into two constituent parts: the seigneurs and the sieurs. Indeed, the king opposed the sieurs seated in the parlement and worked in collusion with the seigneurial families dominating the estates.

Finally, the histories of these three provinces tell us something about the dynamic force of nationalism in seventeenth-century France. Dauphiné was the province in which nationalism played its most important role, though nationalism did have its place in Provence and Brittany. Actually, Provence and Brittany offer classic examples of regionalism, a form of nationalism that is province-wide and crosses social boundaries. Both Provence and Brittany were known for their fierce sense of community and heritage, and the rhetoric of regionalism was expressed especially in the Provençal conflicts, but also in Brittany in 1675. Still, it was in Dauphiné that nationalism and community played their greatest role. Here the attorneys for the third estate expressed an awareness of national identity that aligned the third estate with the monarchy as one community, one nation (*la patrie*), and placed it squarely in opposition to the 'other' that helped to define it – the nobility (or, more precisely, those most recently ennobled). It was the king and the third estate, the nation, pitted against the outsiders, the nobility. By relying on the rhetoric of nationalism, the spokesmen for the third estate offered central government an opportunity it could not refuse. Henry IV had sought to defuse the social conflict inherent in the *procès*. Louis XIII and Richelieu chose to view it and use it as the political opportunity it was. By the resolution of the *procès*, the crown made the only decision it could – it decided in favor of the nation, the third estate, and against those most recently ennobled. In the process, they also allowed the more established noble families (the majority) to continue to enjoy the privileges of their status.

In the future, nationalism would provide the means by which to construct a modern state. In the seventeenth century, however, its presence was still too limited, both temporally and geographically, for it to be such a modernizing and unifying force. Lacking the constancy of national sentiment, the Bourbon state relied instead on the constancy of self-interest as expressed through dependent and vertically constructed man-to-man/woman relationships. The tentacles of central government that grasped at the periphery were only as strong as the self-interest of the nobility on which they fed.

Notes

Introduction

1. Roger Mettam, *Power and Faction in Louis XIV's France* (London, 1988).
2. Sharon Kettering, *Patrons, Brokers, and Clients in Seventeenth-Century France* (Oxford, 1986), and *Judicial Politics and Urban Revolt in Seventeenth-Century France: The Parlement of Aix, 1629–1659* (Princeton, NJ, 1978); James B. Collins, *Classes, Estates, and Order in Early Modern Brittany* (Cambridge, 1994); Daniel Hickey, *The Coming of French Absolutism: The Struggle for Tax Reform in the Province of Dauphiné, 1540–1640* (Toronto, 1986).
3. J. Russell Major, *Representative Government in Early Modern France* (New Haven, Conn., 1980).
4. William Beik, *Absolutism and Society in Seventeenth-Century France: State Power and Provincial Aristocracy in Languedoc* (Cambridge, 1985).
5. David Parker, *Class and State in* Ancien Regime *France: The Road to Modernity?* (London, 1996).
6. Arlette Jouanna, *Le devoir de révolte: La noblesse française et la gestation de l'état moderne (1559–1661)* (Paris, 1989).

Chapter 1: Nobility: Metamorphosis

1. J. R. Hale, *War and Society in Renaissance Europe, 1450–1620* (Baltimore, Md., 1985), Chapter 3.
2. Jeremy Black, *A Military Revolution? Military Change and European Society, 1550–1800* (Atlantic Highlands, NJ, 1991), pp. 79–80.

3. Donna Bohanan, *Old and New Nobility in Aix-en-Provence, 1600–1695: Portrait of an Urban Elite* (Baton Rouge, La., 1992), pp. 114–19.

4. Jonathan Dewald, *Aristocratic Experience and the Origins of Modern Culture: France, 1570–1715* (Berkeley, Calif., 1993), p. 48.

5. J. Russell Major, *From Renaissance Monarchy to Absolute Monarchy: French Kings, Nobles and Estates* (Baltimore, Md., 1994), pp. 318–19.

6. Arlette Jouanna, *Ordre social: Mythes et hiérarchies dans la France du XVIe siècle* (Paris, 1977).

7. Ellery Schalk, *From Valor to Pedigree: Ideas of Nobility in France in the Sixteenth and Seventeenth Centuries* (Princeton, NJ, 1986), pp. 65–74; Bohanan, *Old and New Nobility*, pp. 120–1.

8. Jouanna, *Ordre social*, pp. 192–8, 208–10.

9. Jean-Marie Constant, 'La mobilité sociale dans une province de gentilshommes et de paysans: La Beauce', *XVII Siècle* 122 (1979), pp. 12–13.

10. John David Nordhaus, *Arma et Litterae: The Education of the Noblesse de Race in Sixteenth-Century France* (Ann Arbor, Mich., microfilm, 1974), pp. 150, 152; Joan Simon, *Education and Society in Tudor England* (Cambridge, Mass., 1966); William Harrison Woodward, *Studies in Education During the Age of the Renaissance, 1400–1600* (Cambridge, 1906), p. 246.

11. Dewald, *Aristocratic Experience*, pp. 53–8. Chapter 2 offers a brilliant discussion of the intellectual impact of the profession of arms.

12. Ibid., pp. 62–8.

13. Schalk, *From Valor to Pedigree*, pp. 177–81.

14. Ibid., Chapter 8.

15. Mark Motley, *Becoming a French Aristocrat: The Education of the Court Nobility, 1580–1715* (Princeton, NJ, 1990), p. 79.

16. Norbert Elias, *The Court Society* (New York, 1983), pp. 95–103; Kristen B. Neuschel, *Word of Honor: Interpreting Noble Culture in Sixteenth-Century France* (Ithaca, NY, 1989), pp. 76–7.

17. Roger Chartier, ed., *A History of Private Life* (Cambridge, Mass., 1989), vol. 3, p. 163.

18. Jacques Revel, 'The Uses of Civility', in Chartier, ed., *A History of Private Life*, vol. 3, p. 192.

19. Maurice Magendie, *La politesse mondaine et les théories de l'honnêteté, en France, au XVIIe siècle, de 1600 à 1660* (Paris, 1925), vol. 1, p. 387.

20. Schalk, *From Valor to Pedigree*, pp. 181–96.

21. Dewald, *Aristocratic Experience*, pp. 15–22.

22. Jonathan Dewald, *The Formation of a Provincial Nobility: The Magistrates of the Parlement of Rouen, 1499–1610* (Princeton, NJ, 1980), Chapter 2.

23. Bohanan, *Old and New Nobility*, Chapter 2.

24. Donna Bohanan, 'The Sword as the Robe in Seventeenth-Century Provence and Brittany', in Mack P. Holt, ed., *Society and Institutions in Early Modern France* (Athens, Ga., 1991), p. 57.

25. Bohanan, *Old and New Nobility*, p. 46.

26. James B. Wood, *The Nobility of the Election of Bayeux, 1463–1666: Continuity through Change* (Princeton, NJ, 1980), pp. 108–9.

27. Jonathan Dewald, *The European Nobility, 1400–1600* (Cambridge, 1996), pp. 60–5.

28. Ibid., pp. 69–89; Jonathan Dewald, *Pont-St-Pierre, 1398–1789: Lordship, Community, and Capitalism in Early Modern France* (Berkeley, Calif., 1987), pp. 218–19.

29. Dewald, *The European Nobility*, pp. 69–97; Bohanan, *Old and New Nobility*, pp. 34–5, 85–8.

30. For an excellent discussion of patronage, see 'Forum: Patronage, Language, and Political Culture', *French Historical Studies* 17 (1992), pp. 839–81 (features articles by Sharon Kettering, J. Russell Major, and Arlette Jouanna).

31. Sharon Kettering, 'Patronage in Early Modern France', *French Historical Studies* 17 (1992), p. 844.

32. Kettering, *Patrons, Brokers, and Clients*, pp. 16–18, 27.

33. Ibid., Chapter 1.

34. Mack P. Holt, 'Patterns of *Clientele* and Economic Opportunity at Court during the Wars of Religion: The Household of François, Duke of Anjou', *French Historical Studies* 13 (1984).

35. Kettering, *Patrons, Brokers, and Clients*, p. 27.

36. S. Amanda Eurich, *The Economics of Power: The Private Finances of the House of Foix-Navarre-Albret during the Religious Wars* (Kirksville, Mo., 1994), pp. 85–9.

37. Neuschel, *Word of Honor*, p. 160.

38. Ibid., p. 183.

39. Kettering, *Patrons, Brokers, and Clients*, Chapter 2.

40. Ibid., p. 4.

41. Ibid., pp. 85–97.

42. Ibid., p. 28.

43. Ibid., Chapter 1; Kettering, 'Patronage in Early Modern France', pp. 844–54. Kettering has advanced the most convincing case for self-interest as the driving force in these connections. Although she acknowledges that fidelity and friendship were important to some patron–client relationships, she argues that most were held together

by obligatory reciprocity. It is Roland Mousnier who has maintained a greater role for fidelity-based relationships within the elite of early modern France. See Kettering's discussion of Mousnier in the above cited sources. See Mousnier, *The Institutions of France under the Absolute Monarchy, 1598–1789*, trans. Brian Pearce (Chicago, Ill., 1979), vol. 1, Chapter 3.

44. Kettering, *Patrons, Brokers, and Clients*, pp. 141–2.
45. Ibid.
46. Jean-Marie Constant, 'Un groupe nobiliaire stratégique dans la France de la première moitié du XVIIe siècle: la noblesse seconde', in Philippe Contamine, ed., *L'Etat et les aristocraties (France, Angleterre, Ecosse), XIIe–XVIIe siècles* (Paris, 1994); Laurent Bourquin, *Noblesse seconde et pouvoir en Champagne aux XVIe et XVIIe siècles* (Paris, 1994).
47. Beik, *Absolutism and Society*, p. 42.
48. Ibid., pp. 43–4.
49. Ibid., pp. 50–1.
50. In *Old and New Nobility*, I argue that nobles in the south of France tended to be more urban in their orientation than nobles in the north. In Provence, they usually owned a *hôtel*, or town house, and this was often their primary residence, their *château*, if they had one, being secondary. See Chapter 1.
51. Kristin B. Neuschel, 'Noble Households in the Sixteenth Century: Material Settings and Human Communities', *French Historical Studies* 15 (1988), pp. 599–601.
52. Ibid., pp. 606–7.
53. Ibid., pp. 607–19.
54. AD, Isère, 13B 445. Justice de Grenoble. Inventaire après décès, 1668, Anne de la Croix.
55. AD, Isère, 13B 446. Justice de Grenoble. Inventaire après décès, 1675, Abel de Buffevant.
56. Dewald, *The European Nobility*, pp. 154–5.
57. Henri-Jean Martin, *Print, Power, and People in Seventeenth-Century France*, trans. David Gerard (London, 1993), pp. 609, 627.
58. Bohanan, *Old and New Nobility*, pp. 128–32; AD, Bouches-du-Rhône, Aix. Fonds Lévy-Bram, 303E-562, 303E-563, 303E-564, 303E-566, 303E-568, and 303E-569.
59. AD, Isère, 13B 457. Justice de Grenoble. Inventaire après décès, 1681, François de Simiane de la Coste; Maurice Virieux, *Le Parlement de Grenoble au XVIIe siècle: étude sociale* (Paris: thèse de doctorat d'état, 1986), pp. 274–6.

60. Jouanna, *Le devoir de révolte*; Denis Crouzet, *Les guerriers de Dieu: La violence au temps des troubles de religion (vers 1525–vers 1620)*, 2 vols (Paris, 1990); Jean-Marie Constant, *Les conjurateurs: Le premier libéralisme politique sous Richelieu* (Paris, 1987).
61. Here Jouanna relies on the well-known works of Ernst Kantorowicz and Ralph Giesey. See Kantorowicz, *The King's Two Bodies* (Princeton, NJ, 1957), and Giesey, *The Royal Funeral Ceremony in Renaissance France* (Geneva, 1960).
62. Jouanna, *Le devoir de révolte*, Chapter 10.
63. Ibid.
64. Ibid., pp. 348–60.
65. Ibid., pp. 362–6.
66. Ibid., pp. 395–6.
67. Constant, *Les conjurateurs*, Chapter 6, pp. 262–4.
68. Ibid., pp. 211–15.

Chapter 2: Crown: State-building

1. F. L. Ganshof, *Feudalism* (New York, 1964, rev. edn), pp. 160, 166.
2. Nicholas Henshall, *The Myth of Absolutism: Change and Continuity in Early Modern European Monarchy* (London, 1992), pp. 12–13; Mousnier, *Institutions of France*, vol. 2, pp. 255–60.
3. Major, *From Renaissance Monarchy*, p. 9.
4. Henshall, *The Myth of Absolutism*, pp. 13–14; Major, *From Renaissance Monarchy*, pp. 4–12; see also *Representative Government*, Major's detailed study of the provincial estates.
5. Henshall, *The Myth of Absolutism*, p. 14; James Collins, *The Fiscal Limits of Absolutism: Direct Taxation in Seventeenth-Century France* (Berkeley, Calif., 1988), pp. 90–2.
6. David Potter, *A History of France, 1460–1560: The Emergence of a Nation State* (New York, 1995), p. 39.
7. Ibid., p. 56.
8. Ibid., pp. 43–6.
9. Major, *From Renaissance Monarchy*, p. 47.
10. R. J. Knecht, *Renaissance Warrior and Patron: The Reign of Francis I* (Cambridge, 1994), pp. 537–40.
11. R. J. Knecht, *Francis I and Absolute Monarchy* (London, 1969), p. 5.
12. R. J. Knecht, *Francis I* (Cambridge, 1988, reprint), pp. 130–1.
13. Knecht, *Renaissance Warrior and Patron*, pp. 537–40.

14. Ibid., p. 537.

15. Major, *From Renaissance Monarchy*, pp. 27–8.

16. James B. Collins, *The State in Early Modern France* (Cambridge, 1995), p. xxxi; Major, *From Renaissance Monarchy*, p. 27.

17. Philippe Hamon, *L'argent du roi: Les finances sous François 1er* (Paris, 1994).

18. Potter, *A History of France*, pp. 123–5.

19. The standard work on the sale of offices is Roland Mousnier, *La venalité des offices sous Henri IV et Louis XIII* (Paris, 1971, 2nd edn). Also see Albert N. Hamscher, *The Parlement of Paris after the Fronde, 1653–1673* (Pittsburgh, Pa., 1976), Chapter 1.

20. For an excellent survey of these trends in historical interpretations of the French Wars of Religion, see Mack P. Holt, 'Putting Religion back into the Wars of Religion', *French Historical Studies* 18 (Fall 1993), pp. 524–51.

21. Mack P. Holt, *The French Wars of Religion, 1562–1629* (Cambridge, 1995), p. 2.

22. Robin Briggs, *Early Modern France, 1560–1715* (Oxford, 1977), pp. 14–15.

23. Holt, *Wars of Religion*, p. 51.

24. Crouzet, *Les guerriers de Dieu*; Barbara Diefendorf, *Beneath the Cross: Catholics and Huguenots in Sixteenth-Century Paris* (Oxford, 1991).

25. Denis Crouzet, 'Royalty, Nobility, and Religion: Research on the Wars in Italy', *Proceedings of the Western Society for French History* 18 (1991), pp. 1–14.

26. Major, *From Renaissance Monarchy*, pp. 108–12.

27. Holt, *French Wars of Religion*, pp. 128–9.

28. Ibid., pp. 98–101; Julian Franklin, ed., *Constitutionalism and Resistance in the Sixteenth Century: Three Treatises by Hotman, Beza, and Mornay* (New York, 1969), Introduction.

29. Diefendorf, *Beneath the Cross*, pp. 152–8.

30. Mark Greengrass, *France in the Age of Henri IV: The Struggle for Stability* (London, 1984), pp. 26–9.

31. Holt, *French Wars of Religion*, pp. 163–6.

32. Major, *From Renaissance Monarchy*, pp. 131–3.

33. Ibid., pp. 134–5.

34. Greengrass, *France in the Age of Henry IV*, pp. 97–101.

35. Ibid., p. 101.

36. Ibid., p. 107.

37. Ibid., pp. 155–9; Collins, *The State in Early Modern France*, pp. 24–5; Hamscher, *The Parlement of Paris after the Fronde*, pp. 4–5.

38. Greengrass, *France in the Age of Henri IV*, pp. 202–4.
39. A. Lloyd Moote, *Louis XIII: The Just* (Berkeley, Calif., 1989), pp. 49–50.
40. Ibid., pp. 50–1.
41. Ibid., p. 57.
42. Major, *From Renaissance Monarchy*, p. 184.
43. Ibid., pp. 184–8.
44. *Recueil des cahiers généraux des trois ordres aux Etats-Généraux*, ed. Lalourcé and Duval (Paris, 1789), and as quoted in Major, *From Renaissance Monarchy*, p. 187.
45. R. J. Knecht, *Richelieu* (London, 1991), pp. 13–14.
46. J. Russell Major, 'The Revolt of 1620: A Study in the Ties of Fidelity', *French Historical Studies* 14 (1986), p. 392.
47. Moote, *Louis XIII*, pp. 112–13.
48. Major, 'The Revolt of 1620', pp. 405–7.
49. Knecht, *Richelieu*, pp. 15–16; Moote, *Louis XIII*, pp. 113–14.
50. Collins, *The State in Early Modern France*, p. 47.
51. Major, *From Renaissance Monarchy*, pp. 225–35.
52. Collins, *The State in Early Modern France*, pp. 47–52.
53. Collins, *Classes, Estates, and Order*, pp. 192–3.
54. Victor-L. Tapié, *France in the Age of Louis XIII and Richelieu* (New York, 1975), pp. 197, 264–5.
55. Donald A. Bailey, 'The Family and Career of Michel de Marillac (1560–1632)', in Mack P. Holt, ed., *Society and Institutions in Early Modern France* (Athens, Ga., 1991), p. 170.
56. Bailey, 'Michel de Marillac', p. 171.
57. Holt, *The French Wars of Religion*, pp. 183–8.
58. Collins, *The State in Early Modern France*, pp. 55–8; Moote, *Louis XIII*, pp. 216–19.
59. Moote, *Louis XIII*, p. 161.
60. Richard Bonney, *Political Change in France under Richelieu and Mazarin, 1624–1661* (Oxford, 1978), Chapters 2, 4, and 7; Knecht, *Richelieu*, pp. 141–7; Briggs, *Early Modern France*, pp. 124–8.
61. Major, *Representative Government*, pp. 487–621; Bonney, *Political Change*, pp. 344–83.
62. Knecht, *Richelieu*, pp. 110–14, quotation at p. 112; Henshall, *The Myth of Absolutism*, pp. 26–7.
63. Knecht, *Richelieu*, pp. 136–8; Collins, *The State in Early Modern France*, p. xxvii; Henshall, *The Myth of Absolutism*, p. 24.
64. Moote, *Louis XIII*.

65. Kettering, *Patrons, Brokers, and Clients*, pp. 141–2; Knecht, *Richelieu*, pp. 21–3; Henshall, *The Myth of Absolutism*, pp. 25–6; Briggs, *Early Modern France*, pp. 111–12.

66. Kettering, *Patrons, Brokers, and Clients*, Chapter 5, quotation at p. 178.

67. Mettam, *Power and Faction in Louis XIV's France*, pp. 136–9; Briggs, *Early Modern France*, pp. 132–3; Collins, *The State in Early Modern France*, pp. 67–9.

68. Mettam, *Power and Faction in Louis XIV's France*, pp. 139–40.

69. Briggs, *Early Modern France*, pp. 132–5; Collins, *The State in Early Modern France*, pp. 69–71; Orest Ranum, *The Fronde: A French Revolution* (New York, 1993), Chapter 4.

70. Mousnier, *Institutions of France*, vol. 2, pp. 612–17; Yves-Marie Bercé, *The Birth of Absolutism: A History of France, 1598–1661* (New York, 1996), p. 166.

71. Ranum, *The Fronde*, pp. 121–2, 134–5.

72. Collins, *The State in Early Modern France*, p. 70.

73. A. Lloyd Moote, *The Revolt of the Judges: The Parlement of Paris and the Fronde, 1643–1652* (Princeton, NJ, 1971), pp. 368–72.

74. Hamscher, *The Parlement of Paris after the Fronde*, pp. xviii–xx.

75. Ibid., Chapter 4, pp. 198–9.

76. Briggs, *Early Modern France*, p. 141.

77. Dewald, *The European Nobility*, pp. 122–7.

78. Mettam, *Power and Faction in Louis XIV's France*, pp. 50–2.

79. Ibid., p. 52.

80. Ibid., p. 53.

81. Orest Ranum, 'Courtesy, Absolutism, and the Rise of the French State', *Journal of Modern History* 52 (1980), pp. 426–51.

82. Elias, *Court Society*, pp. 85–7.

83. Jay M. Smith, *The Culture of Merit: Nobility, Royal Service, and the Making of Absolute Monarchy, 1600–1789* (Ann Arbor, Mich., 1996), pp. 127–32.

84. Elias, *Court Society*, pp. 85–7.

85. François Bluche, *Louis XIV* (New York, 1990), p. 354; Henshall, *The Myth of Absolutism*, p. 39.

86. Henshall, *The Myth of Absolutism*, pp. 42–3; Mettam, *Power and Faction in Louis XIV's France*, pp. 210–16.

87. Major, *From Renaissance Monarchy*, pp. 335–58.

88. Henshall, *The Myth of Absolutism*, p. 55.

89. Hamscher, *The Parlement of Paris after the Fronde*, p. 201. See esp. Chapter 5.

90. Ibid., pp. 85, 145–6, 165–6.
91. Ibid., pp. 199–202. For a discussion of venality and the *paulette*, see esp. Chapter 1.
92. Collins, *The State in Early Modern France*, p. 89.
93. Mettam, *Power and Faction in Louis XIV's France*, pp. 81–101.
94. Ibid., p. 90.
95. Ibid., pp. 84–6.
96. For an excellent survey and critique of recent works on nationalism, see David Bell, 'Recent Works on Early Modern French National Identity', *Journal of Modern History* 68 (1996), pp. 84–113.
97. Colette Beaune, *The Birth of an Ideology: Myths and Symbols of Nation in Late-Medieval France* (Berkeley, Calif., 1991), pp. 313–17.
98. Myriam Yardeni, *La conscience nationale en France pendant les guerres de religion (1559–1598)* (Louvain, 1971).
99. William F. Church, 'France', in Orest Ranum, ed., *National Consciousness, History, and Political Culture in Early Modern Europe* (Baltimore, Md., 1975), pp. 46–51.
100. Peter Sahlins, *Boundaries: The Making of France and Spain in the Pyrenees* (Berkeley, Calif., 1989), pp. 8–9.
101. Ibid., pp. 269–71.
102. Benedict Anderson, *Imagined Communities: Reflections on the Origins and Spread of Nationalism* (London, 1983), pp. 15–16.

Chapter 3: Provence: The Opportunities of Factionalism

1. Bohanan, *Old and New Nobility*, pp. 11–13.
2. Jean-Pierre Poly and Eric Bournazel, *La mutation féodale* (Paris, 1980), pp. 315–35; Bohanan, *Old and New Nobility*, p. 13.
3. Bohanan, *Old and New Nobility*, pp. 13–14.
4. Georges Duby, *La Société aux XI et XIIe siècles dans la région mâconnaise* (Paris, 1971), pp. 159–64; Bohanan, *Old and New Nobility*, p. 15.
5. Bohanan, *Old and New Nobility*, pp. 15–20.
6. Ibid., p. 21.
7. Edouard Perroy, 'Social Mobility Among the French *Noblesse* in the Later Middle Ages', *Past and Present* 21 (1962), pp. 25–38.
8. Bohanan, *Old and New Nobility*, p. 22.
9. Jean Paul Coste, *La ville d'Aix en 1695: Structure urbaine et société* (Aix, 1970), vol. 2, pp. 749–816.

10. The list of noble families considered Aixois was compiled from material included in the following sources: 'Jugement de la noblesse de Provence, 1667', Bibliothèque Méjanes, MS 1133; 'Répertoire des jugements de noblesse en l'année 1667...', MS 1134; Artefeuil, *Histoire héroique et universelle de la noblesse de Provence* (Avignon, 1757), *passim*; François-Paul Blanc, *Origines des familles provençales maintenues dans le second ordre sous le règne de Louis XIV: Dictionnaire généalogique* (Aix, 1971), *passim*. I have classified a family as old if its nobility was certain before 1500, which is just prior to the arrival of the sovereign courts in Aix and the period of wholesale ennoblement aided by the purchase of office. Information on officeholding may be found in Balthasar de Clapiers-Collonques, *Chronologie des officiers des cours souverains de Provence*, 2nd edn (Aix, 1904).

11. Monique Cubells, 'A propos des usurpations de noblesse en Provence sous l'Ancien Régime', *Provence historique* 82 (1970), pp. 249, 251–2.

12. Bohanan, *Old and New Nobility*, pp. 26–8; Bibliothèque Méjanes, MS 1143 (630-R.732), 'Etat du florinage, contenant le revenu noble de tous les fiefs et arrière-fiefs de la province, avec les noms des possesseurs, fait par M. le Premier Président d'Oppède en 1668'; MS 1144 (1074), 'Afflorinement des biens nobles possedez par les seigneurs feudataires de Provence'.

13. Kettering, *Judicial Politics*, pp. 221–5.

14. Bohanan, *Old and New Nobility*, pp. 29–32.

15. Ibid., p. 80; Jacqueline Carrière, *La population d'Aix-en-Provence à la fin du XVIIe siècle: Etude de démographie historique d'après le registre de capitation de 1695* (Aix, 1958), p. 96; Coste, *La ville d'Aix en 1695*, vol. 1, pp. 62–5; vol. 2, pp. 1036–51.

16. Bohanan, *Old and New Nobility*; Archives Communales, Aix, BB130, *Catalogue des consuls et assesseurs de la ville d'Aix* (Aix, 1799), *passim*.

17. Kettering, *Judicial Politics*, p. 44.

18. Bohanan, *Old and New Nobility*, pp. 83–4; Archives Communales, Aix, BB99–BB105, 'Délibérations du Conseil', 1600–95.

19. Major, *Representative Government*, pp. 89–90; Jonathan L. Pearl, *Guise and Provence: Political Conflict in the Epoch of Richelieu*, microfilm (Ann Arbor, Mich., 1968), pp. 49–51. For a detailed explanation of the way in which the composition of the estates evolved, see Gaspard H. Coriolis, *Dissertation sur les Etats de Provence* (Aix, 1867), pp. 11–101.

20. Kettering, *Judicial Politics*, pp. 58–9; Major, *Representative Govenment*, p. 90.

21. Major, *Representative Government*, p. 91; Pearl, *Guise and Provence*, p. 96; Bruno Durand, 'Le rôle des consuls d'Aix dans l'administration du pays', *Provence historique* 6 (1956), p. 252.

22. Coriolis, *Dissertation*, p. 122.

23. Kettering, *Judicial Politics*, p. 59; Major, *Representative Government*, p. 91; Durand, 'Rôle', pp. 254–7; A. Bourde, 'La Provence au grand siècle', in *Histoire de Provence*, ed. Edouard Baratier (Toulouse, 1969), p. 312; Louis Blancard, ed., *Inventaire sommaire des archives départementales de Bouches-du-Rhône*, Sér. C (Marseille, 1884–92), vol. 2, pp. 1–3.

24. *Les Bouches-du-Rhône: Encyclopédie départementale*, ed. Paul Masson (Paris, 1913–37), vol. 3, pp. 475–7; Major, *Representative Government*, p. 92.

25. Major, *Representative Government*, p. 92; *Les Bouches-du-Rhône*, vol. 3, p. 477.

26. *Les Bouches-du-Rhône*, vol. 3, pp. 508–14.

27. Bohanan, *Old and New Nobility*, p. 101; Bibliothèque Méjanes, Aix, MS 1144 (1074), 'Etat chronologique et héraldique des messires les syndics du corps de la noblesse de Provence...'; 1144 (1074), 'Etat chronologique et héraldique des messires les commissaires du corps de la noblesse de Provence...'.

28. Major, *Representative Government*, pp. 542–4; Pearl, *Guise and Provence*, pp. 184–97; Kettering, *Judicial Politics*, pp. 54–64; René Pillorget, *Les Mouvements insurrectionnels de Provence entre 1596 et 1715* (Paris, 1975), pp. 314–20; Pillorget, 'The *Cascaveoux*: The Insurrection at Aix in the Autumn of 1630', in *State and Society in Seventeenth-Century France*, ed. Raymond Kierstead (New York, 1975), pp. 96–7. See also Nicolas Claude Fabri de Pieresc, *Lettres aux frères Dupuy*, ed. Philippe Tamizey de Larroque (Paris, 1890), vol. 2, pp. 46–7.

29. Pillorget, *Mouvements insurrectionnels*, pp. 314–15; Bohanan, *Old and New Nobility*, Graph I, p. 30.

30. William Beik, *Urban Protest in Seventeenth-Century France: The Culture of Retribution* (Cambridge, 1997), pp. 40–1.

31. Kettering, *Judicial Politics*, pp. 154–6.

32. Pillorget, *Mouvements insurrectionnels*, pp. 321–2; Bohanan, *Old and New Nobility*, pp. 35–6.

33. Kettering, *Judicial Politics*, pp. 156–7.

34. Pillorget, *Mouvements insurrectionnels*, pp. 136–7.

35. Beik, *Urban Protest*, pp. 62–3.

36. Pillorget, 'The *Cascaveoux*', pp. 111–12.

37. Ibid., pp. 115–16; Pearl, *Guise and Provence*, pp. 204–6.

38. Pillorget, 'The *Cascaveoux*', pp. 115–16.
39. Ibid., p. 117; Major, *Representative Government*, pp. 584–6.
40. Pillorget, 'The *Cascaveoux*', p. 121; Major, *Representative Government*, p. 587; Kettering, *Judicial Politics*, p. 166.
41. Kettering, *Judicial Politics*, p. 175; Pillorget, 'The *Cascaveoux*', pp. 122–3.
42. Kettering, *Patrons, Brokers, and Clients*, p. 159.
43. Ibid., pp. 159–60.
44. Kettering, *Judicial Politics*, pp. 110–18.
45. Ibid., p. 122.
46. Ibid., pp. 118–27.
47. Major, *Representative Government*, pp. 601–2; *Les Bouches-du-Rhône*, vol. 3, p. 514.
48. Kettering, *Judicial Politics*, Chapters 6 and 7.
49. Ibid., pp. 137–9; Kettering, *Patrons, Brokers, and Clients*, pp. 87–93.
50. Pillorget, *Mouvements insurrectionnels*, p. 567.
51. Kettering, *Judicial Politics*, p. 277.
52. Pillorget, *Mouvements insurrectionnels*, pp. 601–2.
53. Kettering, *Judicial Politics*, p. 277.
54. Ibid., pp. 277–80; Pillorget, *Mouvements insurrectionnels*, pp. 621–4.
55. Kettering, *Judicial Politics*, pp. 285–6; Pillorget, *Mouvements insurrectionnels*, pp. 669–71.
56. Kettering, *Judicial Politics*, pp. 286–7; Kettering, *Patrons, Brokers, and Clients*, p. 64; Pillorget, *Mouvements insurrectionnels*, pp. 622–3.
57. Ernst Kossman, *La Fronde* (Leiden, 1954), pp. 242–3; Kettering, *Judicial Politics*, p. 141; Kettering, *Patrons, Brokers, and Clients*, p. 162.
58. Kettering, *Judicial Politics*, pp. 286–97.
59. Kettering, *Patrons, Brokers, and Clients*, p. 45.
60. Ibid., pp. 45–9; Pillorget, *Mouvements insurrectionnels*, pp. 708–15.
61. Pillorget, *Mouvements insurrectionnels*, pp. 784–9.
62. Kettering, *Judicial Politics*, pp. 74–6, 306, 313 (quotation).
63. Ibid., pp. 307–11.
64. Kettering, *Patrons, Brokers, and Clients*, pp. 86–8; Kettering, *Judicial Politics*, pp. 292–5.
65. Kettering, *Patrons, Brokers, and Clients*, pp. 83–4.
66. Kettering, *Judicial Politics*, pp. 315–26.
67. Kettering, *Patrons, Brokers, and Clients*, p. 53.
68. Ibid., pp. 100–1, 86–7.
69. Ibid., pp. 36, 87. Kettering provides a diagram of the major components in Oppède's clientele in ibid., table 2, p. 88.

70. Ibid., pp. 100–2.
71. Ibid., pp. 102–4.
72. Ibid., pp. 104–11.

Chapter 4: Dauphiné: The Potential in Class Conflict

1. Hickey, *The Coming of French Absolutism*, pp. 14–18; Major, *Representative Government*, pp. 69–73.
2. Major, *Representative Government*, p. 73; Hickey, *The Coming of French Absolutism*, pp. 17–18. Hickey notes that the frequency of royal demands for money actually began to increase during the fifteenth century.
3. Major, *Representative Government*, pp. 76–7.
4. Ibid., pp. 77–8; Hickey, *The Coming of French Absolutism*, pp. 19–20.
5. Major, *Representative Government*, pp. 78–9; Hickey, *The Coming of French Absolutism*, pp. 23–5.
6. Hickey, *The Coming of French Absolutism*, p. 25.
7. Ibid., pp. 31–2.
8. Liewain Scott Van Doren, 'Revolt and Reaction in the City of Romans, Dauphiné, 1579–1580', *Sixteenth-Century Journal* 5 (1974), pp. 76–85; Emmanuel Le Roy Ladurie, *Carnival in Romans* (New York, trans. 1979, repr. 1980), p. 101.
9. Van Doren, 'Revolt and Reaction', pp. 86–8.
10. Ibid., pp. 89–91.
11. Eustache Piémond, *Mémoires de Eustache Piémond, Notaire royal-delphinal de la ville de Saint Antoine en Dauphiné, 1572–1608* (Geneva, repr. 1973), pp. 88–9.
12. Van Doren, 'Revolt and Reaction', p. 97.
13. Le Roy Ladurie, *Carnival*, pp. 214–16.
14. Hickey, *The Coming of French Absolutism*, pp. 68–9; Vital Chomel, 'La monarchie, "Etat de justice", et le conflit des ordres en Dauphiné. Autour du procès des tailles, 1540–1640', *Cahiers d'histoire* 33 (1988), pp. 74–5.
15. Hickey, *The Coming of French Absolutism*, pp. 66–9.
16. Ibid., pp. 77–8.
17. Ibid., pp. 78–9; Major, *Representative Government*, p. 326; Chomel, 'La monarchie', p. 79.
18. Hickey, *The Coming of French Absolutism*, pp. 79–80.
19. Ibid., p. 80; Major, *Representative Government*, p. 326.

20. Hickey, *The Coming of French Absolutism*, pp. 88–92.

21. Ibid., pp. 94–8.

22. Ibid., pp. 80–93.

23. William Bouwsma, 'Lawyers and Early Modern Culture', in William Bouwsma, ed., *A Usable Past: Essays in European Cultural History* (Berkeley, Calif., 1990), pp. 129–34.

24. Hickey, *The Coming of French Absolutism*, pp. 105–12.

25. Dewald, *Aristocratic Experience*, Chapter 1.

26. Hickey, *The Coming of French Absolutism*, pp. 113–16.

27. Ibid., pp. 116–17.

28. Jean Vincent, *Discours en forme de plaidoyé pour le tiers estat de Dauphiné* (Paris, 1598), p. 41.

29. Ibid., pp. 26–7.

30. Ibid., pp. 25–6.

31. Ibid., p. 36.

32. Antoine Rambaud, *Plaidoyé pour le tiers estat de Dauphiné* (Lyon, 1598), pp. 68–9.

33. Ibid., pp. 72–3.

34. Ibid., pp. 90–1.

35. Hickey, *The Coming of French Absolutism*, pp. 106–7.

36. Jean Aquin, *Le plaidé des docteurs et avocats consistoriaux du Parlement du Dauphiné, defendeurs contre les demandes et pretentions du tiers estat dudit pais* (Grenoble, 1599).

37. Vincent, *Discours*, p. 38.

38. Ibid.

39. Hickey, *The Coming of French Absolutism*, p. 118; Jules Ollivier, 'Expilly', *Revue de Dauphiné* 6 (1839), p. 78; Jouanna, *Ordre social*, p. 42.

40. *Premières escritures, pour la defence des Nobles du Dauphiné, contre les demandes et injures du tiers Estat dudit païs*, BM, Grenoble.

41. Anon., *Second Escritures pour l'estat des nobles du Dauphiné; contenant contredicts contre la production, et responses aux invectives injurieuses de tiers estat* (Grenoble, 1602), pp. 88–9; P. Boissat, *Remerciement au roy par les anoblis du Dauphiné* (Vienne, 1602), pp. 65–6.

42. Jean-Claude Audeyer, *Très-humbles remonstrances en forme d'avertissement au roy par les officiers de la cour de parlement de Dauphiné sur le procès intenté par le tiers estat* (Grenoble, 1601), p. 57.

43. Anon., *Secondes Escritures*, pp. 31–2.

44. Dewald, *Aristocratic Experience*, Chapter 1.

45. Hickey, *The Coming of French Absolutism*, pp. 121–3.

46. Major, *Representative Government*, p. 236; Major, *From Renaissance Monarchy to Absolute Monarchy*, p. 126.

47. Hickey, *The Coming of French Absolutism*, p. 121; Major, *Representative Government*, p. 330; Charles Dufayard, *Le Connétable de Lesdiguières* (Paris, 1892), p. 286.

48. Le Comte Douglas et J. Roman, *Actes et correspondance du Connétable de Lesdiguières* (Grenoble, 1878), vol. 1, p. 371; Antoine Boniel de Catilhon, *La vie de Messire Claude Expilly, chevalier, conseiller du roy en son Conseil d'Etat et President au Parlement de Grenoble* (Grenoble, 1640), p. 41; Ollivier, 'Expilly', pp. 74–82.

49. Hickey, *The Coming of French Absolutism*, pp. 132–3; Major, *Representative Government*, pp. 330–1.

50. Hickey, *The Coming of French Absolutism*, pp. 123–39.

51. Ibid., pp. 139–41.

52. Dufayard, *Le Connétable de Lesdiguières*, pp. 267–78.

53. Ibid., p. 270.

54. Ibid., p. 268; Bercé, *Birth of Absolutism*, p. 17.

55. Kettering, *Patrons, Brokers, and Clients*, p. 27.

56. Major, *Representative Government*, p. 333.

57. Hickey, *The Coming of French Absolutism*, pp. 139–44; Major, *Representative Government*, p. 332.

58. Hickey, *The Coming of French Absolutism*, pp. 144–5.

59. Major, *Representative Government*, pp. 525–6.

60. Hickey, *The Coming of French Absolutism*, pp. 161, 166; Major, *Representative Government*, pp. 526–9; Bernard Bonnin, 'Autorité royale et pouvoirs locaux sous Louis XIV: L'exemple du "Pays de Dauphiné"', *Revue Marseille* 101 (1975), p. 60.

61. Major, *Representative Government*, pp. 529–30.

62. Virieux, *Le Parlement de Grenoble au XVIIe siècle*, p. 53.

63. Ibid.

64. Ibid., *passim*. The figure of 10 per cent is my calculation based on the family biographies contained in Virieux's work.

65. Bibliothèque Municipale, Grenoble, R. 7426, Hyacinthe Gariel, 'Dénombrement des familles annoblis depuis l'an 1587 jusques en 1634 que ceste province fut cadastré et leur revenu', *Statistique Nobiliaire* (Mélanges Guy Allard).

66. Briggs, *Early Modern France*, p. 94; Moote, *Louis XIII*, p. 134.

67. Holt, *The French Wars of Religion*, Chapter 7.

68. Hickey, *The Coming of French Absolutism*, pp. 161–6.

69. Ibid., p. 167; Major, *Representative Government*, p. 614.

70. Hickey, *The Coming of French Absolutism*, pp. 167–9; Major, *Representative Government*, p. 614.
71. Major, *Representative Government*, pp. 614–15.
72. Hickey, *The Coming of French Absolutism*, pp. 170–1.
73. Ibid., pp. 171–2.
74. Ibid., p. 172.
75. René Favier, 'Les Assemblées du Dauphiné après la suspension des Etats en 1628', *Cahiers d'histoire* 24 (1979), pp. 59–66.
76. Bonnin, 'Autorité royale', p. 60.

Chapter 5: Brittany: The Limits of Elite Solidarity

1. Potter, *History of France*, p. 113; Major, *Representative Government*, pp. 94–5.
2. Collins, *Classes, Estates, and Order*, pp. 118–21.
3. Ibid., pp. 122–6.
4. Ibid., pp. 126–8.
5. Ibid., pp. 132–5.
6. Major, *Representative Government*, pp. 342–4.
7. Ibid., pp. 344–5.
8. Ibid., pp. 345–7; Collins, *Classes, Estates, and Order*, pp. 168–9.
9. Major, *Representative Government*, p. 347.
10. Jean Meyer, *La noblesse bretonne au XVIII siècle* (Paris, 1966), vol. 1, p. 57. This material is included in my article 'The Sword as the Robe' in Holt, ed., *Society and Institutions in Early Modern France*, pp. 51–62.
11. Meyer, *La noblesse bretonne*, vol. 1, p. 57.
12. Michael Jones, *The Creation of Brittany: A Late Medieval State* (London, 1988), pp. 228–9.
13. Ibid., p. 230.
14. Frédéric Saulnier, *Le Parlement de Bretagne, 1554–1790: Répertoire alphabétique et biographique de tous les membres de la cour* (Rennes, 1909), vol. 2, pp. 766–7; Bibliothèque Nationale, MS FR 30121: Dossiers bleus, 576.
15. Saulnier, *Le Parlement de Bretagne*, vol. 2, pp. 548–9; BN, MS FR 29919: Dossiers bleus, 374.
16. Meyer, *La noblesse bretonne*, vol. 1, pp. 57–9.
17. Bohanan, 'The Sword as the Robe', p. 57. This assessment is based on material in Saulnier, *Le Parlement de Bretagne*, vols. 1–2.

18. Bibliothèque Nationale, MS FR 29688: Dossiers bleus, 143, fols. 1–7; Saulnier, *Le Parlement de Bretagne*, vol. 1, pp. 180–2.

19. P. S. Lewis, 'Breton Estates', in his *Essays in Later Medieval French History* (London, 1985), pp. 128–9, 134; Major, *Representative Government*, pp. 93–4.

20. Jean Kerhervé, *Finances et gens de finances des Ducs de Bretagne, 1365–1491* (Paris: thèse d'état, 1986), pp. 854–65.

21. John H. Hurt, 'The Parlement of Brittany and the Crown: 1665–1675', in Raymond F. Kierstead, ed., *State and Society in Seventeenth-Century France* (New York, 1975), p. 47.

22. Saulnier, *Le Parlement de Bretagne*, vol. 1, pp. 65–6; vol. 2, p. 662; Henri Frotier de la Messelière, *La noblesse en Bretagne avant 1789* (Rennes, thèse de droit, 1902), p. 46.

23. Saulnier, *Le Parlement de Bretagne*, vols. 1 and 2, *passim*.

24. Collins, *Classes, Estates, and Order*, pp. 157–63; Armand Rébillon, *Les états de Bretagne de 1661–1789* (Rennes, 1932), pp. 94–5.

25. Collins, *Classes, Estates, and Order*, pp. 174–5; Rébillon, *Les états de Bretagne*, pp. 83–6.

26. Major, *Representative Government*, pp. 436–40.

27. Ibid., pp. 478–9.

28. Joseph Bergin, *Cardinal Richelieu: Power and the Pursuit of Wealth* (New Haven, Conn., 1985), pp. 94–7; Kenneth M. Dunkley, *Richelieu and the Estates of Brittany, 1624–1640* (Ph.D. dissertation, Emory University, 1972), Chapter 3; Collins, *Classes, Estates, and Order*, pp. 187–91; Major, *Representative Government*, pp. 564–5.

29. Collins, *Classes, Estates, and Order*, p. 191.

30. Dunkley, *Richelieu and the Estates of Brittany*, pp. 182–6.

31. Ibid., pp. 187–9, 198.

32. Ibid., pp. 194–5.

33. Kettering, *Patrons, Brokers, and Clients*, pp. 70–2; Collins, *Classes, Estates, and Order*, pp. 192–3.

34. Collins, *Classes, Estates, and Order*, pp. 206–7.

35. Ibid., pp. 189–96.

36. Ibid., pp. 196, 217.

37. Ibid., pp. 215–17.

38. Ibid., pp. 205–7.

39. Ibid., pp. 209–11.

40. Major, *Representative Government*, pp. 646–7.

41. Major, *Representative Government*, p. 648; Kettering, *Patrons, Brokers, and Clients*, p. 170.

42. Collins, *Classes, Estates, and Order*, p. 223.

43. Major, *Representative Government*, p. 648; Rébillon, *Les états de Bretagne*, pp. 234–5.

44. Collins, *Classes, Estates, and Order*, p. 220; Rébillon, *Les états de Bretagne*, p. 236.

45. Collins, *Classes, Estates, and Order*, p. 220.

46. Hurt, 'The Parlement of Brittany and the Crown', pp. 45–8.

47. Ibid., pp. 53–8. See also Hurt, 'La politique du parlement de Bretagne (1661–1675)', *Annales de Bretagne et des pays de l'Ouest* 81 (1974), pp. 105–30.

48. Beik, *Urban Protest*, pp. 159–60.

49. Yvon Garlan and Claude Nières, *Les révoltes bretonnes de 1675: Papier Timbré et Bonnets Rouges* (Paris, 1975), p. 37; A. de la Borderie and B. Pocquet, *Histoire de la Bretagne* (Rennes, 1905–14), vol. 5, pp. 482–3.

50. Beik, *Urban Protest*, pp. 161–2; Garlan and Nières, *Les révoltes bretonnes*, p. 40.

51. Beik, *Urban Protest*, pp. 162–3; Garlan and Nières, *Les révoltes bretonnes*, pp. 50–1.

52. Beik, *Urban Protest*, p. 163.

53. Ibid., pp. 163–8; Borderie and Pocquet, *Histoire de la Bretagne*, vol. 5, pp. 488–9.

54. Collins, *Classes, Estates, and Order*, pp. 264–81; Borderie and Pocquet, *Histoire de la Bretagne*, vol. 5, pp. 495, 501–5.

55. Borderie and Pocquet, *Histoire de la Bretagne*, vol. 5, pp. 495–500, 505–16.

56. Ibid., pp. 519–22.

57. Ibid., pp. 522–6.

58. Ibid., p. 526; Hurt, 'The Parlement of Brittany and the Crown', pp. 59–60.

59. Hurt, 'La politique du parlement de Bretagne', pp. 112–13.

60. Collins, *Classes, Estates, and Order*, *passim*.

61. Hurt, 'La politique du parlement de Bretagne', pp. 116–17.

62. Ibid., pp. 118–20.

63. Ibid., pp. 120–1.

64. Ibid., pp. 121–2; Rébillon, *Les états de Bretagne*, pp. 216–17.

65. Hurt, 'La politique du parlement de Bretagne', pp. 123–5.

66. Ibid., pp. 126–7.

67. Major, *Representative Government*, p. 664.

68. Collins, *Classes, Estates, and Order*, *passim*.

69. Borderie and Pocquet, *Histoire de la Bretagne*, vol. 5, pp. 528–9; Major, *Representative Government*, p. 649.
70. Collins, *Classes, Estates, and Order, passim*.
71. I have compiled these figures based on information contained in Saulnier's study of the parlement.
72. Rébillon, *Les états de Bretagne*, p. 86.

Bibliography

Archival Sources

Paris

Bibliothèque Nationale
Dossiers généalogique:
  Dossiers bleus
  Cabinet d'Hozier
  Carrés d'Hozier
  Nouveau d'Hozier
MS FR 18711–18713. Dom Lobineau, 'Mémoires touchant la noblesse de
  Bretagne'.

Aix

Archives Départementales, Bouches-du-Rhône, Annexe d'Aix

  IVB, Les Insinuations, 1598–1700.
  Fonds Lévy-Bram, 303E-562, 303E-563, 303E-564, 303E-566,
    303E-568, 303E-569. Inventaires après décès. 305E, Contrats
    de mariage.
  Fonds Berlie, 301E. Contrats de mariage.
  Fonds Bertrand, 302E. Contrats de mariage.
  Fonds Vachier, 305E. Contrats de mariage.
  Fonds Laucagne, 306E. Contrats de mariage.
  Fonds Mouravit, 307E. Contrats de mariage.
  Fonds Muraire, 308E. Contrats de mariage.

Archives Communales

BB130, *Catalogue des consuls et assesseurs de la ville d'Aix*. Aix, 1799.
BB99–BB105, 'Délibérations du Conseil', 1600–95.

Bibliothèque Méjanes

MS 1133 (R.A.32), 'Jugement de la noblesse de Provence, 1667'.
MS 1134 (R.A.32), 'Répertoire des jugements de noblesse en l'année 1667'.
MS 1143 (630-R.732), 'Etat du florinage, contenant le revenu noble de tous les fiefs et arrière-fiefs de la province... en 1668'.
MS 1144 (1074), 'Afflorinement des biens nobles possedez par les seigneurs feudataires de Provence'.
 'Etat chronologique et héraldique des messires les commissaires du corps de la noblesse de Provence...'.
 'Etat chronologique et héraldique des messires les syndics du corps de la noblesse de Provence...'.

Grenoble

Archives Départementales, Isère

Séries B
13B 445. Justice de Grenoble. Inventaire après décès, 1668, Anne de la Croix.
13B 446. Justice de Grenoble. Inventaire après décès, 1675, Abel de Buffevant.
13B 457. Justice de Grenoble. Inventaire après décès, 1681, François de Simiane de la Coste.

Bibliothèque Municipale, Grenoble

Unpublished:
R. 7426. Mélanges Guy Allard: Statistique Nobiliaire, edited by Hyacinthe Gariel.
 'Dénombrement des familles annoblis depuis l'an 1587 jusques en 1634 que ceste province fut cadastré et leur revenu.'
 'Familles qui ont usurpé la noblesse et qui n'ont point eu de certificat de M. Dugué.'
R80, t9, f776. Guy Allard. 'Rolle des annoblis dans le Dauphiné depuis 1582 et la valleur de leurs biens.'
U474. 'Traité de la noblesse de Dauphiné.'

Published:

Anon. *Abregé des escritures fournies de la part de la noblesse du Dauphiné, contre le Tiers Estat dudit pais.* n.p., 1600.

——. *Premières escritures, pour la defence des Nobles du Dauphiné, contre les demandes et injures du tiers Estat dudit pais.* n.p., 1600.

——. *Second Escritures pour l'estat des nobles du Dauphiné; contenant contredicts contre la production, et responses aux invectives injurieuses de tiers estat.* Grenoble, 1602.

——. *Très humbles remonstrances faites au roy par les Deputez de la Noblesse du Dauphiné, pour la deffence de leurs droicts et franchises.* Paris, 1633.

Aquin, Jean. *Le plaidé des docteurs et avocats consistoriaux du Parlement du Dauphiné, defendeurs contre les demandes et pretentions du tiers estat dudit pais.* Grenoble, 1599.

Audeyer, Jean-Claude. *Très-humbles remonstrances en forme d'avertissement au roy par les officiers de la cour de parlement de Dauphiné sur le procès intenté par le tiers estat.* Grenoble, 1601.

Boissat, P. *Remerciement au roy par les anoblis du Dauphiné.* Vienne, 1602.

Catilhon, Antoine Boniel de. *La vie de Messire Claude Expilly, chevalier, conseiller du roy en son Conseil d'Etat et President au Parlement de Grenoble.* Grenoble, 1640.

Vincent, Jean. *Discours en forme de plaidoyé pour le tiers estat de Dauphiné.* Paris, 1598.

Rambaud, Antoine. *Plaidoyé pour le tiers estat de Dauphiné.* Lyon, 1598.

Rennes

Archives Départementales, Ile et Vilaine

1 Bi 6. Chambre pour la Réformation de la noblesse de Bretagne.

2 F 11. Liste des anoblis de Bretagne 1300 à 1663.

2 F 33. Moustre du ban et de l'arrière-ban de l'Eveché de Rennes en 1557.

Published Sources

Allard, Guy. *Dictionnaire historique, chronologique, géographique, généalogique, héraldique, juridique, politique et botanographique du Dauphiné.* 3 vols. Grenoble, 1864.

Artefeuil, *Histoire héroique et universelle de la noblesse de Provence.* Avignon, 1757.

Blancard, Louis, ed. *Inventaire sommaire des archives départementales de Bouches-du-Rhône*. Séries C, Vol. 2. Marseille, 1884–92.

Chorier, Nicolas. *Histoire générale de Dauphiné*. Grenoble, 1661. Repr. Valence, 1878.

Clapiers-Collonques, Balthasar de. *Chronologie des officiers des cours souverains de Provence*. Aix, 2nd edn, 1904.

Coste, Jean Paul. *La ville d'Aix en 1695: Structure urbaine et société*. 2 vols. Aix, thèse de doctorat, 1970.

Douglas, Le Cte et Roman, J. *Actes et correspondance du Connétable de Lesdiguières*. 3 vols. Grenoble, 1878.

Piémond, Eustache. *Mémoires de Eustache Piémond, Notaire royal-delphinal de la ville de Saint Antoine en Dauphiné, 1572–1608*. Geneva, reprint, 1973.

Pieresc, Nicolas Claude Fabri de. *Lettres aux frères Dupuy*. Ed. Philippe Tamizey de Larroque. Vol. 2. Paris, 1890.

Pilot-Dethorey, M. and Prudhomme, M.A. *Inventaire-sommaire des Archives Départementales d'Isère*. Grenoble, 1884.

Rosmorduc, M. Le Comte de. *La Noblesse de Bretagne devant la Chambre de Réformation 1668–1671. Arrêts de maintenue de noblesse*. 4 vols. Saint Brieuc, 1896–1905.

Saulnier, Frédéric. *Le Parlement de Bretagne, 1554–1790: Répertoire alphabétique et biographique de tous les membres de la cour*. Rennes, 1909.

Videl, Louis. *Histoire du Connestable de Lesdiguières contenant toute sa vie, avec plusieurs choses memorables servant à l'histoire générale*. Paris, 1666.

Virieux, Maurice. *Le Parlement de Grenoble au XVIIe siècle: étude sociale*. Paris, thèse de doctorat d'état, 1986.

Literature

Anderson, Benedict. *Imagined Communities: Reflections on the Origins and Spread of Nationalism*. London, 1983.

Bailey, Donald A. 'The Family and Career of Michel de Marillac (1560–1632)'. In *Society and Institutions in Early Modern France*, ed. Mack P. Holt. Athens, Ga., 1991.

Beaune, Colette. *The Birth of an Ideology: Myths and Symbols of Nation in Late-Medieval France*. Berkeley, Calif., trans., 1991.

Beik, William. *Absolutism and Society in Seventeenth-Century France: State Power and Provincial Aristocracy in Languedoc*. Cambridge, 1985.

——. *Urban Protest in Seventeenth-Century France: The Culture of Retribution*. Cambridge, 1997.

Bell, David. 'Recent Works on Early Modern French National Identity'. *Journal of Modern History* 68 (1996), pp. 84–113.

Bercé, Yves-Marie. *The Birth of Absolutism: A History of France, 1598–1661*. Trans. Richard Rex. New York, 1996.

Bergin, Joseph. *Cardinal Richelieu: Power and the Pursuit of Wealth*. New Haven, Conn., 1985.

Black, Jeremy. *A Military Revolution? Military Change and European Society, 1550–1800*. Atlantic Highlands, NJ, 1991.

Blanc, François-Paul. *Annoblissement par lettres en Provence à l'époque de réformations de Louis XIV, 1630–1730*. Aix, thèse de droit, 1971.

———. *Origines des familles provençales maintenues dans le second ordre sous le règne de Louis XIV: Dictionnaire généalogique*. Aix, thése de droit, 1971.

Bluche, François. *Louis XIV*. Trans. Mark Greengrass. New York, 1990.

Bohanan, Donna. *Old and New Nobility in Aix-en-Provence, 1600–1695: Portrait of an Urban Elite*. Baton Rouge, La., 1992.

———. 'The Sword as the Robe in Seventeenth-Century Provence and Brittany'. In *Society and Institutions in Early Modern France*, ed. Mack P. Holt. Athens, Ga., 1991, pp. 51–62.

Bonney, Richard. *Political Change in France under Richelieu and Mazarin, 1624–1661*. Oxford, 1978.

Bonnin, Bernard. 'Autorité royale et pouvoirs locaux sous Louis XIV: L'exemple du "Pays de Dauphiné"'. *Revue Marseille* 101 (1975), pp. 59–64.

Borderie, A. de la and Pocquet, B. *Histoire de la Bretagne*. Vol. 5. Rennes, 1905–14.

Bourde, A. 'La Provence au grand siècle'. In *Histoire de Provence*, ed. Edouard Baratier. Toulouse, 1969.

Bourquin, Laurent. *Noblesse seconde et pouvoir en Champagne aux XVIe et XVIIe siècles*. Paris, 1994.

Bouwsma, William. 'Lawyers and Early Modern Culture'. In *A Usable Past: Essays in European Cultural History*, ed. William Bouwsma. Berkeley, Calif., 1990, pp. 129–53.

Briggs, Robin. *Early Modern France, 1560–1715*. Oxford, 1977.

Carrière, Jacqueline. *La population d'Aix-en-Provence à la fin du XVIIe siècle: Etude de démographie historique d'après le registre de capitation de 1695*. Aix, 1958.

Chartier, Roger. *A History of Private Life*. Vol. 3. Cambridge, Mass., 1989.

Chomel, Vital. 'La monarchie, "Etat de justice", et le conflit des ordres en Dauphiné. Autour du procès des tailles, 1540–1640'. *Cahiers d'histoire* 33 (1988), pp. 71–81.

Church, William F. 'France'. *National Consciousness, History, and Political Culture in Early Modern Europe*, ed. Orest Ranum. Baltimore, Md., 1975, pp. 43–66.

Collins, James B. *Classes, Estates, and Order in Early Modern Brittany.* Cambridge, 1994.

———. *The Fiscal Limits of Absolutism: Direct Taxation in Seventeenth-Century France.* Berkeley, Calif., 1988.

———. *The State in Early Modern France.* Cambridge, 1995.

Constant, Jean-Marie. *Les conjurateurs: Le premier libéralisme politique sous Richelieu.* Paris, 1987.

———. 'Un groupe nobiliaire stratégique dans la France de la première moitié du XVIIe siècle: la noblesse seconde'. In *L'Etat et les aristocraties (France, Angleterre, Ecosse), XIIe–XVIIe siècles*, ed. Philippe Contamine. Paris, 1994, pp. 279–304.

———. 'La mobilité sociale dans une province de gentilshommes et de paysans: La Beauce'. *XVII Siècle* 122 (1979), pp. 7–20.

———. *La noblesse française aux XVIe–XVIIe siècles.* Paris, 1985.

Coriolis, Gaspard H. *Dissertation sur les Etats de Provence.* Aix, 1867.

Crouzet, Denis. *Les guerriers de Dieu: La violence au temps des troubles de religion (vers 1525–vers 1620).* 2 vols. Paris, 1990.

———. 'Royalty, Nobility, and Religion: Research on the Wars in Italy'. *Proceedings of the Western Society for French History* 18 (1991), pp. 1–14.

Cubells, Monique. 'A propos des usurpations de noblesse en Provence sous l'Ancien Régime'. *Provence historique* 82 (1970), pp. 224–301.

———. *La Provence des Lumières: Les Parlementaires d'Aix au XVIIIe siècle.* Paris, 1984.

Dewald, Jonathan. *Aristocratic Experience and the Origins of Modern Culture: France, 1570–1715.* Berkeley, Calif., 1993.

———. *The European Nobility, 1400–1600.* Cambridge, 1996.

———. *The Formation of a Provincial Nobility: The Magistrates of the Parlement of Rouen, 1499–1610.* Princeton, NJ, 1980.

———. *Pont-St-Pierre, 1398–1789: Lordship, Community, and Capitalism in Early Modern France.* Berkeley, Calif., 1987.

Diefendorf, Barbara. *Beneath the Cross: Catholics and Huguenots in Sixteenth-Century Paris.* Oxford, 1991.

Duby, Georges. *La Société aux XI et XIIe siècles dans la région mâconnaise.* Paris, 1971.

Dufayard, Charles. *Le Connétable de Lesdiguières.* Paris, 1892.

Dunkley, Kenneth M. *Richelieu and the Estates of Brittany, 1624–1640.* Emory University, doctoral dissertation, 1972.

Durand, Bruno. 'Le rôle des consuls d'Aix dans l'administration du pays'. *Provence historique* 6 (1956), pp. 244–59.

Dussert, A. *Les Etats du Dauphiné aux XIVe et XVe siècles*. Grenoble, 1915.

Elias, Norbert. *The Court Society*. Trans. Edmund Jephcott. New York, 1983.

Escalier, Emile. 'La noblesse des avocats consistoriaux au Parlement de Dauphiné'. *Bulletin de la Société d'Etudes des Hautes-Alpes* 70 (1973), pp. 49–59.

Eurich, S. Amanda. *The Economics of Power: The Private Finances of the House of Foix-Navarre-Albret during the Religious Wars*. Kirksville, Mo., 1994.

Favier, René. 'Les Assemblées du Dauphiné après la suspension des Etats en 1628'. *Cahiers d'histoire* 24 (1979), pp. 59–69.

Franklin, Julian, ed. *Constitutionalism and Resistance in the Sixteenth Century: Three Treatises by Hotman, Beza, and Mornay*. New York, 1969.

Frotier de la Messelière, Henri. *La noblesse en Bretagne avant 1789*. Rennes, thèse de droit, 1902.

Ganshof, F. L. *Feudalism*. New York, 1964, rev. edn.

Garlan, Yvon and Nières, Claude. *Les révoltes bretonnes de 1675: Papier Timbré et Bonnets Rouges*. Paris, 1975.

Greengrass, Mark. *France in the Age of Henri IV: The Struggle for Stability*. London, 1984.

Hale, J. R. *War and Society in Renaissance Europe, 1450–1620*. Baltimore, Md., 1985.

Hamon, Philippe. *L'argent du roi: Les finances sous François 1er*. Paris, 1994.

Hamscher, Albert N. *The Parlement of Paris after the Fronde, 1653–1673*. Pittsburgh, Pa., 1976.

Henshall, Nicholas. *The Myth of Absolutism: Change and Continuity in Early Modern European Monarchy*. London, 1992.

Hickey, Daniel. *The Coming of French Absolutism: The Struggle for Tax Reform in the Province of Dauphiné, 1540–1640*. Toronto, 1986.

Holt, Mack P. *The French Wars of Religion, 1562–1629*. Cambridge, 1995.

———. 'Patterns of *Clientele* and Economic Opportunity at Court during the Wars of Religion: The Household of François, Duke of Anjou'. *French Historical Studies* 13 (1984), pp. 305–22.

———. 'Putting Religion back into the Wars of Religion'. *French Historical Studies* 18 (Fall 1993), pp. 524–51.

———, ed. *Society and Institutions in Early Modern France*. Athens, Ga., 1991.

Hurt, John H. 'The Parlement of Brittany and the Crown: 1665–1675'. In *State and Society in Seventeenth-Century France*, ed. Raymond F. Kierstead. New York, 1975.

——. 'La politique du parlement de Bretagne (1661–1675)'. *Annales de Bretagne et des pays de l'Ouest* 81 (1974), pp. 105–30.

Jones, Michael. *The Creation of Brittany: A Late Medieval State*. London, 1988.

Jouanna, Arlette. *Le devoir de révolte: La noblesse française et la gestation de l'état moderne (1559–1661)*. Paris, 1989.

——. *Ordre social: Mythes et hiérarchies dans la France du XVIe siècle*. Paris, 1977.

——. 'Réflexions sur les relations internobiliaires en France aux XVIe et XVIIe siècles'. *French Historical Studies* 17 (1992), pp. 872–81.

Kerhervé, Jean. *Finance et gens de finances des Ducs de Bretagne, 1365–1491*. Paris, thèse d'état, 1986.

Kettering, Sharon. *Judicial Politics and Urban Revolt in Seventeenth-Century France: The Parlement of Aix, 1629–1659*. Princeton, NJ, 1978.

——. 'Patronage in Early Modern France'. *French Historical Studies* 17 (1992), pp. 839–62.

——. *Patrons, Brokers, and Clients in Seventeenth-Century France*. Oxford, 1986.

Knecht, R. J. *Francis I*. Repr. Cambridge, 1988.

——. *Francis I and Absolute Monarchy*. London, 1969.

——. *Renaissance Warrior and Patron: The Reign of Francis I*. Cambridge, 1994.

——. *Richelieu*. London, 1991.

Kossman, Ernst. *La Fronde*. Leiden, 1954.

Le Roy Ladurie, Emmanuel. *Carnival in Romans*. Trans. Mary Feeney. New York, 1979, repr. 1980.

Lewis, P. S. 'Breton Estates'. In *Essays in Later Medieval French History*, ed. P. S. Lewis. London, 1985.

Magendie, Maurice. *La politesse mondaine et les théories de l'honnêteté, en France, au XVIIe siècle, de 1600 à 1660*. 2 vols. Paris, 1925.

Major, J. Russell. *From Renaissance Monarchy to Absolute Monarchy: French Kings, Nobles and Estates*. Baltimore, Md., 1994.

——. *Representative Government in Early Modern France*. New Haven, Conn., 1980.

——. 'The Revolt of 1620: A Study in the Ties of Fidelity'. *French Historical Studies* 14 (1986), pp. 319–408.

——. 'Vertical Ties Through Time'. *French Historical Studies* 17 (1992), pp. 863–71.

Martin, Henri-Jean. *Print, Power, and People in Seventeenth-Century France*. Trans. David Gerard. London, 1993.

Masson, Paul, ed. *Les Bouches-du-Rhône: Encyclopédie départementale*. Vol. 3. Paris, 1913–37.

Mettam, Roger. *Power and Faction in Louis XIV's France*. London, 1988.

Meyer, Jean. *La noblesse bretonne au XVIII siècle*. Paris, 1966.

Moote, A. Lloyd. *Louis XIII: The Just*. Berkeley, Calif., 1989.

Motley, Mark. *Becoming a French Aristocrat: The Education of the Court Nobility, 1580–1715*. Princeton, NJ, 1990.

Mousnier, Roland. *The Institutions of France under the Absolute Monarchy, 1598–1789*. Trans. Brian Pearce. 2 vols. Chicago, 1979.

——. *La venalité des offices sous Henri IV et Louis XIII*. 2nd edn. Paris, 1971.

Neuschel, Kristen B. 'Noble Households in the Sixteenth Century: Material Settings and Human Communities'. *French Historical Studies* 15 (1988), pp. 599–601.

——. *Word of Honor: Interpreting Noble Culture in Sixteenth-Century France*. Ithaca, NY, 1989.

Nordhaus, John David. *Arma et Litterae: The Education of the Noblesse de Race in Sixteenth-Century France*. Ann Arbor, Mich.: university microfilm, 1974.

Ollivier, Jules. 'Expilly'. *Revue de Dauphiné* 6 (1839), pp. 65–94.

Parker, David. *Class and State in* Ancien Régime *France: The Road to Modernity?* London, 1996.

Pearl, Jonathan L. *Guise and Provence: Political Conflict in the Epoch of Richelieu*. Microfilm. Ann Arbor, Mich., 1968.

Perroy, Edouard. 'Social Mobility Among the French *Noblesse* in the Later Middle Ages'. *Past and Present* 21 (1962), pp. 25–38.

Pillorget, René. 'The *Cascaveoux*: The Insurrection at Aix in the Autumn of 1630'. In *State and Society in Seventeenth-Century France*, ed. Raymond Kierstead. New York, 1975.

——. *Les Mouvements insurrectionnels de Provence entre 1596 et 1715*. Paris, 1975.

Poly, Jean-Pierre and Bournazel, Eric. *La mutation féodale*. Paris, 1980.

Potter, David. *A History of France, 1460–1560: The Emergence of a Nation State*. New York, 1995.

Ranum, Orest. 'Courtesy, Absolutism, and the Rise of the French State'. *Journal of Modern History* 52 (1980), pp. 426–51.

——. *The Fronde: A French Revolution*. New York, 1993.

Rébillon, Armand. *Les états de Bretagne de 1661–1789*. Rennes, 1932.

Revel, Jacques. 'The Uses of Civility'. In *A History of Private Life*, ed. Roger Chartier. Vol. 3. Cambridge, Mass., 1989, pp. 167–205.

Sahlins, Peter. *Boundaries: The Making of France and Spain in the Pyrenees*. Berkeley, Calif., 1989.

Schalk, Ellery. *From Valor to Pedigree: Ideas of Nobility in France in the Sixteenth and Seventeenth Centuries.* Princeton, NJ, 1986.

Simon, Joan. *Education and Society in Tudor England.* Cambridge, Mass., 1966.

Smith, Jay M. *The Culture of Merit: Nobility, Royal Service, and the Making of Absolute Monarchy, 1600–1789.* Ann Arbor, Mich., 1996.

Tapié, Victor-L. *France in the Age of Louis XIII and Richelieu.* Trans. D. McN. Lockie. New York, 1975.

Van Doren, Liewain Scott. 'Revolt and Reaction in the City of Romans, Dauphiné, 1579–1580'. *Sixteenth-Century Journal* 5 (1974), pp. 71–100.

Wood, James B. *The Nobility of the Election of Bayeux, 1463–1666: Continuity through Change.* Princeton, NJ, 1980.

Woodward, William Harrison. *Studies in Education during the Age of the Renaissance, 1400–1600.* Cambridge, 1906.

Yardeni, Myriam. *La conscience nationale en France pendant les guerres de religion (1559–1598).* Louvain, 1971.

Index

185